Microsoft®

2030A: Creating Reporting Solutions Using Microsoft® SQL Server™ 2000 Reporting Services

Course Number: 2030A
Part Number: X10-42472
Released: 02/2004

END-USER LICENSE AGREEMENT FOR OFFICIAL MICROSOFT LEARNING PRODUCTS – STUDENT EDITION

PLEASE READ THIS END-USER LICENSE AGREEMENT ("EULA") CAREFULLY. BY USING THE MATERIALS AND/OR USING OR INSTALLING THE SOFTWARE THAT ACCOMPANIES THIS EULA (COLLECTIVELY, THE "LICENSED CONTENT"), YOU AGREE TO THE TERMS OF THIS EULA. IF YOU DO NOT AGREE, DO NOT USE THE LICENSED CONTENT.

1.   **GENERAL.** This EULA is a legal agreement between you (either an individual or a single entity) and Microsoft Corporation ("Microsoft"). This EULA governs the Licensed Content, which includes computer software (including online and electronic documentation), training materials, and any other associated media and printed materials. This EULA applies to updates, supplements, add-on components, and Internet-based services components of the Licensed Content that Microsoft may provide or make available to you unless Microsoft provides other terms with the update, supplement, add-on component, or Internet-based services component. Microsoft reserves the right to discontinue any Internet-based services provided to you or made available to you through the use of the Licensed Content. This EULA also governs any product support services relating to the Licensed Content except as may be included in another agreement between you and Microsoft. An amendment or addendum to this EULA may accompany the Licensed Content.

2.   **GENERAL GRANT OF LICENSE.** Microsoft grants you the following rights, conditioned on your compliance with all the terms and conditions of this EULA. Microsoft grants you a limited, non-exclusive, royalty-free license to install and use the Licensed Content solely in conjunction with your participation as a student in an Authorized Training Session (as defined below). You may install and use one copy of the software on a single computer, device, workstation, terminal, or other digital electronic or analog device ("Device"). You may make a second copy of the software and install it on a portable Device for the exclusive use of the person who is the primary user of the first copy of the software. A license for the software may not be shared for use by multiple end users. An "Authorized Training Session" means a training session conducted at a Microsoft Certified Technical Education Center, an IT Academy, via a Microsoft Certified Partner, or such other entity as Microsoft may designate from time to time in writing, by a Microsoft Certified Trainer (for more information on these entities, please visit www.microsoft.com). WITHOUT LIMITING THE FOREGOING, COPYING OR REPRODUCTION OF THE LICENSED CONTENT TO ANY SERVER OR LOCATION FOR FURTHER REPRODUCTION OR REDISTRIBUTION IS EXPRESSLY PROHIBITED.

3.   **DESCRIPTION OF OTHER RIGHTS AND LICENSE LIMITATIONS**

    3.1   *Use of Documentation and Printed Training Materials.*

        3.1.1   The documents and related graphics included in the Licensed Content may include technical inaccuracies or typographical errors. Changes are periodically made to the content. Microsoft may make improvements and/or changes in any of the components of the Licensed Content at any time without notice. The names of companies, products, people, characters and/or data mentioned in the Licensed Content may be fictitious and are in no way intended to represent any real individual, company, product or event, unless otherwise noted.

        3.1.2   Microsoft grants you the right to reproduce portions of documents (such as student workbooks, white papers, press releases, datasheets and FAQs) (the "Documents") provided with the Licensed Content. You may not print any book (either electronic or print version) in its entirety. If you choose to reproduce Documents, you agree that: (a) use of such printed Documents will be solely in conjunction with your personal training use; (b) the Documents will not republished or posted on any network computer or broadcast in any media; (c) any reproduction will include either the Document's original copyright notice or a copyright notice to Microsoft's benefit substantially in the format provided below; and (d) to comply with all terms and conditions of this EULA. In addition, no modifications may made to any Document.

        Form of Notice:

        Copyright undefined.

        © 2004. Reprinted with permission by Microsoft Corporation. All rights reserved.

        Microsoft and Windows are either registered trademarks or trademarks of Microsoft Corporation in the US and/or other countries. Other product and company names mentioned herein may be the trademarks of their respective owners.

    3.2   *Use of Media Elements.* The Licensed Content may include certain photographs, clip art, animations, sounds, music, and video clips (together "Media Elements"). You may not modify these Media Elements.

    3.3   *Use of Sample Code.* In the event that the Licensed Content include sample source code ("Sample Code"), Microsoft grants you a limited, non-exclusive, royalty-free license to use, copy and modify the Sample Code; if you elect to exercise the foregoing rights, you agree to comply with all other terms and conditions of this EULA, including without limitation Sections 3.4, 3.5, and 6.

    3.4   *Permitted Modifications.* In the event that you exercise any rights provided under this EULA to create modifications of the Licensed Content, you agree that any such modifications: (a) will not be used for providing training where a fee is charged in public or private classes; (b) indemnify, hold harmless, and defend Microsoft from and against any claims or lawsuits, including attorneys' fees, which arise from or result from your use of any modified version of the Licensed Content; and (c) not to transfer or assign any rights to any modified version of the Licensed Content to any third party without the express written permission of Microsoft.

3.5   *Reproduction/Redistribution Licensed Content.* Except as expressly provided in this EULA, you may not reproduce or distribute the Licensed Content or any portion thereof (including any permitted modifications) to any third parties without the express written permission of Microsoft.

4.   **RESERVATION OF RIGHTS AND OWNERSHIP.** Microsoft reserves all rights not expressly granted to you in this EULA. The Licensed Content is protected by copyright and other intellectual property laws and treaties. Microsoft or its suppliers own the title, copyright, and other intellectual property rights in the Licensed Content. You may not remove or obscure any copyright, trademark or patent notices that appear on the Licensed Content, or any components thereof, as delivered to you. **The Licensed Content is licensed, not sold.**

5.   **LIMITATIONS ON REVERSE ENGINEERING, DECOMPILATION, AND DISASSEMBLY.** You may not reverse engineer, decompile, or disassemble the Software or Media Elements, except and only to the extent that such activity is expressly permitted by applicable law notwithstanding this limitation.

6.   **LIMITATIONS ON SALE, RENTAL, ETC. AND CERTAIN ASSIGNMENTS.** You may not provide commercial hosting services with, sell, rent, lease, lend, sublicense, or assign copies of the Licensed Content, or any portion thereof (including any permitted modifications thereof) on a stand-alone basis or as part of any collection, product or service.

7.   **CONSENT TO USE OF DATA.** You agree that Microsoft and its affiliates may collect and use technical information gathered as part of the product support services provided to you, if any, related to the Licensed Content. Microsoft may use this information solely to improve our products or to provide customized services or technologies to you and will not disclose this information in a form that personally identifies you.

8.   **LINKS TO THIRD PARTY SITES.** You may link to third party sites through the use of the Licensed Content. The third party sites are not under the control of Microsoft, and Microsoft is not responsible for the contents of any third party sites, any links contained in third party sites, or any changes or updates to third party sites. Microsoft is not responsible for webcasting or any other form of transmission received from any third party sites. Microsoft is providing these links to third party sites to you only as a convenience, and the inclusion of any link does not imply an endorsement by Microsoft of the third party site.

9.   **ADDITIONAL LICENSED CONTENT/SERVICES.** This EULA applies to updates, supplements, add-on components, or Internet-based services components, of the Licensed Content that Microsoft may provide to you or make available to you after the date you obtain your initial copy of the Licensed Content, unless we provide other terms along with the update, supplement, add-on component, or Internet-based services component. Microsoft reserves the right to discontinue any Internet-based services provided to you or made available to you through the use of the Licensed Content.

10.   **U.S. GOVERNMENT LICENSE RIGHTS**. All software provided to the U.S. Government pursuant to solicitations issued on or after December 1, 1995 is provided with the commercial license rights and restrictions described elsewhere herein. All software provided to the U.S. Government pursuant to solicitations issued prior to December 1, 1995 is provided with "Restricted Rights" as provided for in FAR, 48 CFR 52.227-14 (JUNE 1987) or DFAR, 48 CFR 252.227-7013 (OCT 1988), as applicable.

11.   **EXPORT RESTRICTIONS**. You acknowledge that the Licensed Content is subject to U.S. export jurisdiction. You agree to comply with all applicable international and national laws that apply to the Licensed Content, including the U.S. Export Administration Regulations, as well as end-user, end-use, and destination restrictions issued by U.S. and other governments. For additional information see <http://www.microsoft.com/exporting/>.

12.   **TRANSFER.** The initial user of the Licensed Content may make a one-time permanent transfer of this EULA and Licensed Content to another end user, provided the initial user retains no copies of the Licensed Content. The transfer may not be an indirect transfer, such as a consignment. Prior to the transfer, the end user receiving the Licensed Content must agree to all the EULA terms.

13.   **"NOT FOR RESALE" LICENSED CONTENT.** Licensed Content identified as "Not For Resale" or "NFR," may not be sold or otherwise transferred for value, or used for any purpose other than demonstration, test or evaluation.

14.   **TERMINATION.** Without prejudice to any other rights, Microsoft may terminate this EULA if you fail to comply with the terms and conditions of this EULA. In such event, you must destroy all copies of the Licensed Content and all of its component parts.

15.   <u>**DISCLAIMER OF WARRANTIES.**</u> **TO THE MAXIMUM EXTENT PERMITTED BY APPLICABLE LAW, MICROSOFT AND ITS SUPPLIERS PROVIDE THE LICENSED CONTENT AND SUPPORT SERVICES (IF ANY)** *AS IS AND WITH ALL FAULTS,* **AND MICROSOFT AND ITS SUPPLIERS HEREBY DISCLAIM ALL OTHER WARRANTIES AND CONDITIONS, WHETHER EXPRESS, IMPLIED OR STATUTORY, INCLUDING, BUT NOT LIMITED TO, ANY (IF ANY) IMPLIED WARRANTIES, DUTIES OR CONDITIONS OF MERCHANTABILITY, OF FITNESS FOR A PARTICULAR PURPOSE, OF RELIABILITY OR AVAILABILITY, OF ACCURACY OR COMPLETENESS OF RESPONSES, OF RESULTS, OF WORKMANLIKE EFFORT, OF LACK OF VIRUSES, AND OF LACK OF NEGLIGENCE, ALL WITH REGARD TO THE LICENSED CONTENT, AND THE PROVISION OF OR FAILURE TO PROVIDE SUPPORT OR OTHER SERVICES, INFORMATION, SOFTWARE, AND RELATED CONTENT THROUGH THE LICENSED CONTENT, OR OTHERWISE ARISING OUT OF THE USE OF THE LICENSED CONTENT. ALSO, THERE IS NO WARRANTY OR CONDITION OF TITLE, QUIET ENJOYMENT, QUIET POSSESSION, CORRESPONDENCE TO DESCRIPTION OR NON-INFRINGEMENT WITH REGARD TO THE LICENSED CONTENT. THE ENTIRE RISK AS TO THE QUALITY, OR ARISING OUT OF THE USE OR PERFORMANCE OF THE LICENSED CONTENT, AND ANY SUPPORT SERVICES, REMAINS WITH YOU.**

16.   <u>**EXCLUSION OF INCIDENTAL, CONSEQUENTIAL AND CERTAIN OTHER DAMAGES.**</u> **TO THE MAXIMUM EXTENT PERMITTED BY APPLICABLE LAW, IN NO EVENT SHALL MICROSOFT OR ITS SUPPLIERS BE LIABLE FOR ANY SPECIAL, INCIDENTAL, PUNITIVE, INDIRECT, OR CONSEQUENTIAL DAMAGES WHATSOEVER (INCLUDING, BUT NOT**

LIMITED TO, DAMAGES FOR LOSS OF PROFITS OR CONFIDENTIAL OR OTHER INFORMATION, FOR BUSINESS INTERRUPTION, FOR PERSONAL INJURY, FOR LOSS OF PRIVACY, FOR FAILURE TO MEET ANY DUTY INCLUDING OF GOOD FAITH OR OF REASONABLE CARE, FOR NEGLIGENCE, AND FOR ANY OTHER PECUNIARY OR OTHER LOSS WHATSOEVER) ARISING OUT OF OR IN ANY WAY RELATED TO THE USE OF OR INABILITY TO USE THE LICENSED CONTENT, THE PROVISION OF OR FAILURE TO PROVIDE SUPPORT OR OTHER SERVICES, INFORMATION, SOFTWARE, AND RELATED CONTENT THROUGH THE LICENSED CONTENT, OR OTHERWISE ARISING OUT OF THE USE OF THE LICENSED CONTENT, OR OTHERWISE UNDER OR IN CONNECTION WITH ANY PROVISION OF THIS EULA, EVEN IN THE EVENT OF THE FAULT, TORT (INCLUDING NEGLIGENCE), MISREPRESENTATION, STRICT LIABILITY, BREACH OF CONTRACT OR BREACH OF WARRANTY OF MICROSOFT OR ANY SUPPLIER, AND EVEN IF MICROSOFT OR ANY SUPPLIER HAS BEEN ADVISED OF THE POSSIBILITY OF SUCH DAMAGES. BECAUSE SOME STATES/JURISDICTIONS DO NOT ALLOW THE EXCLUSION OR LIMITATION OF LIABILITY FOR CONSEQUENTIAL OR INCIDENTAL DAMAGES, THE ABOVE LIMITATION MAY NOT APPLY TO YOU.

17.   LIMITATION OF LIABILITY AND REMEDIES. NOTWITHSTANDING ANY DAMAGES THAT YOU MIGHT INCUR FOR ANY REASON WHATSOEVER (INCLUDING, WITHOUT LIMITATION, ALL DAMAGES REFERENCED HEREIN AND ALL DIRECT OR GENERAL DAMAGES IN CONTRACT OR ANYTHING ELSE), THE ENTIRE LIABILITY OF MICROSOFT AND ANY OF ITS SUPPLIERS UNDER ANY PROVISION OF THIS EULA AND YOUR EXCLUSIVE REMEDY HEREUNDER SHALL BE LIMITED TO THE GREATER OF THE ACTUAL DAMAGES YOU INCUR IN REASONABLE RELIANCE ON THE LICENSED CONTENT UP TO THE AMOUNT ACTUALLY PAID BY YOU FOR THE LICENSED CONTENT OR US$5.00. THE FOREGOING LIMITATIONS, EXCLUSIONS AND DISCLAIMERS SHALL APPLY TO THE MAXIMUM EXTENT PERMITTED BY APPLICABLE LAW, EVEN IF ANY REMEDY FAILS ITS ESSENTIAL PURPOSE.

18.   APPLICABLE LAW. If you acquired this Licensed Content in the United States, this EULA is governed by the laws of the State of Washington. If you acquired this Licensed Content in Canada, unless expressly prohibited by local law, this EULA is governed by the laws in force in the Province of Ontario, Canada; and, in respect of any dispute which may arise hereunder, you consent to the jurisdiction of the federal and provincial courts sitting in Toronto, Ontario. If you acquired this Licensed Content in the European Union, Iceland, Norway, or Switzerland, then local law applies. If you acquired this Licensed Content in any other country, then local law may apply.

19.   ENTIRE AGREEMENT; SEVERABILITY. This EULA (including any addendum or amendment to this EULA which is included with the Licensed Content) are the entire agreement between you and Microsoft relating to the Licensed Content and the support services (if any) and they supersede all prior or contemporaneous oral or written communications, proposals and representations with respect to the Licensed Content or any other subject matter covered by this EULA. To the extent the terms of any Microsoft policies or programs for support services conflict with the terms of this EULA, the terms of this EULA shall control. If any provision of this EULA is held to be void, invalid, unenforceable or illegal, the other provisions shall continue in full force and effect.

Should you have any questions concerning this EULA, or if you desire to contact Microsoft for any reason, please use the address information enclosed in this Licensed Content to contact the Microsoft subsidiary serving your country or visit Microsoft on the World Wide Web at http://www.microsoft.com.

Si vous avez acquis votre Contenu Sous Licence Microsoft au CANADA :

DÉNI DE GARANTIES. Dans la mesure maximale permise par les lois applicables, le Contenu Sous Licence et les services de soutien technique (le cas échéant) sont fournis *TELS QUELS ET AVEC TOUS LES DÉFAUTS* par Microsoft et ses fournisseurs, lesquels par les présentes dénient toutes autres garanties et conditions expresses, implicites ou en vertu de la loi, notamment, mais sans limitation, (le cas échéant) les garanties, devoirs ou conditions implicites de qualité marchande, d'adaptation à une fin usage particulière, de fiabilité ou de disponibilité, d'exactitude ou d'exhaustivité des réponses, des résultats, des efforts déployés selon les règles de l'art, d'absence de virus et d'absence de négligence, le tout à l'égard du Contenu Sous Licence et de la prestation des services de soutien technique ou de l'omission de la 'une telle prestation des services de soutien technique ou à l'égard de la fourniture ou de l'omission de la fourniture de tous autres services, renseignements, Contenus Sous Licence, et contenu qui s'y rapporte grâce au Contenu Sous Licence ou provenant autrement de l'utilisation du Contenu Sous Licence. PAR AILLEURS, IL N'Y A AUCUNE GARANTIE OU CONDITION QUANT AU TITRE DE PROPRIÉTÉ, À LA JOUISSANCE OU LA POSSESSION PAISIBLE, À LA CONCORDANCE À UNE DESCRIPTION NI QUANT À UNE ABSENCE DE CONTREFAÇON CONCERNANT LE CONTENU SOUS LICENCE.

EXCLUSION DES DOMMAGES ACCESSOIRES, INDIRECTS ET DE CERTAINS AUTRES DOMMAGES. DANS LA MESURE MAXIMALE PERMISE PAR LES LOIS APPLICABLES, EN AUCUN CAS MICROSOFT OU SES FOURNISSEURS NE SERONT RESPONSABLES DES DOMMAGES SPÉCIAUX, CONSÉCUTIFS, ACCESSOIRES OU INDIRECTS DE QUELQUE NATURE QUE CE SOIT (NOTAMMENT, LES DOMMAGES À L'ÉGARD DU MANQUE À GAGNER OU DE LA DIVULGATION DE RENSEIGNEMENTS CONFIDENTIELS OU AUTRES, DE LA PERTE D'EXPLOITATION, DE BLESSURES CORPORELLES, DE LA VIOLATION DE LA VIE PRIVÉE, DE L'OMISSION DE REMPLIR TOUT DEVOIR, Y COMPRIS D'AGIR DE BONNE FOI OU D'EXERCER UN SOIN RAISONNABLE, DE LA NÉGLIGENCE ET DE TOUTE AUTRE PERTE PÉCUNIAIRE OU AUTRE PERTE

DE QUELQUE NATURE QUE CE SOIT) SE RAPPORTANT DE QUELQUE MANIÈRE QUE CE SOIT À L'UTILISATION DU CONTENU SOUS LICENCE OU À L'INCAPACITÉ DE S'EN SERVIR, À LA PRESTATION OU À L'OMISSION DE LA 'UNE TELLE PRESTATION DE SERVICES DE SOUTIEN TECHNIQUE OU À LA FOURNITURE OU À L'OMISSION DE LA FOURNITURE DE TOUS AUTRES SERVICES, RENSEIGNEMENTS, CONTENUS SOUS LICENCE, ET CONTENU QUI S'Y RAPPORTE GRÂCE AU CONTENU SOUS LICENCE OU PROVENANT AUTREMENT DE L'UTILISATION DU CONTENU SOUS LICENCE OU AUTREMENT AUX TERMES DE TOUTE DISPOSITION DE LA U PRÉSENTE CONVENTION EULA OU RELATIVEMENT À UNE TELLE DISPOSITION, MÊME EN CAS DE FAUTE, DE DÉLIT CIVIL (Y COMPRIS LA NÉGLIGENCE), DE RESPONSABILITÉ STRICTE, DE VIOLATION DE CONTRAT OU DE VIOLATION DE GARANTIE DE MICROSOFT OU DE TOUT FOURNISSEUR ET MÊME SI MICROSOFT OU TOUT FOURNISSEUR A ÉTÉ AVISÉ DE LA POSSIBILITÉ DE TELS DOMMAGES.

LIMITATION DE RESPONSABILITÉ ET RECOURS. MALGRÉ LES DOMMAGES QUE VOUS PUISSIEZ SUBIR POUR QUELQUE MOTIF QUE CE SOIT (NOTAMMENT, MAIS SANS LIMITATION, TOUS LES DOMMAGES SUSMENTIONNÉS ET TOUS LES DOMMAGES DIRECTS OU GÉNÉRAUX OU AUTRES), LA SEULE RESPONSABILITÉ 'OBLIGATION INTÉGRALE DE MICROSOFT ET DE L'UN OU L'AUTRE DE SES FOURNISSEURS AUX TERMES DE TOUTE DISPOSITION DEU LA PRÉSENTE CONVENTION EULA ET VOTRE RECOURS EXCLUSIF À L'ÉGARD DE TOUT CE QUI PRÉCÈDE SE LIMITE AU PLUS ÉLEVÉ ENTRE LES MONTANTS SUIVANTS : LE MONTANT QUE VOUS AVEZ RÉELLEMENT PAYÉ POUR LE CONTENU SOUS LICENCE OU 5,00 $US. LES LIMITES, EXCLUSIONS ET DÉNIS QUI PRÉCÈDENT (Y COMPRIS LES CLAUSES CI-DESSUS), S'APPLIQUENT DANS LA MESURE MAXIMALE PERMISE PAR LES LOIS APPLICABLES, MÊME SI TOUT RECOURS N'ATTEINT PAS SON BUT ESSENTIEL.

À moins que cela ne soit prohibé par le droit local applicable, la présente Convention est régie par les lois de la province d'Ontario, Canada. Vous consentez Chacune des parties à la présente reconnaît irrévocablement à la compétence des tribunaux fédéraux et provinciaux siégeant à Toronto, dans de la province d'Ontario et consent à instituer tout litige qui pourrait découler de la présente auprès des tribunaux situés dans le district judiciaire de York, province d'Ontario.

Au cas où vous auriez des questions concernant cette licence ou que vous désiriez vous mettre en rapport avec Microsoft pour quelque raison que ce soit, veuillez utiliser l'information contenue dans le Contenu Sous Licence pour contacter la filiale de succursale Microsoft desservant votre pays, dont l'adresse est fournie dans ce produit, ou visitez écrivez à : Microsoft sur le World Wide Web à http://www.microsoft.com

Contents

About This Course

This section provides you with a brief description of the course and its audience, suggested prerequisites, and objectives.

Description

This two-day instructor-led course provides students with the knowledge and skills to develop and deploy reporting solutions using Microsoft® SQL Server™ 2000 Reporting Services. The course focuses on Reporting Services architecture, report development and enhancement, data retrieval using SQL Server 2000, and the administration of a report server.

This course is provided in conjunction with the released version of Microsoft SQL Server Reporting Services.

Audience

This course is intended for database administrators and developers who have SQL Server 2000 experience and have developed simple applications using Microsoft Visual Studio® .NET. Students should have some experience using reporting tools, such as Crystal Reports.

Student prerequisites

This course requires that students meet the following prerequisites:

- Some exposure to the Visual Studio .NET environment. This includes being able to:
  - Navigate the Visual Studio .NET development environment.
  - Build a simple project.
  - Create simple Web or Microsoft Windows® forms.
  - Use SQL Server as a data source.
- Exposure to creating reports in Microsoft Access or other third-party reporting products, such as Crystal Reports
- Conceptual understanding of the push and pull distribution/subscription paradigm
- Experience navigating the Microsoft Windows Server™ environment
- Experience with Windows services (starting and stopping)
- Experience creating service accounts and permissions
- Experience with SQL Server, including:
  - SQL Server Agent
  - SQL Server query language (SELECT, UPDATE, INSERT, and DELETE)
  - SQL Server System tables
  - SQL Server accounts (users and permissions)

Course objectives   After completing this course, students will be able to:

- Describe the key features of Reporting Services.
- Use Visual Studio .NET to develop and deploy reports through the Report Designer.
- Understand deployment scenarios and architecture.
- Use Report Definition Language (RDL).
- Query a SQL Server 2000 database.
- Create simple reports, including:
    - Add controls and data regions to a report, including Table, Chart, List, and Matrix data regions and subreports.
    - Add expressions and aggregates to a report.
    - Add interactive controls to aid navigation and to provide drill-through functionality between reports and drill-down functionality from summary to detail data.
    - Structure and format reports.
    - Use report and query parameters.
    - Use filters.
- Publish reports to a report server.
- Execute reports on demand.
- Create cached report instances.
- Create snapshot reports.
- Deliver reports using the publish/subscribe model.
- Use configuration files to administer the report server.
- Monitor the performance and reliability of the report server.
- Administer the ReportServer and ReportServerTempDB databases.
- Administer the Reporting Services security model.
- Automate report management tasks.
- Render reports programmatically using the Report Server Web Service.
- Create custom code and call custom functionality from reports.

Student Materials Compact Disc Contents

The Student Materials compact disc contains the following files and folders:

- *Autorun.inf.* When the compact disc is inserted into the compact disc drive, this file opens StartCD.exe.

- *Default.htm.* This file opens the Student Materials Web page. It provides you with resources pertaining to this course, including additional reading, review and lab answers, lab files, multimedia presentations, and course-related Web sites.

- *Readme.txt.* This file explains how to install the software for viewing the Student Materials compact disc and its contents and how to open the Student Materials Web page.

- *StartCD.exe.* When the compact disc is inserted into the compact disc drive, or when you double-click the StartCD.exe file, this file opens the compact disc and allows you to browse the Student Materials or Trainer Materials compact disc.

- *StartCD.ini.* This file contains instructions to launch StartCD.exe.

- *Democode.* This folder contains demonstration code.

- *Fonts.* This folder contains fonts that may be required to view the Microsoft Word documents that are included with this course.

- *Labfiles.* This folder contains files that are used in the hands-on labs. These files are used to prepare the student computers for the hands-on labs.

- *Mplayer.* This folder contains the setup file to install Microsoft Windows Media® Player.

- *Practices.* This folder contains files that are used in the hands-on practices.

- *Setup.* This folder contains the lab database files required to complete this course.

- *Webfiles.* This folder contains the files that are required to view the course Web page. To open the Web page, open Windows Explorer, and in the root directory of the compact disc, double-click **StartCD.exe**.

- *Wordview.* This folder contains the Word Viewer that is used to view any Word document (.doc) files that are included on the compact disc.

Document Conventions

The following conventions are used in course materials to distinguish elements of the text.

Convention	Use
Bold	Represents commands, command options, and syntax that must be typed exactly as shown. Bold also indicates commands on menus and buttons, dialog box titles and options, and icon and menu names.
Italic	In syntax statements or descriptive text, indicates argument names or placeholders for variable information. Italic is also used for introducing new terms, for book and course titles, and for emphasis in the text.
Title Capitals	Indicate domain names, user names, computer names, directory names, and folder and file names, except when specifically referring to case-sensitive names. Unless otherwise indicated, you can use lowercase letters when you type a directory name or file name in a dialog box or at a command prompt.
ALL CAPITALS	Indicate the names of keys, key sequences, and key combinations—for example, ALT+SPACEBAR
`monospace`	Represents code samples or examples of on-screen text
[ ]	In syntax statements, enclose optional items. For example, [*filename*] in command syntax indicates that you can choose to type a file name with the command. Type only the information within the brackets, not the brackets themselves.
{ }	In syntax statements, enclose required items. Type only the information within the braces, not the braces themselves.
|	In syntax statements, separates an either/or choice
▶	Indicates a procedure with sequential steps
...	In syntax statements, specifies that the preceding item may be repeated
.	Represents an omitted portion of a code sample

Introduction

Contents

Introduction

- Name
- Company affiliation
- Title/function
- Job responsibility
- Report design experience
- Database design and administration experience
- Expectations for the course

Course Materials

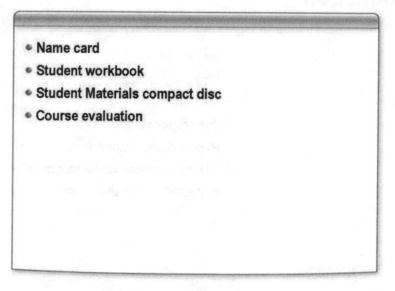

The following materials are included in your kit:

- *Name card.* Write your name on both sides of the name card.

- *Student workbook.* The student workbook contains the material covered in class, including the hands-on lab exercises.

- *Student Materials compact disc.* The Student Materials compact disc contains a Web page that provides you with links to resources pertaining to this course, including additional readings, review and lab exercise answers, lab files, multimedia presentations, and course-related Web sites.

Note   To open the Web page, insert the Student Materials compact disc into the CD-ROM drive, and then in the root directory of the compact disc, double-click **Start.exe**.

- *Course evaluation.* You will have the opportunity to provide feedback on the course, training facility, and instructor by completing an online evaluation near the end of the course.

To submit additional comments or inquire about the Microsoft® Certified Professional program, e-mail mcphelp@microsoft.com.

Prerequisites

- Exposure to the Visual Studio .NET environment
- Experience creating reports in Microsoft Access or other products, such as Crystal Reports
- Conceptual understanding of the push and pull distribution/subscription paradigm
- Experience with Windows services (starting and stopping)
- Experience creating service accounts and permissions
- Experience with Microsoft SQL Server

This course requires that you meet the following prerequisites:

- Some exposure to the Microsoft Visual Studio® .NET environment. You should be able to:
  - Navigate the Visual Studio .NET development environment
  - Build a simple project
  - Create simple Web or Microsoft Windows® forms
  - Use SQL Server as a data source
- Exposure to creating reports in Microsoft Access or other third-party reporting products, such as Crystal Reports
- Conceptual understanding of the push and pull distribution/subscription paradigm
- Experience navigating the Microsoft Windows Server™ environment
- Experience with Windows services (starting and stopping)
- Experience creating service accounts and permissions
- Experience with Microsoft SQL Server™, including:
  - SQL Server Agent
  - SQL Server query language (SELECT, UPDATE, INSERT, and DELETE)
  - SQL Server System tables
  - SQL Server accounts (users and permissions)

Course Outline

- **Module 1: Introduction to Microsoft SQL Server Reporting Services**
- **Module 2: Authoring Basic Reports**
- **Module 3: Enhancing Basic Reports**
- **Module 4: Manipulating Data Sets**
- **Module 5: Managing Content**
- **Module 6: Administering Reporting Services**
- **Module 7: Programming Reporting Services**

Module 1, "Introduction to Microsoft SQL Server Reporting Services," introduces the role that Reporting Services plays in an organization's reporting life cycle, the key features offered by Reporting Services, and the components that make up the Reporting Services architecture. After completing this module, you will be able to describe the scenarios in which Reporting Services can be used.

Module 2, "Authoring Basic Reports," introduces the fundamentals of report authoring, including configuring data sources and data sets, creating tabular reports, summarizing data, and applying basic formatting. After completing this module, you will be able to create a basic report.

Module 3, "Enhancing Basic Reports," introduces navigational controls and some additional types of data regions and discusses how to use them to enhance a basic report. After completing this module, you will be able to create interactive navigation using report links and display data using data regions.

Module 4, "Manipulating Data Sets," explores data sets to a greater depth, including the use of alternative data sources and interacting with a data set through the use of parameters. You will learn how to dynamically modify the data set underlying a data region by allowing parameters to be sent to the underlying query, as well as learn to use best practices to deal with static and dynamic parameter lists when interacting with queries and stored procedures. After completing this module, you will be able to describe the features of a data set.

Module 5, "Managing Content," explains how to manage content stored in the report server database. After completing this module, you will be able to publish content to the report server.

Module 6, "Administering Reporting Services," discusses how to administer the Reporting Services server, how to monitor and optimize the performance of the report server, how to maintain the Reporting Services databases, and how to keep the system secure. After completing this module, you will be able to administer a report server.

Module 7, "Programming Reporting Services," explains how to query Reporting Services information programmatically and how to automate your report management tasks. You will also learn how to render reports without relying on Report Manager. Finally, you will learn how creating custom code can extend the feature set of your report server. After completing this module, you will be able to retrieve information about the report server programmatically.

Initial Logon Procedure

- Passwords in Microsoft Official Courses must be complex
- Log in as Administrator
- Password is P@ssw0rd

Complex passwords

To meet the complexity requirements for the password that you will use in this course, you must include characters in your password from at least three of the following four categories:

- Uppercase letters (A to Z)
- Lowercase letters (a to z)
- Numbers (0 to 9)
- Symbols (! @ # $)

You must log in as **Administrator** to perform labs and demonstrations.

Tasks

▶ **Log in to your account**

1. Press **CTRL+ALT+DEL** to open the **Log On to Windows** dialog box.
2. In the **Username** text box, type **Administrator**.
3. In the **Password** text box, type **P@ssw0rd**.

Microsoft Learning

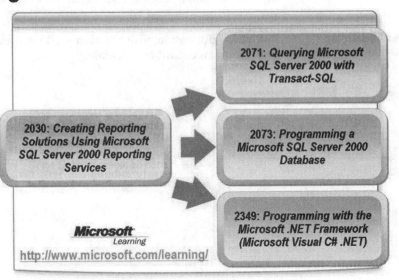

Microsoft Learning develops Official Microsoft Learning Products for computer professionals who design, develop, support, implement, or manage solutions by using Microsoft products and

After taking Course 2030, *Creating Reporting Solutions Using Microsoft SQL Server 2000 Reporting Services*, you can take the following courses in any order:

- 2071, *Querying Microsoft SQL Server 2000 with Transact-SQL*

- 2073, *Programming a Microsoft SQL Server 2000 Database*

- 2349, *Programming with the Microsoft .NET Framework (Microsoft Visual C# .NET)*

> **Note**   Course 2415, *Programming with the Microsoft .NET Framework (Microsoft Visual Basic .NET)*, is the Visual Basic version of Course 2349.

Course	Title and description
2071	*Querying Microsoft SQL Server 2000 with Transact-SQL* Updated, two-day, instructor-led course teaches the technical skills required to write basic Transact-SQL queries for Microsoft SQL Server 2000
2073	*Programming a Microsoft SQL Server 2000 Database* This course provides students with the technical skills required to program a database solution by using Microsoft SQL Server 2000
2349	*Programming with the Microsoft .NET Framework (Microsoft Visual C# .NET)* This course provides a hands-on tour of the Microsoft .NET Framework for C# developers. An overview of key concepts is followed by an in-depth tutorial on areas including the common type system, base class libraries, assemblies, delegates, and events.

Other related courses may become available in the future, so for up-to-date information about recommended courses, visit the Microsoft Learning Web site.

Microsoft Learning information

For more information, visit the Microsoft Learning Web site at http://www.microsoft.com/learning/.

Microsoft Learning Product Types

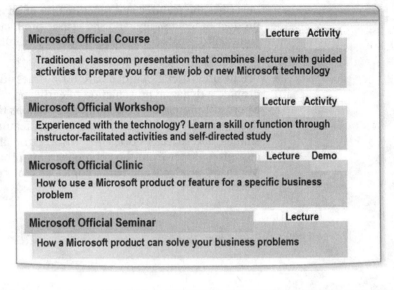

Microsoft Learning offers four instructor-led product types. Each type is specific to a particular audience type and level of experience. The different product types also tend to suit different learning styles. These types are as follows:

- Microsoft Official Courses are for information technology (IT) professionals and developers who are new to a particular product or technology and for experienced individuals who prefer to learn in a traditional classroom format. Courses provide a relevant and guided learning experience that combines lecture and practice to deliver thorough coverage of a Microsoft product or technology. Courses are designed to address the needs of learners engaged in planning, design, implementation, management, and support phases of the technology adoption lifecycle. They provide detailed information by focusing on concepts and principles, reference content, and in-depth hands-on lab activities to ensure knowledge transfer. Typically, the content of a course is broad, addressing a wide range of tasks necessary for the job role.

- Microsoft Official Workshops are for knowledgeable IT professionals and developers who learn best by doing and exploring. Workshops provide a hands-on learning experience by using Microsoft products in a safe and collaborative environment based on real-world scenarios.

- Workshops are the learning products where students learn by doing through scenario and troubleshooting hands-on labs, targeted reviews, information resources, and best practices, with instructor facilitation.

- Microsoft Official Clinics are for IT professionals, developers and technical decision makers. Clinics offer a detailed "how to" presentation that describes the features and functionality of an existing or new Microsoft product or technology, and showcases product demonstrations and solutions. Clinics focus on how specific features will solve business problems.

- Microsoft Official Seminars are for business decision makers. Seminars provide a dynamic presentation of early and relevant information on Microsoft products and technology solutions that enable decision makers to make critical business decisions through featured business scenarios, case studies, and success stories. Microsoft Official Seminars are concise, engaging, direct-from-the-source learning products that show how emerging Microsoft products and technologies help our customers serve their customers.

Microsoft Certified Professional Program

Microsoft Learning offers a variety of certification credentials for developers and IT professionals. The Microsoft Certified Professional program is the leading certification program for validating your experience and skills, keeping you competitive in today's changing business environment.

MCP certifications

The Microsoft Certified Professional program includes the following certifications.

- MCSA on Microsoft Windows Server™ 2003

  The Microsoft Certified Systems Administrator (MCSA) certification is designed for professionals who implement, manage, and troubleshoot existing network and system environments based on the Windows Server 2003 platform. Implementation responsibilities include installing and configuring parts of the systems. Management responsibilities include administering and supporting the systems.

- MCSE on Microsoft Windows Server 2003

  The Microsoft Certified Systems Engineer (MCSE) credential is the premier certification for professionals who analyze the business requirements and design and implement the infrastructure for business solutions based on the Windows Server 2003 platform. Implementation responsibilities include installing, configuring, and troubleshooting network systems.

- MCAD

  The Microsoft Certified Application Developer (MCAD) for Microsoft .NET credential is appropriate for professionals who use Microsoft technologies to develop and maintain department-level applications, components, Web or desktop clients, or back-end data services or work in teams developing enterprise applications. The credential covers job tasks ranging from developing to deploying and maintaining these solutions.

- MCSD

  The Microsoft Certified Solution Developer (MCSD) credential is the premier certification for professionals who design and develop leading-edge business solutions with Microsoft development tools, technologies, platforms, and the Microsoft Windows DNA architecture. The types of applications MCSDs can develop include desktop applications and multi-user, Web-based, N-tier, and transaction-based applications. The credential covers job tasks ranging from analyzing business requirements to maintaining solutions.

- MCDBA on Microsoft SQL Server™ 2000

  The Microsoft Certified Database Administrator (MCDBA) credential is the premier certification for professionals who implement and administer Microsoft SQL Server databases. The certification is appropriate for individuals who derive physical database designs, develop logical data models, create physical databases, create data services by using Transact-SQL, manage and maintain databases, configure and manage security, monitor and optimize databases, and install and configure SQL Server.

- MCP

  The Microsoft Certified Professional (MCP) credential is for individuals who have the skills to successfully implement a Microsoft product or technology as part of a business solution in an organization. Hands-on experience with the product is necessary to successfully achieve certification.

- MCT

  Microsoft Certified Trainers (MCTs) demonstrate the instructional and technical skills that qualify them to deliver Official Microsoft Learning Products through Microsoft Certified Technical Education Centers (Microsoft CTECs).

Certification requirements

The certification requirements differ for each certification category and are specific to the products and job functions addressed by the certification. To become a Microsoft Certified Professional, you must pass rigorous certification exams that provide a valid and reliable measure of technical proficiency and expertise.

For More Information See the Microsoft Learning Web site at http://www.microsoft.com/learning/.

You can also send e-mail to mcphelp@microsoft.com if you have specific certification questions.

Acquiring the skills tested by an MCP exam

Official Microsoft Learning Products can help you develop the skills that you need to do your job. They also complement the experience that you gain while working with Microsoft products and technologies. However, no one-to-one correlation exists between Official Microsoft Learning Products and MCP exams. Microsoft does not expect or intend for the courses to be the sole preparation method for passing MCP exams. Practical product knowledge and experience is also necessary to pass the MCP exams.

To help prepare for the MCP exams, use the preparation guides that are available for each exam. Each Exam Preparation Guide contains exam-specific information, such as a list of the topics on which you will be tested. These guides are available on the Microsoft Learning Web site at http://www.microsoft.com/learning/.

Facilities

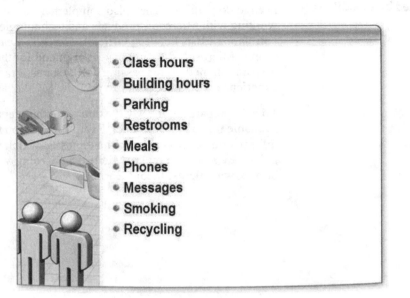

- Class hours
- Building hours
- Parking
- Restrooms
- Meals
- Phones
- Messages
- Smoking
- Recycling

Microsoft®

Module 1: Introduction to Microsoft SQL Server Reporting Services

Contents

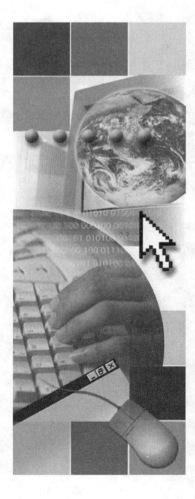

Overview

- Overview of Microsoft SQL Server Reporting Services
- Tour of Reporting Services
- Overview of Reporting Services Architecture

Introduction

Microsoft® SQL Server™ 2000 Reporting Services extends the Microsoft Business Intelligence (BI) vision by providing a comprehensive, server-based reporting platform. Reporting Services provides a report repository (Report Server), a report authoring tool (Report Designer), and centralized management (Report Manager). Authoring and management services are made available as Web services.

Report developers can author reports using the Report Designer, accessible through Visual Studio® .NET 2003 or any third- party tool that supports Report Definition Language (RDL). Reports are published and managed on the report server through a Web service. Execution of reports can occur either on demand or on a specified schedule, and the reports can be cached for consistency and performance.

Reporting services supports a wide-range of data sources and output formats. Integration with Web services means that organizations can leverage existing information sources, such as mainframe or custom applications.

In this module, you will learn about the role Reporting Services plays in an organization's reporting life cycle, the key features offered by Reporting Services, and the components that make up the Reporting Services architecture.

Objectives

After completing this module, you will be able to:

- Describe the scenarios in which Reporting Services can be used.
- Describe the process of scheduling a report.
- Describe the architecture of Reporting Services.

Lesson: Overview of Microsoft SQL Server Reporting Services

- The Reporting Life Cycle
- Highlights of Reporting Services
- Reporting Services Scenarios

Introduction

Many organizations struggle with gathering and analyzing data within a heterogeneous enterprise environment. Reporting Services provides a coherent platform for the authoring, management, and delivery of reports within an organization and across multiple organizations.

This lesson introduces the role of Reporting Services in an organization's reporting life cycle and highlights the key features of the technology.

Lesson objectives

After completing this lesson, you will be able to:

- Describe the reporting life cycle.
- Describe the key features of Reporting Services.
- Describe the scenarios in which Reporting Services can be used.

The Reporting Life Cycle

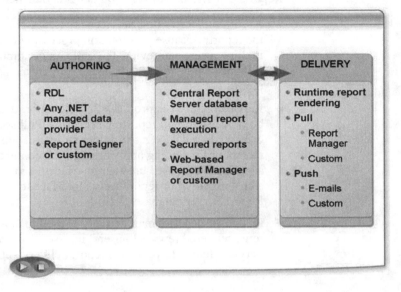

The analysis and presentation of information is critical to informing decision making at all levels of an organization. The process of report creation, administration, and dissemination (known collectively as the *reporting life cycle*) can be broken down into three stages: authoring, management, and delivery. These stages might be performed by different people within the organization. Reporting Services provides a single platform that supports the reporting lifecycle:

Authoring

In the authoring stage, the report author defines the report data and presentation:

- Reporting Services uses RDL to provide an Extensible Markup Language (XML) representation of the report definition. RDL defines a common schema to promote the interchange of report definitions.

- Reporting Services uses ADO.NET-managed data providers to access OLE DB, open database connectivity (ODBC), and XMLA (XML for Analysis) data sources.

- Report Designer is the supplied design tool for Reporting Services. Report Designer is integrated with the Visual Studio .NET 2003 development environment.

Management

In the management stage, the author publishes the report to a central location where the report manager can administer its security and execution schedule:

- Reporting Services uses the central Report Server database for report storage, public consumption, and report sharing.

- After the reports are published to the Report Server database, Reporting Services allows an execution schedule to be established and security options to be set.

- Report Manager is the supplied Web-based content management tool for administering reports. You can also use a custom or third-party management tool.

Delivery

In the delivery stage, reports can be made available in a number of formats. Reports can also be delivered on demand or scheduled based on an event:

- At runtime, Reporting Services processes or renders the presentation style of the report. Because presentation processing occurs after data is retrieved, multiple users can review the same report simultaneously in formats designed for different devices, or quickly change the viewing format of the report.

- Reporting Services provides flexible report delivery mechanisms to support both push and pull reporting scenarios. Pull scenarios typically involve browser-based access to a folder structure, which provides a familiar metaphor for finding and working with content. Report Manager is the supplied Web-based browser interface for viewing reports. You can also use a custom portal or report access interface to access reports stored in the Report Server database.

- In a push scenario, mail delivery is used to automate report processing and route rendered reports to users' inboxes. You can also extend Reporting Services to create your own report delivery vehicles.

Highlights of Reporting Services

- **Authoring**
  - Wide range of supported data sources
  - Open report authoring options
  - Flexible report designs
- **Management**
  - Parameterized reports
  - Execution properties
  - Report scheduling and history
  - Role-based security
- **Delivery**
  - Range of rendering options
  - Flexible and extensible delivery

Introduction

As a component of SQL Server 2000, Reporting Services provides a number of key features. In this module, you will explore some of those features in the context of the reporting life cycle.

In the authoring stage of the reporting life cycle, Reporting Services supports the following important features and functionality:

Authoring

- Reporting Services uses ADO.NET-managed data providers to access OLE DB, ODBC, and XMLA data sources.

- RDL can be created by using the Report Designer within the Visual Studio .NET 2003 development environment or by using third-party tools.

- Data regions provide a wide range of formatting options during report design. Supported data regions include Matrix, Table, List, and Chart. Further flexibility can be gained through the use of drill-through, where the user can navigate to hidden, detailed information, and the linking of reports.

Management

In the management stage of the reporting life cycle, Reporting Services supports following important features and functionality:

- Reports are published to the Report Server. Report Manager is used to configure report settings once a report has been published. Parameterized reports allow users to specify values such as month or salesperson to generate specific reports, or they can use default values provided by in reports.

- The execution properties of a report can be configured to be on-demand, multiuser shared cache, or snapshots.

- Report scheduling is integrated with SQL Server Agent. The Report History feature maintains an archive of copies of processed reports.

- Role-based security allows security to be tailored to individual users. Administrators can delegate content management functions for different reports to specific individuals.

Delivery

In the delivery stage of the reporting life cycle, Reporting Services supports the following important features and functionality:

- Reporting Services supplies the following formats for rendering a report:
  - Web formats (HTML)
  - Print formats (PDF, TIFF)
  - Data Formats (Microsoft Excel, XML, CSV)

  Additionally, Reporting Services provides an open application programming interface (API) to extend the rendering options.

- Reporting Services supports scheduled or event-driven delivery mechanisms. The Subscription feature allows individual users to subscribe to receive a particular report, such as updated reports when the report data has been updated (data-driven). Reports can be delivered as rendered reports or as URLs.

Reporting Services Scenarios

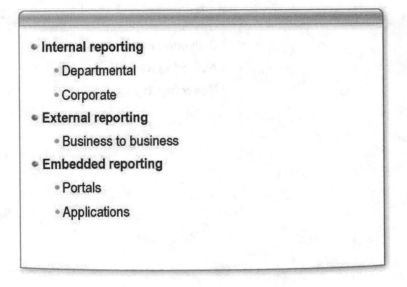

- Internal reporting
  - Departmental
  - Corporate
- External reporting
  - Business to business
- Embedded reporting
  - Portals
  - Applications

Introduction

Reporting Services can be used to support multiple scenarios that include an organization's internal and external business reporting needs.

Internal reporting

Internal reporting typically supports the reporting needs of departments within your organization. Order detail reports for the Customer Support department, financial statements for the Finance department, and salesperson performance for the Sales department are all examples of internal reporting scenarios.

External reporting

External reporting supports the business-to-business exchange of information by allowing users to access reports via extranet connections. Customer invoices and shareholder reports are both examples of external reporting scenarios.

Embedded reporting

Embedded reporting provides report integration for portals and applications. It can apply to corporate IT or to third-party applications. Embedded reports in corporate portals and in line-of-business applications, such as customer relations management (CRM) or manufacturing control systems, are an example of embedded reporting scenarios.

Lesson: Tour of Reporting Services

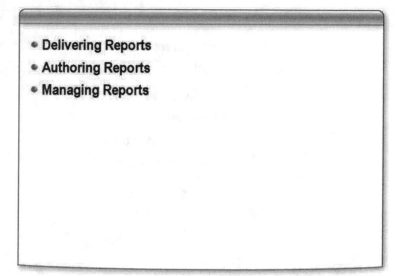

- Delivering Reports
- Authoring Reports
- Managing Reports

Introduction

This lesson takes a practical approach to exploring the functionality provided by Reporting Services in supporting the reporting life cycle.

In this lesson, you will learn how to render a pre-existing report in a number of formats, author a report, and change the execution properties of a report in order to make it a snapshot report.

Lesson objectives

After completing this lesson, you will be able to:

- Describe the process of report delivery.
- Describe the authoring process.
- Describe the process of managing reports.

Delivering Reports

> - **Runtime rendering**
>   - Web – HTML, MHTML
>   - Print – PDF, TIFF
>   - Data – CSV, Excel, XML
> - **Pull delivery – User issues report request**
>   - Report Manager
>   - Custom
> - **Push delivery – Report is automatically distributed to user**
>   - E-mail
>   - File
>   - Custom

Introduction

Reporting Services allows a user to alter the rendering format of a report at runtime. Therefore, a single report can have multiple representations and formats.

Delivery of reports can be achieved using a pull or push delivery mechanism.

Runtime rendering

At runtime, Reporting Services processes, or renders, the presentation style of the report. Because presentation processing occurs after the data is retrieved, multiple users can review the same report simultaneously in formats designed for different devices, or quickly change the viewing format of the report. Reporting Services supports the following formats:

- Web formats, such as Hypertext Markup Language (HTML) and Multipurpose Internet Mail Extensions (MIME)–encapsulated HTML (MHTML)

- Print formats, such as Portable Document Format (PDF)

- Data formats, such as comma separated values (CSV)

Pull delivery

Reporting Services provides flexible report delivery mechanisms to support both push and pull reporting scenarios. Pull scenarios typically involve browser-based access to a folder structure, which provides a familiar metaphor for finding and working with content. Report Manager is a Web-based browser interface for viewing reports. You can also use a custom portal or report access interface to access reports stored in the Report Server database.

Push delivery

Reporting Services provides various mechanisms for push delivery of reports. For example, mail delivery provides a mechanism to automate report processing and route rendered reports to user inboxes. You can also extend Reporting Services to create your own report delivery vehicles.

Demonstration: Delivering a Report

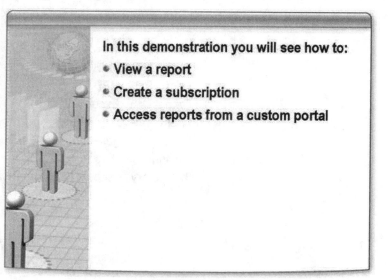

Introduction

In this demonstration, you will see how to use Report Manager to view and render reports, create a subscription, and access reports from a custom portal site.

A number of reports relating to the company Adventure Works have already been deployed. These reports will form the basis for the demonstration.

Procedures

▶ **Launch the Report Manager**

1. Click **Start**, point to **All Programs**, and then click **Internet Explorer**.

2. Go to **http://localhost/Reports**.

   The home page for Report Manager is displayed.

▶ **View the Sales Summary Report**

1. Click the **Example Reports** folder link.

   Note that the Example Reports folder contains eight reports:

   - Actual Vs Quota
   - Employee Product Sales
   - Order Details
   - Product Catalog
   - Product Detail
   - Product Profitability
   - Reseller Sales
   - Sales Summary

   Note that the folder also contains two shared data sources:

   - AdventureWorks
   - AdventureWorksDW

2. Click the **Sales Summary** report link.

3. Browse the report. Note that it is a tabular report that displays yearly sales data organized by employee, sales territory country, and sales territory group. Also note that each calendar year starts a new page of the report and that totals are displayed per Sales Territory Country and per Sales Territory Group.

4. In the HTML viewer toolbar, navigate through the report by clicking the **Next Page** icon.

5. In the **Page Number** text box, type **3** and then press **Enter**.

6. In the **Find Text** text box, type **Australia** and then click **Find**.

▶ **Render the Sales Summary Report to PDF**

1. In the **Export** drop-down list, click **Acrobat (PDF) file**, and then click **Export**.

2. In the **File Download** dialog box, click **Open**, and click **Accept** if the **End User License Agreement** dialog box appears.

   The Actual Vs Quota report is now displayed as an Acrobat PDF file and can be printed or saved.

3. Close Adobe Acrobat Reader.

▶ **View the Actual Vs Quota Report**

1. Click the **Home** link on the top left-hand side of the page.

2. Click the **Example Reports** folder link, and then click the **Actual Vs Quota** link. The Actual Vs Quota report is displayed.

▶ **Create an e-mail subscription**

1. Click **New Subscription**. Note that subscriptions allow administrators as well as end users to automate the process of delivering reports.

2. In the **To** text box, type **NADirector@adventure-works.msft**

Important   Make sure to not type any spaces in the **NADirector@adventure-works.msft** e-mail address.

---

3. Verify that the **Include Link** and **Include Report** check boxes are selected. Note that for e-mail subscriptions, the report can be delivered as a hyperlink or as an attached/embedded file.

4. Verify that **Render Format** is set to **Web archive**.

5. Click the **Select Schedule** button.

6. Under **Schedule details**, select the **Once** check box.

7. Set the **Start time** to be two minutes later than the current time and then click **OK**.

Caution   Be sure to select the correct AM or PM option.

---

8. On the **Subscription:Actual Vs Quota** page, set the **CalendarYear** and **Group** parameters to **2003** and **North America** respectively, and then click **OK**.

▶ **Configure Security**

1. On the **Properties** tab, click **Security** and then click **Edit Item Security** and click **OK** in the Microsoft Internet Explorer message.

2. Click **New Role Assignment**.

3. **In the Group or user name** text box, type **NADirector**

4. Select the **Browser** check box, and then click **OK**.

5. Close Internet Explorer.

▶ **View the e-mail output**

1. On the **Start** menu, click **Log Off**, and then in the **Log Off Windows** dialog box, click **Log Off**.

2. Press **CTRL+ALT+DELETE**. In the **User name** text box, type **NADirector** and in the **Password** text box, type **P@ssw0rd** and then click **OK**.

3. On the **Start** menu, click **Outlook Express**.

4. In the Folders pane, click **Inbox**.

5. Click the **Actual Vs Quota** message and view its contents.

Note The report information might not display properly. The default Outlook Express security settings cause the report information to appear in a single, unformatted column.

---

6. Click the report link at the end of the message. The report is displayed in Internet Explorer.

7. Close Internet Explorer and Outlook Express.

8. On the **Start** menu, click **Log Off,** and then log back on using the user name **Administrator** and the password **P@ssw0rd**.

▶ **Launch the Adventure Works Portal**

1. Click **Start**, point to **All Programs**, and then click **Internet Explorer**.

2. On the **Favorites** menu, click **Adventure Works Portal**.

Note You can also access the Adventure Works Portal by typing the following web address in the Internet Explorer address bar: **http://localhost/Portal/home.htm**

The Adventure Works Portal is an intranet site with access to several reports, as well as company news, product announcements, and other corporate information.

3. Under **Available Reports**, click the **Sales Summary** link and examine the report. Note that the rendering of the report is the same as the rendering of the report by Report Manager.

4. Close Internet Explorer.

Authoring Reports

Report Definition Language

- List / Table / Matrix / Chart
- Sorting / Filtering / Grouping / Aggregates
- Interactivity (drill-down, drill-through)
- Parameters
- Full Visual Basic .NET Expression Language

Access through ADO.NET managed data providers

- OLE DB
- ODBC
- OLE DB for OLAP

Development options

- Report Designer
- Third Party

Introduction

Through Report Designer, Reporting Services provides a rich authoring environment integrated within Visual Studio .NET. Because Reporting Services uses a standard XML schema to represent reports, any development environment that supports RDL can be used to author reports.

RDL

Reporting Services uses RDL to provide an XML representation of the report definition. RDL defines a common schema to promote the interchange of report definitions—it is not a proprietary report definition language. It supports a full feature set for design, including a collection of report display types (List, Table, Matrix, and Chart), parameters for dynamic content, and rich formatting options.

Access using ADO.NET managed data providers

Reporting Services uses ADO.NET-managed data providers to access OLE DB, ODBC, and XMLA data sources.

Development options

Reporting Services uses Report Designer as a design tool for authoring reports. Again, Report Designer is integrated with the Visual Studio .NET 2003 development environment.

Demonstration: Authoring a Report

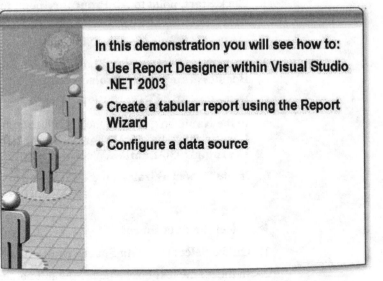

In this demonstration you will see how to:
- Use Report Designer within Visual Studio .NET 2003
- Create a tabular report using the Report Wizard
- Configure a data source

Introduction

In this demonstration, the instructor will explore the report design functionality of Reporting Services by recreating the Sales Summary Report for the fictitious company Adventure Works.

Before creating the report, the instructor will open the report's query using Notepad. This query specifies the data that will be used in the report. The source of this query is the Adventure Works data warehouse.

Procedures

▶ **Copy the report query**

1. Click **Start**, point to **All Programs**, point to **Accessories**, and then click **Notepad**.

2. On the **File** menu, click **Open**, navigate to the C:\Program Files\ Microsoft Learning\2030\Democode\Mod01 directory, click **Sales Summary.txt**, and then click **Open**.

3. In **Notepad**, select all by using **CTRL+A** and then copy by using **CTRL+C**.

   You will paste the query to its destination later in the exercise.

4. Close Notepad.

▶ **Launch the report design environment**

1. Click **Start**, point to **All Programs**, point to **Microsoft Visual Studio .NET 2003**, and then click **Microsoft Visual Studio .NET 2003**.

2. On the **File** menu, point to **New**, and then click **Project**.

3. In the **New Project** dialog box, in the Project Types pane, click the **Business Intelligence Projects** folder.

4. In the Templates pane, click **Report Project Wizard**.

5. In the **Name** box, replace the default name with **Sales Summary**. In the **Location** box, type **C:\Program Files\Microsoft Learning\2030\Labfiles\Workspace** and then click **OK**.

6. In the **Report Wizard**, on the **Welcome to the Report Wizard** page, click **Next**.

▶ **Select the data source**

1. On the **Select the Data Source** page, click **New data source**.

2. In the **Name** text box, type the default name, **DataSource1**.

3. In the **Type** drop-down list, click **Microsoft SQL Server**.

4. To the right of the **Connection string** text box, click **Edit**.

5. In the **Data Link Properties** dialog box, on the **Connection** tab, in the **Select or enter a server name** box, type **localhost**

Caution   Do not click the down arrow for the server name list as this may take a long time.

---

6. Under **Enter information to log on to the server**, click **Use Windows NT Integrated security**.

7. In the **Select the database on the server** drop-down list, click **AdventureWorksDW**.

8. Click **Test Connection**, and then in the **Microsoft Data Link** dialog box, click **OK**.

9. Click **OK** to close the **Data Link Properties** dialog box, and then click **Next**.

▶ **Design the query**

1. Paste the Sales Summary report query into the **Query string** text box by using **CTRL+V**.

Note   If you do not have anything on your Clipboard to paste, repeat the **Copy the report query** procedure above.

---

2. Click the **Edit** button to open and view the Query Builder.

3. Click **OK**, and on the **Design the Query** page, click **Next**.

▶ **Select the report type**

1. On the **Select the Report Type** page, click **Tabular**, and then click **Next**.

2. On the **Design the Table** page, move the data fields to the following report data areas, and then click **Next**:

   - Page: **CalendarYear**

   - Group: **SalesTerritoryGroup, SalesTerritoryCountry**

   - Details: **Employee, ActualSales**

▶ **Finish and preview the completed report**

1. On the **Choose the Table Layout** page, click **Block**, select the **Include subtotals** check box, and then click **Next**.

2. On the **Choose the Table Style** page, click **Bold,** and then click **Next**.

3. On the **Choose the Deployment Location** page, verify the following, and then click **Next**:

   a. **Report server** text box displays **http://localhost/ReportServer**

   b. **Deployment folder** text box displays **Sales Summary**

4. On the **Completing the Report Wizard** page, in the **Report name** text box, type **Sales Summary** and select the **Preview report** check box, and then click **Finish**.

   Verify that the report displays the correct columns—Sales Territory Group, Sales Territory Country, Employee, and Actual Sales with one page per calendar year for a total of four pages.

▶ **Refine the report formatting**

1. In **Visual Studio .NET**, click the **Layout** tab.

2. Click the table data region (the area containing the rows and columns) and use the mouse to click and drag the line between the column headers to make the first column (Sales Territory Group) approximately 1 inch wide.

3. Use the mouse to click and drag the line between the column headers to make the second column (Sales Territory Country) approximately 1.25 inches wide.

4. Use the mouse to click and drag the line between the column headers to make the third column (Employee) approximately 1.75 inches wide.

5. Use the mouse to click and drag the line between the columns to make the forth column (Actual Sales) approximately 1 inch wide.

6. Click the gray cell above the **Actual Sales** text box. In the **Properties** window, in the **Format** property, type **C0** to format the field as currency with no decimal places.

▶ **Save and preview the report**

1. On the **File** menu, click **Save All**.

2. Click the **Preview** tab.

3. Browse through the remaining pages of the report by clicking the **Next Page** button.

4. Close Visual Studio .NET.

Managing Reports

- Publish reports to a centralized report server database
- General report management tasks:
  - Define execution schedule–on demand or in advance
  - Set up security
  - Maintain report folders
  - Administer user features
- Management roles
  - Content manager
  - System administrator

Introduction

Reporting Services supports end-to-end management of reports and the reporting environment. Report Manager can be used to configure end-user access to reports and report server folders, set options that determine how and when reports are run, manage report distribution, and manage report processing.

Centralized report server database

Reports are published to a centralized SQL Server 2000 reports database. A combination of tools can be used to administer this report server database. SQL Server tools can be used to back up and restore the database. Report server command line utilities can be used to manage the connection and copy data.

Content management

Content management includes the following tasks:

- Securing the report server site and items in the report server database by applying the role-based security provided with Reporting Services.

- Structuring the report server folder hierarchy by adding, modifying, and deleting folders.

- Setting defaults and properties that apply to items managed by the report server. For example, you can set baseline maximum values that determine report history storage policies.

- Creating shared data source items that can be used in place of report-specific data source connections. A publisher or content manager can select a data source that is different from the one originally defined for a report; for example, a reference to a test database can be replaced with a reference to a production database.

- Creating data-driven subscriptions that generate recipient lists by retrieving data from a data store.

- Balancing report-processing demands that are placed on the server by scheduling report processing and specifying which ones can be run on demand and which ones are loaded from cache.

Management roles

Management tasks are organized into two predefined roles: Content Manager and System Administrator. By default, a user who is a local system administrator is automatically assigned to both roles. He or she can assign additional users to either role to delegate management responsibilities.

The Content Manager role includes a complete set of item-level tasks. Initially, the role assignment that maps a local system administrator to a Content Manager role is in effect for the root folder of the report server (Home) and all child folders and content.

The System Administrator role includes tasks that provide access to site-level settings.

Practice: Managing a Report

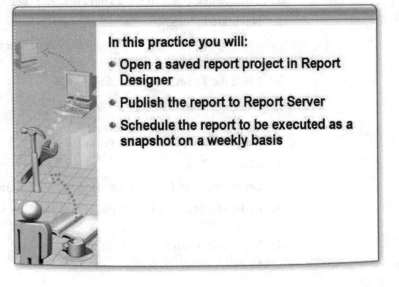

In this practice you will:

- Open a saved report project in Report Designer
- Publish the report to Report Server
- Schedule the report to be executed as a snapshot on a weekly basis

Introduction

In this practice, you will play the role of an Adventure Works report manager who is in charge of publishing reports to the Report Server database and managing execution of those reports.

You will first deploy the Sales Summary report to the Report Server database. You will then configure the report to run in advance of end-user browsing.

▶ **Open a saved project and report**

1. Click **Start**, point to **All Programs**, point to **Microsoft Visual Studio .NET 2003**, and then click **Microsoft Visual Studio .NET 2003**.

2. On the **File** menu, point to **Open**, and then click **Project**.

3. In the **Open Project** dialog box, navigate to the C:\Program Files\ Microsoft Learning\2030\Practices\Mod01\ folder.

4. Click **Practice1.rptproj**, and then click **Open**.

▶ **Deploy the solution to the Report Server database**

1. In **Solution Explorer**, right-click the solution, and then click **Properties**.

2. In the **Solution Property Pages** dialog box, in the left-hand pane, click **Configuration Properties**.

3. In the right-hand pane, select the **Deploy** check box, and then click **OK**.

4. On the **Build** menu, click **Deploy Solution**.

5. Close Visual Studio .NET.

▶ **Browse the Sales Summary report**

1. Click **Start**, point to **All Programs**, and then click **Internet Explorer**.

2. Navigate to http://localhost/Reports/.

   The Report Manager is displayed. Notice that a folder has been created for your newly deployed solution.

3. Click the **Practice1** folder link.

4. Click the **Sales Summary** report link.

▶ **Add a description to the report**

1. Click the **Properties** tab.

2. On the left-hand side of the window, click **General**.

3. In the **Description** box, type **Actual sales by sales person by year** and then click **Apply**.

4. In the upper-left hand side of the screen, click the **Practice1** folder link and view the description.

▶ **Specify the login credentials**

1. Click the **Sales Summary** report link.

2. Click the **Properties** tab.

3. On the left-hand side of the screen, click the **Data Sources** tab.

   In this scenario, you will use a generic SQL Server account, Report Execution, to connect to the data source.

4. Under **Connect Using**, select **Credentials stored securely in the report server**.

5. In the **User name** text box, type **ReportExecution**

6. In the **Password** text box, type **P@ssw0rd**

Caution   Do *not* select the **Use as Windows credentials when connecting to the data source** check box.

---

7. Click **Apply**.

8. Verify that you can execute the report with the new credentials by clicking the **View** tab.

▶ **Schedule a snapshot to run everyday**

1. Click the **Properties** tab.

2. On the left-hand side of the screen, click the **Execution** tab.

3. Click **Render this report from an execution snapshot**, click **Use the following schedule to create execution snapshots**, click **Report-specific schedule**, and then click the **Configure** button.

4. Under **Schedule details**, click **Week**.

5. Under **Weekly Schedule**, specify the following values.

Setting	Value
Repeat after this number of weeks	1
On day(s)	Sun
Start time	05:00 AM

6. Click **OK**.

7. Verify that the **Create a snapshot of the report when the apply button is selected** check box is selected. This will create an initial snapshot report.

8. Click **Apply**.

9. Click the **View** tab to view the report one last time.

10. On the **File** menu, click **Close** to close the Report Manager.

Lesson: Overview of Reporting Services Architecture

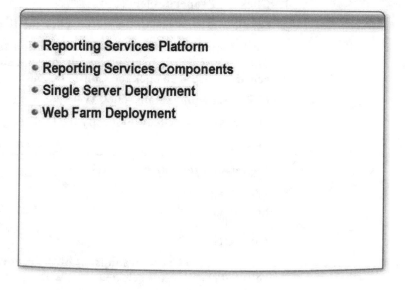

- Reporting Services Platform
- Reporting Services Components
- Single Server Deployment
- Web Farm Deployment

Introduction

Reporting Services is a .NET-based platform that includes a complete set of tools for integrating a reporting solution into any centrally-managed technical environment.

In this lesson, you will learn about the architectural components of Reporting Services, including the components that make up Report Server, the software components required for an install, and the single server and Web farm deployment configurations.

Lesson objectives

After completing this lesson, you will be able to:

- Describe the Reporting Services platform.
- Describe Reporting Services components and software prerequisites.
- Describe single server deployment.
- Describe Web farm deployment.

Reporting Services Platform

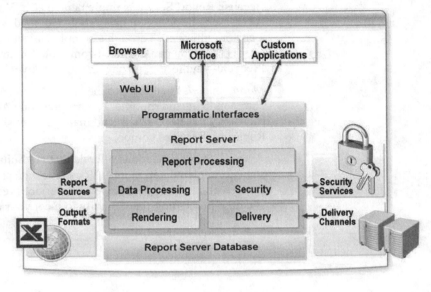

Introduction

Reporting Services is a .NET-based platform that includes a comprehensive set of tools that you can use to integrate a reporting solution into any centrally-managed technical environment.

Key components

The key server components of the Reporting Services architecture include the following:

- **Report Server**

  Report Server is a Web service that includes several subcomponents to manage report processing: data processing, report rendering, security policies, and report delivery.

  - Data processing: Retrieves data from the report data source
  - Rendering: Transforms the report layout and data into a device-specific format
  - Delivery: Delivers reports to specific devices or rendering formats
  - Security: Specifies the authorization model of Reporting Services

- **Report Server Database**

  Report Server performs stateless storing of all information in a Report Server database. This means that Report Server treats each interaction request solely on information in that request. The Report Server database is a SQL Server database that stores information used by Report Server to manage reports and resources. You can have one or more Report Servers that all point to the same Report Server database.

■ **Programmatic Interfaces**

Because Report Server is implemented as a Web service using published APIs, it can be accessed using tools included with Reporting Services or via a custom interface. Through a Simple Object Access Protocol (SOAP) API over HTTP, you can create custom tools for any stage of the reporting lifecycle—authoring, management, or delivery.

Managed code is code that runs on the Microsoft .NET Framework's common language runtime. A managed code API is available so that you can easily develop, install, and manage extensions consumed by many Reporting Services components.

Assemblies are collections of code that are built, versioned, and deployed as a single implementation unit. You can create assemblies using the .NET Framework and add new Reporting Services rendering, security, delivery, and data-processing functionality to meet your evolving business needs.

Reporting Services Components

	Component	Prerequisites
Server	Report Server Report Manager	IIS .NET Framework
	Report Server Database	SQL Server SQL Server Agent
	E-mail Delivery Extension	SMTP Server
Client	Report Designer	Visual Studio .NET
	Utilities	Windows Management Instrumentation

Introduction

The Reporting Services installation has specific software and hardware prerequisites for both server and client components. When a prerequisite for a Reporting Services component is missing, that component cannot be installed.

Server components

All server components must be installed on a server running one of the following operating systems:

- Microsoft Windows® 2000 Advanced Server or Windows 2000 Data Center
- Microsoft Windows Server™ 2003 (All editions)
- Windows XP

The Reporting Services server components include:

- **Report Server and Report Manager**

  These components have the following requirements:

  - An existing installation of Internet Information Services (IIS)
  - .NET Framework.

    The Setup process will install this component if not already installed and will register ASP.NET in IIS.

Note When installing components on separate servers, the Report Server database must be installed first, followed by Report Server and Report Manager. All other components can be installed in any order.

■ **Report Server Database**

Installation of the Report Server database requires an existing installation of SQL Server and SQL Server Agent. If both a default instance and a named instance exist, the Setup process will prompt for selection of the instance to be used for the installation of the Report Server database.

Important If using Reporting Services Standard Edition, the SQL Server instance must be local. Remote instances are supported only by Reporting Services Enterprise Edition.

■ **Delivery Extensions**

If the Delivery Extensions component is installed, the Setup process will prompt for the location of a Simple Mail Transfer Protocol (SMTP) server. This server can be a local or remote server, but must be on the same network as Report Server.

Client components

To view published reports or manage Report Server, the choice of browser will determine the minimum operating system and hardware requirements. The Reporting Services client components include:

■ **Report Designer**

The Report Designer client component must be installed on a workstation running one of the following operating systems with the most current service pack applied:

- Windows 2000

- Windows Server 2003

- Windows XP

In addition, Report Designer requires an existing installation of Visual Studio .NET 2003.

■ **Utilities**

Windows Management Instrumentation (WMI) is required for the Reporting Services utilities as well as network connectivity to the Report Server.

Single Server Deployment

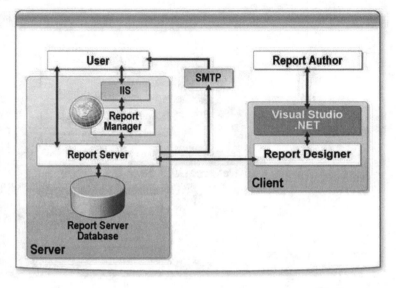

Introduction

The simplest deployment configuration is to install all server components on a single server and install Report Designer on a client workstation. This deployment configuration is also known as the *standard deployment model*.

Server components

If you are deploying Reporting Services in a corporate workgroup or in a small- to medium-sized business, consider installing and running the server components in a standard deployment configuration. The standard deployment model describes a configuration in which the Report Server and Report Manager components are installed on a single computer running a Windows server-based operating system. The Report Server database requires a SQL Server instance, which may be located on the local computer or on a remote computer. A standard configuration supports the following server-side components:

- Report Server
- Report Manager
- Report Server database (on a local or remote server)
- Report Server and Report Manager components have a combination of prerequisites that must be satisfied by a single computer.

Client components

The client component Report Designer should be installed on a separate client workstation. Before installing Report Designer, this client workstation must have Visual Studio .NET 2003 installed.

Choosing a standard configuration

The standard deployment topology is required if you are running Reporting Services Standard Edition. It is also recommended if you are evaluating the product or developing an application based on the Reporting Services platform.

This deployment model is not intended for organizations that have high availability or high-volume reporting requirements.

Web Farm Deployment

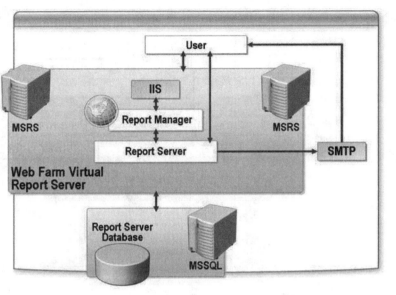

Introduction

There is another deployment model that you can implement to support a large installation, known as the *Web farm deployment model*.

Clustering support in Reporting Services

Reporting Services supports clustering so that you can create a highly available and scalable report server installation. A report server Web farm consists of multiple report servers that share a single report server database (or a cluster of report server databases). You must use additional software to configure and manage the cluster. You can cluster report servers, report server databases, or both.

A report server database can be part of a SQL Server failover cluster. After you install Reporting Services, you can use features in SQL Server 2000 to create a cluster based on the existing Report Server database. Whether you use a single database or a database cluster, the configuration you use is transparent to a report server.

Microsoft recommends the use of Microsoft Application Center 2000 or third-party software to create and maintain a report server Web farm. Although you can create a report server Web farm by running Reporting Services Setup, Reporting Services does not include tools for managing a Web farm configuration.

Review

- Overview of Microsoft SQL Server Reporting Services
- Tour of Reporting Services
- Overview of Reporting Services Architecture

1. What are the stages in the reporting life cycle?

2. What does Reporting Services use to create a representation of a report?

3. What are data regions?

4. How is a report rendered?

Microsoft®

Module 2: Authoring Basic Reports

Contents

Overview

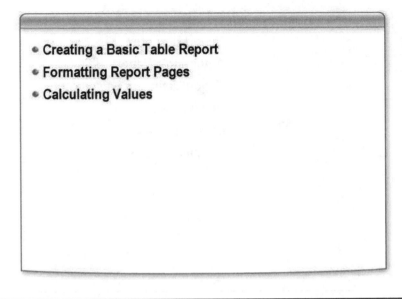

- Creating a Basic Table Report
- Formatting Report Pages
- Calculating Values

Introduction

Using Reporting Services, you can create and deliver sophisticated reporting solutions. The report authoring process is fully integrated with Microsoft® Visual Studio® .NET 2003, providing drag-and-drop development through Report Designer. Data regions can be used to control both the format and structure of data within a report.

In this module, you will learn about the fundamentals of report authoring, including configuring data sources and data sets, creating tabular reports, summarizing data, and applying basic formatting.

Objectives

After completing this module, you will be able to:

- Create a basic report.
- Apply basic report formatting.
- Use calculated values in a report.

Lesson: Creating a Basic Table Report

- Report Designer
- Authoring a Report
- Report Definition Language
- Accessing Data
- Creating a Table
- Creating Groups

Introduction

Visual Studio .NET 2003 enables the developer to create Reporting Services solutions. Each solution can contain many projects, and each project can contain one or many reports.

In this lesson, you will learn how to author basic reports using Visual Studio .NET 2003 and how to construct and use data sources and data sets.

Lesson objectives

After completing this lesson, you will be able to:

- Use Report Designer.
- Describe the options for creating a report.
- Describe the purpose of Report Definition Language (RDL).
- Access data using a data source and a data set.
- Create a table.
- Create groups.

Report Designer

- **Integrated with Visual Studio .NET 2003**
- **Full report authoring capabilities**
- **Generates Report Definition Language (RDL)**
- **Provides deployment directly to Report Server**

Introduction

Report Designer is the Microsoft SQL Server Reporting Services tool for authoring reports. It provides a drag-and-drop environment for authoring reports and provides a mechanism for report deployment.

Visual Studio .NET 2003 integration

Report Designer is integrated with Visual Studio .NET 2003, enabling you to take full advantage of the Visual Studio development environment. You can create report projects manually by using the Report Template. Alternatively, can by use the Report Wizard.

Full authoring capabilities

Report Designer provides a graphical designer interface with which you can configure all aspects of a final report. Three views are provided:

- The data view: Allows the creation of data sources and data sets
- The layout view: Allows the creation of data regions for displaying data in various formats
- The preview view: Allows previewing of the rendered report

RDL

A *report definition* contains data retrieval and layout information for a report. RDL is an XML representation of this report definition. It is an open schema; developers can extend RDL with additional attributes and elements. Report Designer automatically translates between the graphical representation of the report layout and RDL.

Deployment

Report Designer provides deployment functionality, allowing you to deploy reports, projects, or entire solutions to the report server directly from Report Designer. Multiple deployment configurations can be created to enable easy deployment to a number of environments. For example, a deployment schema can be configured to deploy to test and production environments.

Three deployment properties can be set for a report project:

- **OverwriteDataSources** republishes data sources to the server when set to **True**.

- **TargetFolder** specifies the name of the folder to which reports are published.

- **TargetServerURL** specifies the URL of the report server.

Authoring a Report

- **Report Designer**
  - Create a blank report
  - Use the Report Wizard
  - Import an existing report
- **Third-party tools can be used to create RDL**

Introduction

Because RDL defines a report independently of the authoring tool, reports can be created using Report Designer or any third-party tool that supports RDL. Deployment can be achieved through the use of Report Designer, Report Manager, or a third-party tool that uses the Reporting Services Simple Object Access Protocol (SOAP) application programming interface (API) to interact with the report server.

Report Designer

In Report Designer, you can create a report three different ways:

- Create a blank report and manually add queries and layout.
- Use Report Wizard, which automatically creates a table or matrix report based on information you provide.
- Import an existing report from Microsoft Access.

Reports can be deployed using Report Designer or Report Manager, which is a Web-based tool hosted on the report server itself.

When manually creating a report, you typically complete the following process:

1. Create a new report project contained within a Visual Studio .NET solution.
2. Create a data source to provide a connection to the underlying data source.
3. Create a data set. This is a SQL query that defines the data items available to the report from the data source.
4. Choose a data region type, add it to the report, and then provide the data region with relevant fields from the data set.
5. Determine grouping and aggregate values. For example, data can be grouped into categories and subcategories, with relevant summary calculations.
6. Add formatting to enhance the look of the report, if so desired. Conditional formatting can be used to highlight certain data values.
7. Publish the report to the report server.

Third-party tool

Because a report definition is an XML document, you can create and edit reports using other tools. You can edit RDL code using a text editor or a third-party tool designed for editing Reporting Services reports. If you use a tool that does not publish reports directly to a report server, you can upload reports using Report Manager.

Report Definition Language

- Provides an XML representation of the report definition
- Validated against an XML schema definition (XSD)
- Common schema
- Designed to be output format neutral
- Has an open and extensible schema

Introduction

The definition of a report is stored in a structured XML document, specified by using RDL. An RDL schema is used to validate reports. Only valid reports may be published to a report server. RDL is automatically created by Report Designer, but can be created or modified directly through the use of a text editor, and saved using a suffix of .rdl.

RDL characteristics

RDL has the following characteristics:

- RDL provides the XML representation of the report definition—data and layout. RDL is not a programmatic interface or protocol.

- The RDL for a particular report is validated using an XML schema definition (XSD). The XSD defines the accepted elements of the XML document. When a report is published using Report Designer, the XSD is used to validate the report. Again, only valid reports may be published to a report server.

- RDL defines a common schema to promote the interchange of report definitions. It is not a proprietary report definition language, and can be used by vendors who wish to create either report design tools or report execution and rendering tools.

- RDL is designed to be output format neutral. This means that a report written in RDL can be rendered in any of several output formats.

- RDL is an open schema, allowing developers to extend and add custom functionality. The **<Custom></Custom>** element can be used to insert any XML structure into the RDL document. The rendering extensions included with Reporting Services do not use the **Custom** element, though a custom rendering extension can use it.

Accessing Data

- **Data source**
  - Any .NET-managed data provider
  - Optionally store user credentials
  - Shared or report specific
- **Data set**
  - Query retrieves a row set from a data source
  - Query language specific to the source database
  - Dynamic query can accept parameters
  - Contains fields

Introduction

A Reporting Services *data source* contains information about a connection to a database. This includes such information as a server name, a database name, and user credentials. A Reporting Services *data set* contains information about the query to be used by a report. The fields contained in a data set are used as the basis for creating a report.

Data source

Within a reporting solution, a data source represents a connection to an external data source. Data sources have the following characteristics:

- A data source can be used to access data from any .NET-managed data provider. Reporting Services directly supports SQL Server 2000/ SQL Server 7.0, OLE DB data sources (including SQL Server Analysis Services), open database connectivity (ODBC) data sources, and Oracle. A report can retrieve values from multiple data sources.

   Reporting Services is also extensible; developers can create additional data processing extensions that data sources can use to connect to other sources of data.

- A data source can be one of two types:

  - Shared: A data source that can be referenced in multiple reports. The data source definition for a shared data source is stored in a separate file stored on the report server. Using a single shared data source allows you to administer the data source in a single location.

  - Report specific: A data source specific to a particular report. The definition for a report-specific data source is stored within the report itself.

Data source configuration can be modified after a report solution has been deployed by using Report Manager.

Data set

A data set retrieves rows of data from a data source based on an SQL query. Queries can be constructed by creating SQL statements or by using the Query Builder. Data sets have the following characteristics:

- Data sets are created by queries that access data sources. A single report can retrieve data from multiple data sets. The fields in a data set become the building blocks for creating a report.

- Data sets are based on queries that must be written in the necessary query language for the source database. T-SQL and PL/SQL are two examples of such query languages.

- Data sets can be made dynamic by adding SQL parameters to the WHERE clause of the query and mapping them to report parameters. Report parameters are discussed in a Module 4, "Manipulating Data Sets," in Course 2030, *Creating Reporting Solutions Using Microsoft SQL Server 2000 Reporting Services*.

Fields

Each data set in a report contains a list of fields. Typically, the fields refer to columns or fields returned by the query in the data set. Fields that refer to database fields contain a pointer to the database field and a name property. You can use the name property to provide a user-friendly name in place of the name of the database field.

In addition to database fields, a fields list can contain calculated fields. Calculated fields contain a name and an expression. Column names can be aliased within the SQL query or can be renamed within Report Designer.

Creating a Table

Product	Sales Amount
=Fields!Product.Value	=Fields!SalesAmount.Value
Total	=Sum(Fields!SalesAmount.Value)

Layout view

Product	Sales Amount
Component	$14,565,123
Clothing	$1,968,428
Bike	$80,861,815
Accessory	$583,136
Total	$97,978,503

Report preview

Introduction

Typically, the body of a report contains repeating data retrieved from an underlying data set. A *data region* is a control that is capable of both displaying data in a structured fashion and displaying database fields, custom fields, and expressions. The simplest type of data region is a table.

Table data region

A *table* is a type of data region and is made up of a group of cells organized into fixed columns with repeating rows. Each cell in a table contains one report item, such as a text box. The value displayed in the text box can be a string constant, a field from the current row of the data set, or a more complex expression.

The slide shows a table report item in the body of a simple report, shown in layout and preview views from within Report Designer. The layout view is a design view used to author the report, while report preview is used to view the rendering of the report.

Notice that the report contains two columns, **Product** and **Sales Amount**, and a **Total** row. Within Report Designer, fields may be added to a table from the Fields window or typed in as an expression. For example, a field may be referenced by **=Fields!SalesAmount.Value**.

Aggregate expressions may be added to create total entries. For example the Sales Amount Total field contains the expression **=Sum(Fields!SalesAmount.Value)**.

Note that all expressions begin with an = symbol, and that a table may reference a single data set. Aggregate functions are discussed in more detail in Module 3, "Enhancing Basic Reports," in Course 2030, *Creating Reporting Solutions Using Microsoft SQL Server 2000 Reporting Services*.

Creating Groups

- **Grouping Levels**
  - Table header
  - Category header
  - Detail
  - Category footer
  - Table Footer

Product	Sales Amount
=Fields!Category.Value	
=Fields!Product.Value	=Fields!SalesAmount.Value
= Fields!Category.Value +"Total"	=Sum(Fields!SalesAmount.Value)
Grand Total	=Sum(Fields!SalesAmount.Value)

Introduction

Table data regions provide a grouping mechanism that enables the display of detail rows, as well as header and footer rows for each grouping level contained within the report. Reports can therefore contain multiple levels of totaling.

Grouping table rows

Each table row is associated with one of the following:

- A detail row in the data set
- A header or footer for a single grouping
- A header or footer for the table

The default table consists of a table header row, a detail row, and a table footer row. Numeric fields placed in the header or footer row summarize values from all the rows of the data set, giving a grand total.

Header and footer rows for categories and subcategories may be added. Categories and subcategories provide grouping of detail rows based on values in other fields.

Table columns make it easy to create reports where captions and summary values align vertically, but they also can be more rigid than you may prefer. There are two ways to make column alignment less rigid:

- *Merging cells*. Two or more adjacent cells in a single row can be merged, spanning the original columns. You can merge cells to allow longer text for headings at some grouping levels or to center a caption across columns.
- *Cell padding*. Padding is the minimum space between the edge of a text box and its contents.

Demonstration: Creating a Basic Table Report

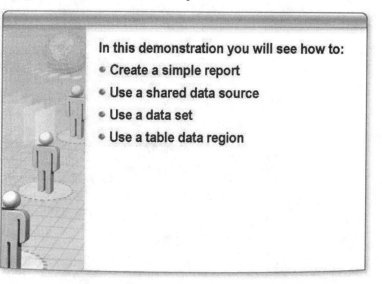

In this demonstration you will see how to:
- Create a simple report
- Use a shared data source
- Use a data set
- Use a table data region

Introduction

In this demonstration, the instructor will create the Adventure Works Reseller Sales report. To do this, the instructor will define a data source and data set, and then add groupings and basic formatting to the report table.

Procedures

▶ **Create a new report named "Reseller Sales"**

1. Click **Start**, point to **All Programs**, point to **Microsoft Visual Studio .NET 2003**, and then click **Microsoft Visual Studio .NET 2003**.

2. On the **File** menu, point to **New**, and then click **Project**.

3. In the **New Project** dialog box, in the Project Types pane, click the **Business Intelligence Projects** folder.

4. In the Templates pane, click **Report Project**.

5. In the **Name** text box, type **Reseller Sales**. In the **Location** text box, type **C:\Reporting Services Training\Workspace** and then click **OK**.

6. In **Solution Explorer**, right-click the **Reports** folder, point to **Add**, and then click **Add New Item**.

7. In the **Add New Item** dialog box, in the Templates pane, click **Report**. In the **Name** box, type **Reseller Sales** and then click **Open**.

▶ **Create a shared data source**

1. In **Solution Explorer**, right-click the **Shared Data Sources** folder, and then click **Add New Data Source**.

2. In the **Data Link Properties** dialog box, on the **Connection** tab, in the **Select or enter a server name** text box, type **localhost**.

Caution   Do not click the down arrow for the server name list as it may take a long time to populate the list.

---

3. Under **Enter information to log on to the server**, ensure the **Use Windows NT Integrated security** option is selected.

4. In the **Select the database on the server** drop-down list, click **AdventureWorksDW**.

5. Click **Test Connection**, and then click **OK** to close the **Microsoft Data Link** dialog box.

6. Click **OK** to close the **Data Link Properties** dialog box.

▶ **Add a data set**

1. In design view, in the **Dataset** drop-down list, click **<New Dataset...>**.

2. In the **Dataset** dialog box, type **DataDetail** in the **Name** text box on the **Query** tab.

Caution   Be sure that there are no spaces in the name of your data set.

---

3. In the **Data source** text box, verify that the data source is **AdventureWorksDW (shared)**.

4. In the **Query string** text box, type (press **CTRL+ENTER** at the end of a line):

```
SELECT *
FROM vResellerSales
WHERE Year = 2003 AND MonthNumberOfYear = 1
```

5. Click **OK**.

6. On the **Data** tab, click the **Run** button. A data set containing the query results is displayed.

7. On the **File** menu, click **Save All**.

▶ **Add a table data region**

1. Click the **Layout** tab.

2. In the **Toolbox**, double-click **Table**. A table is added to the report. Notice that it has placeholder rows for the table header, table detail row, and table footer.

Tip You can display a table row name and description by hovering your mouse over the icon to the left of each row.

▶ **Add fields to the detail**

1. Drag the **Reseller** field from the **Fields** window and drop it into the first cell in the detail row.

Tip By default, the **Fields** window is located on the left side of the screen. If the **Fields** window is not visible, on the **View** menu, click **Fields**.

---

2. In the **Fields** window, drag the **SalesAmount** field and drop it into the second cell in the **Detail** row.

3. In the **Fields** window, drag the **OrderQuantity** field and drop it into the third cell in the **Detail** row.

▶ **To add fields to the table footer**

1. In the **Fields** window, drag the **SalesAmount** field and drop it into the second cell in the **Table Footer** row. Note that when you add a numeric field to a header or footer row, the Report Designer automatically adds a sum function to aggregate the values.

2. In the **Fields** window, drag the **OrderQuantity** field and drop it into the third cell in the **Table Footer** row.

3. Click the first cell of the **Table Footer** row, type **Grand Total** and then press **Enter**.

▶ **To save and preview the report**

1. On the **File** menu, click **Save All**.

2. Click the **Preview** tab. Notice that the report shows a header for each column and detail values from the source data set.

▶ **To create the table1_Category group**

1. Click the **Layout** tab.

2. Click the table, right-click the icon to the left of the **Detail** row (the second row), and then click **Insert Group**.

3. In the **Grouping and Sorting Properties** dialog box, set the **Name** to **table1_Category**.

Important   Group names are case sensitive.

---

4. Under **Group on**, click the first row, and from the **Expression** drop-down list, click **=Fields!Country.Value**, and then click **OK**.

5. In the **Fields** window, drag the **Country** field and drop in into the first cell in the **table1_Category Header** row, directly beneath the **Reseller** title cell.

6. In the first cell in the **table1_Category Footer** row (directly above the **Grand Total** cell), type **Country Total** and then press **Enter**.

7. In the **Table Footer** row, click the cells that contain the **SalesAmount** total and the **OrderQuantity** total, right-click, and then click **Copy**.

8. Right-click the second cell in the **table1_Category Footer** row (next to the **Category Total** cell), and then click **Paste**.

9. Click the **Preview** tab. Notice that the country total and the grand total are displayed at the end of the report.

▶ **To apply basic formatting to the table**

1. Click the **Layout** tab.

2. Click the column handle (the gray box above the column) for the **Sales Amount** column.

3. In the **Properties** window, in the **Format** property text box, type **C0** and then press **Enter**. The cell's format is set to currency with no decimal places.

Note Locale settings are taken from the client's browser settings when deployed.

---

4. Click the column handle for the **Order Quantity** column.

5. In the **Properties** window, in the **Format** property text box, type **N0** and then press **Enter**. The cell's format is set to numeric with no decimal places.

6. Click the **Table Header** row icon, and then press **CTRL** and the **Table Footer** row icon. The header and footer rows are selected.

7. On the **Report Formatting** toolbar, perform the following tasks:

   - Click **12** in the **Font Size** drop-down list

   - Click the **Bold** button to boldface the cells.

   - Click the **Background Color** button, click the **Web** tab, click **Black**, and then click **OK**.

   - Click the **Foreground Color** button, click the **Web** tab, click **White**, and then click **OK**.

8. Click the **table1_Category Footer** row icon, click the **Background Color** button, click the **Web** tab, click **LightGrey**, and then click **OK**.

▶ **To indent row captions**

1. In the **Detail** row, click the first cell.

2. In the **Properties** window, expand the **Padding** property group.

3. In the padding **Left** property text box, type **22pt**.

4. Click the first cell in the **table1_Category Header** row, press **CTRL** and click the first cell in the **table1_Category Footer** row, and then click the **Bold** button.

▶ **To save and preview the report**

1. On the **File** menu, click **Save All**.

2. Click the **Preview** tab, and verify that the report is rendered correctly.

Lesson: Formatting Report Pages

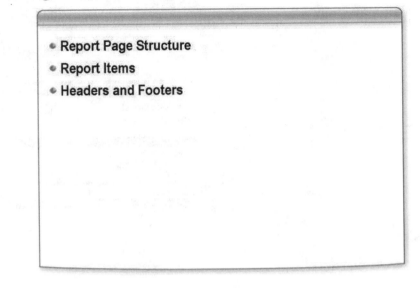

- Report Page Structure
- Report Items
- Headers and Footers

Introduction

A report page is made up of a header, a body and a footer area. Within the body area of a report, report items can be used to format and structure information.

In this lesson, you will use Report Designer to organize the report page layout. You will learn how to use data regions and independent report items and how to format report headers and footers.

Lesson objectives

After completing this lesson, you will be able to:

- Describe the report page structure.
- Add items to a report.
- Create report headers and footers.

Report Page Structure

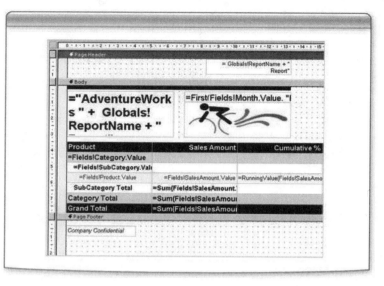

Introduction

Report pages can contain different sections. Understanding these sections will help you design your reports by taking full advantage of all the Report Designer capabilities.

Header and footers

A report can contain a header and footer that run along the top and bottom of each page. Headers and footers can contain text, images, and other report items, but they cannot contain data regions, subreports, or an item that refers directly to a field. Report headers and footers structure the report page; headers and footers within a data region provide category headers and footers.

In Report Designer, page headers and footers are displayed on the first and last page of a report by default. It is possible to suppress page headers and footers. To change this setting, change the **PrintOnFirstPage** or **PrintOnLastPage** property for the header or footer.

One of the most common uses for a footer is to display a page number. To display a page number in the footer of a report, create a text box in the footer and add the following expression:

```
="Page " & Globals.PageNumber
```

Report Items

```
● Data regions                      ● Independent items
    ●Link to data set                   ●Constant or expression
    ●Repeat for detail or group         ●Repeat if in a data region
● Types                             ● Types
    ●List                               ●Line
    ●Table                              ●Text box
    ●Matrix                             ●Image
    ●Chart                              ●Rectangle
                                        ●Subreport
```

Introduction

Report items are used to add data, structure, and formatting to a report. Report items come in two varieties: data regions and independent items. You can add these to a report page by using the Toolbox within Report Designer.

Data regions

As mentioned earlier in this module, a data region is used within a report to render data from an underlying data set. Tables and matrices provide multiple levels of grouping within a single data region; lists provide a single grouping. All data regions may be nested.

Data region types

Data region types include the following:

- A *list* is a data region that presents data arranged in a free-form fashion. You can arrange report items to create a form, with text boxes, images, and other data regions placed anywhere within the list.

- A *table* is a data region that presents data row by row. Table columns are static. Table rows expand downwards to accommodate data. You can add groups to tables, to organize data by selected fields or expressions.

- A *matrix*, also known as a *crosstab*, is a data region that contains both columns and rows that expand to accommodate data. A matrix can have dynamic columns and rows, which are repeated with groups of data, and static columns and rows, which are fixed. Columns or rows can be contained within other columns or rows, to group data.

- A *chart* is a data region that presents data graphically. Examples of charts include bar, pie, and line charts, but many more styles are supported.

For more information about list, matrix, and chart data regions see Module 3, "Enhancing Basic Reports," in Course 2030, *Creating Reporting Solutions Using Microsoft SQL Server 2000 Reporting Services*.

Independent items and item types

Independent report items are items that are not associated with a data set. The independent item types are as follows:

- Line: Horizontal, vertical or diagonal straight line

- Text box: Control that enables the displaying of textual information and can take input from the user

- Image: Graphic from a file, URL, or database field used within a table. Most common compression types are supported (e.g., jpg, png, gif, tif). Images can be added to a project and shared across all reports within the project.

- Rectangle: Rectangular box for graphical shape or to group other items. Grouping items can make things more convenient when formatting a report within Report Designer. Page breaks can be added before and/or after a group.

Note   To repeat an image over the background of a report, do not use an image independent report item. Rather, specify the image as the **BackgroundImage** property of the report body.

- A subreport references the body of another report. Because most reports contain a data region, the subreport appears to be a data region, although technically it is an independent item.

Headers and Footers

> ● **Report header/footer**
>   ○ Area of report above or below data region
> ● **Page header/footer**
>   ○ Add to page definition
>   ○ Optional for First and Last pages
> ● **Table header/footer**
>   ○ Optional repeat on each page
> ● **Group header/footer**
>   ○ Force page break before or after
>   ○ Optional repeat on each page

Introduction

Page headers and footers give context to a report. When you create headings, you often need to deal with the first and last pages differently than the pages in the main body of the report.

Report

Report headers and footers appear only on the first and last pages, respectively, of a report. To create a report header or footer in Reporting Services, simply place report items above or below the data region.

Page

Page headers and footers appear on all pages, optionally excluding the first or last page. To include page headers or footers in a report, add page header or page footer sections, and set the **PrintOnFirstPage** and **PrintOnLastPage** options appropriately.

Table

Table headers and footers appear at the beginning and end of a table. You can choose to have table headers and footers repeat on new pages. This allows you to create headers and footers that are the same for all pages, even if the headers and footers exclude the first or last page. To do this, set the **RepeatHeaderOnNewPage** and **RepeatFooterOnNewPage** options of the report to **True**.

Group

Group headers and footers appear at the beginning and end of grouping levels within a table. As with table headers and footers, you can choose to have group headers and footers repeat on new pages. The group header and footer, however, can each have different values, depending on current values of the grouping. To control the printing of group headers and footers, set the **Repeat Group Header** and **Repeat Group Footer** options within the **Grouping/Sorting** dialog box for each grouping level.

Reporting Services can render the final report in a number of formats, such as printed document, HTML, PDF, or Microsoft Excel. When rendering a printed report, for example, page breaks are automatically added as needed, while an HTML report will create a new page only where the author specifies.

Demonstration: Formatting Report Pages

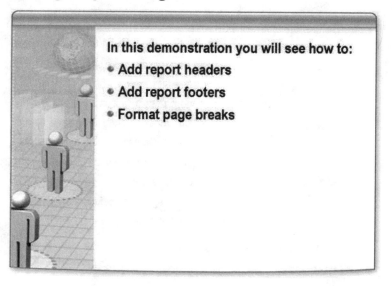

In this demonstration you will see how to:
- Add report headers
- Add report footers
- Format page breaks

Introduction

In this demonstration, the instructor will add further formatting to the report created in the first demonstration. The instructor will add headers, footers, and page breaks.

Procedures

▶ **Open a saved project**

1. In **Visual Studio .NET 2003**, on the **File** menu, point to **Open**, and then click **Project**.

2. In the **Open Project** dialog box, navigate to C:\Program Files\ Microsoft Learning\2030\Democode\Mod02\Demo02\Starter\Reseller Sales, and then double-click **Reseller Sales.sln**.

3. In **Solution Explorer**, double-click the **Reseller Sales.rdl** report.

▶ **Add a page break at the end of each Country group**

1. Click the **Layout** tab.

2. Click in the table, click the **table1_Category Footer** row icon to select the row, and right-click the group footer handle button.

3. Select **Edit Group**.

4. Select the **Page break at end** check box and then click **OK**.

▶ **Add a report header to the first page of the report**

1. Click in the table so that you see the row and column handles, and then click the handle in the top left corner to select the table item.

2. Drag the table down to the bottom of the **Body** design area.

3. In the **Toolbox** window, click **Line**. Drag a horizontal line across the very top of the report, aligned with the width of the table.

4. In the **Properties** window, change the **LineWidth** property of the line (**line1**) to a value of **12pt**.

5. In the **Toolbox** window, click **Textbox**. Drag the text box to fill the area between the line and the top of the table.

6. Click inside the text box, type **AdventureWorks Reseller Sales Report January 2003** and then press **Enter**.

7. On the **Report Formatting** toolbar, in the **Font Size** drop-down list, click **18**, and then click the **Bold** button to format the text box.

▶ **Save and preview the report**

1. On the **File** menu, click **Save All**.

2. Click the **Preview** tab. Notice that:

   • The report header appears on the first page only

   • Each country appears on its own page.

▶ **Add a repeating table header**

1. Click the **Layout** tab.

2. In the **Properties** window drop-down list, click **table1**.

3. In the **RepeatHeaderOnNewPage** property drop-down list, click **True**.

4. Click the **Preview** tab, and notice that the table header appears in black on each report page.

▶ **Add a page header to the report**

1. Click the **Layout** tab.

2. Right-click the margin to the left of the report body, and then click **Page Header**. Notice that a new section, labeled **Page Header**, appears at the top of the report.

3. In the **Toolbox** window, click **Textbox**.

4. Click inside the **Page Header** and size the text box to fit the available space.

5. With the text box selected, in the **Properties** window, in the **Appearance** section, in the **TextAlign** property drop-down list, click **Right**.

6. Click inside the text box, type **Reseller Sales Report**, and then press **Enter**.

7. In the **Properties** window drop-down list, click **PageHeader**.

8. In the **PrintOnFirstPage** property drop-down list, set the value to **False**.

9. In the **PrintOnLastPage** property drop-down list, set the value to **True**.

10. Click the **Preview** tab. Notice that the page header is printed on every page except for the first page.

► **Add a page footer to the report**

1. Click the **Layout** tab.

2. Right-click the margin to the left of the report body and then click **Page Footer**.

3. In the **Toolbox** window, click **Textbox**.

4. Click inside the page footer and size the text box to fit the available space.

5. Click inside the text box and type **Company Confidential**.

6. On the **Report Formatting** toolbar, click the **Italic** button.

7. In the **Properties** window drop-down list, click **PageFooter**.

8. Verify that the **PrintOnFirstPage** and **PrintOnLastPage** properties are set to **True**.

► **Save and preview the report**

1. On the **File** menu, click **Save All**.

2. Click the **Preview** tab. Notice that each country is on a different page and that the table header and page footer are repeated on all pages of the report. The page header is also on all pages except the first page.

Lesson: Calculating Values

- Creating Custom Fields
- Adding Expressions to a Report
- Aggregate Functions
- Common Aggregate Functions
- Conditional Formatting

Introduction

Most non-trivial reports require some sort of calculated values, such as running totals, sums, and averages. Adding calculated values to a report allows summary information to be displayed, as well as aggregated values per grouping category. Conditional formatting can be added to a report to highlight certain data values or ranges of values.

Lesson objectives

After completing this lesson, you will be able to:

- Create new fields based on data set fields.
- Create expressions as the values of individual text boxes.
- Use aggregate functions.
- Describe the common aggregate functions.
- Use conditional expressions to create dynamic formatting.

Creating Custom Fields

- **Database**
  - Report Designer automatically creates fields from data set columns
  - You can change name (alias) of database field
- **Calculated**
  - Based on database fields
  - Evaluated for every record returned in the data set
  - Create expressions by using Visual Basic .NET

Introduction

When creating a data region within a report, you can utilize all the fields contained within the underlying data set. Custom fields can be created with Report Designer to provide calculated values based on data fields and/or global data held within the report.

Database fields

Database fields originate from the query used to generate the underlying data set. Field names default to those found in the data set, but they may be changed by creating an alias within Report Manager.

Calculated fields

Any database fields referenced in calculated fields must come from the same source data set. You can reference calculated fields in the same manner as database fields. Calculated fields are evaluated for each record in the data set.

Important   When creating a calculated field, if you use the wrong capitalization when typing the name of a source field, no error will be reported. However, no data will be displayed in the calculated field.

Calculated fields can also be built into the underlying query, by using SQL aggregate functions or simple expressions. Aliases should be used with the query to provide appropriate field names. The SQL query only has access to database values and not the global report variables found within the report.

Adding Expressions to a Report

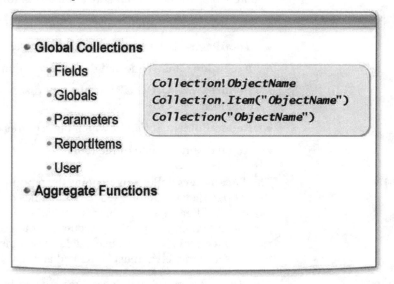

- **Global Collections**
  - Fields
  - Globals
  - Parameters
  - ReportItems
  - User
- **Aggregate Functions**

```
Collection!ObjectName
Collection.Item("ObjectName")
Collection("ObjectName")
```

Introduction

There are five global collections that can be used to reference data values in a report. These global collections are used within report items that are capable of displaying data—for example, data regions and text boxes.

Fields

The **Fields** collection contains the fields within the current data set. These fields typically are used to display data in text boxes in a report, but they can also be used in other report items, properties, and functions. Items within the **Fields** collection have two properties: **Value** and **IsMissing**. The **Value** property returns the value that was retrieved for the field in the data set. The **IsMissing** property indicates whether the field exists in the data set. (This is useful for queries that return variable sets of fields.) The **Value** property of missing fields is **Null**.

If the data provider does not support the current property, or if the field is not found when the query is executed, the value for the property is **Null** for properties of type **String** and **Object**, and zero for properties of type **Integer**.

A report contains one virtual **Fields** collection for each data set in the report. Fields must be unique within a collection, but the same field name can exist in multiple collections. When referring to a field within a data region, the data set for the data region determines which collection is used. When referring to a field within an aggregate expression, the data set for the scope determines which collection is used.

Globals

The **Globals** collection contains the global variables for the report. The members of the **Global** collection are as follows:

- **PageNumber**: Current page number
- **TotalPages**: Total number of pages in a report
- **ExecutionTime**: Time and date of execution of the report
- **ReportServerURL**: URL of the report server on which the report has been deployed
- **ReportFolder**: Folder in which the report is stored
- **ReportName**: Name of the report

Parameters

The **Parameters** collection contains the report parameters within the report. Report parameters can be used to pass values to an underlying query, pass values to a filter, or as variables for calculating data within the report. A report parameter text box is usually presented to the user when he or she runs the report, but a report can also use a default parameter and not present the choice to the user. Parameters must be named and have a defined data type.

ReportItems

The **ReportItems** collection contains the text boxes within the report. A text box can reference values in other text boxes from within an expression. For example, to refer to the value from a text box named **Category**, use the expression **=ReportItems!Category.Value**. You can refer to text boxes at the same level or at a container level. To refer to the value of the current text box, use **Me.Value**.

User

The **User** collection contains data on the user who is running the report. The members of the **User** collection are as follows:

- **UserID**: Fully qualified user name (such as London\Administrator)
- **UserLanguage**: Culture identifier for report (such as en-US). This can be used to retrieve localized information depending on the user's locale.

Aggregate functions

Aggregations provide summary data based on detail rows from a data set. Examples of aggregate functions are Sum and Average. These are discussed in more detail in the next topic.

Aggregate Functions

- Syntax
  - Function(Expression, Scope)
  - For example:
    Sum(Fields!SalesAmount.Value, "Category")
- Scope – grouping name specifying level for applying aggregate

---

Introduction

Aggregate functions allow you to return a single value from multiple rows in a data set.

Syntax

Most aggregate functions have a similar pattern for the arguments:

`Function(Expression, Scope)`

This syntax is composed of the following parts:

- *Expression* is typically a numeric field from the data set, but it can be any valid expression. The expression is calculated for each detail row accessed by the aggregate function.

- *Scope* determines which detail rows from the data set are accessed by the function. The aggregate applies only to rows that share a common value at the specified scope.

Scope

The scope argument for an Aggregate function allows three possibilities:

- If you omit the argument, the expression uses the current grouping level when the expression is on a group header or footer, and the lowest available grouping when the expression is used in a detail row.

- If you use the name of a grouping level, the expression uses all of the rows that have the same value for that grouping level. The grouping level name must be entered as a string (in quotation marks), it must be from the current or higher level within the report, and it is case sensitive. This allows you to do percent of group calculations.

Common Aggregate Functions

Avg	Average of non-null values
Count	Count of values
CountDistinct	Count of all distinct values
First	First value
Min	Minimum non-null value
RunningValue	Running aggregate (specify function)
StDev	Standard deviation of non-null values
Sum	Sum of the values

Introduction

Reporting Services includes a small but useful set of aggregate functions. These functions allow you to encapsulate information from a large number of rows into a single, high-level value that can be displayed on a report.

Common aggregate functions

The most commonly used aggregate functions are described as follows:

- **Avg**: Retrieves the sum of all values divided by the count of non-null values

- **Count**: Retrieves the count of all non-null values. This counts all the rows of the data source, not just distinct values.

  Count is useful as a denominator when you want to create a customized average, or when you want to have visibility to the number of rows in the data set.

- **CountDistinct**: Retrieves the count of distinct values for a field

  This function is useful when counting identifiers that can repeat. For example, if you have multiple orders for each customer, you can use **CountDistinct** to count the customers.

- **First**: Retrieves the first value from a field over the scope.

  This is typically the value you get from the data set if you do not use an aggregate function, but explicitly using the **First** function makes the intent of the expression clearer. If you reference a database field from outside the data region in a report that contains multiple data sets, you must use the **First** function so that you can specify the desired data set. If the data set is sorted by date, the **First** function can be used for retrieving the starting inventory value.

- **Last**: Retrieves the last value from a field over the scope. This can be used for retrieving the final inventory value.

- **Max**: Retrieves the largest value from a field over the scope. This is useful for finding exceptions in values that cannot be summed.

- **Min**: Retrieves the smallest value from a field over the scope. Similar to the **Max** function, **Min** is useful for finding exceptions.

- **RowNumber**: Retrieves an identity column (an automatically incrementing integer) on the data set.

  The row number increments for each row of the data set, not for each row of the report. It resets to 1 when the value at the specified scope changes. The **RowNumber** function can be used with conditional formatting to create alternating colors for detail rows. This is the only function that can be used as a grouping expression. When used as a grouping expression, it creates a grouping for the detail rows of the report.

- **RunningValue**: Accumulates the results of any aggregate function (except **RowNumber** or **RunningValue**). A generalized form of **RowNumber**, It can be used with **CountDistinct** to create alternating colors at non-detail levels.

- **StDev**: Returns the standard deviation based on a sample.

  This is useful to determine whether higher level averages are truly representative of detailed values. Use this version when the data is a random sample.

- **StDevP** – Returns the standard deviation based on data that represents the entire population. Use this version of StDev when the data represents everyone, not just a sample (as when examining logs from transaction systems).

- **Sum**: Returns a simple summation. This is the most commonly used aggregate. Be sure that the values are additive (that is, they can be logically summed). For example, prices are not additive, and inventory counts cannot be summed over time.

- **Var**: Returns the variance of all non-null values of the specified expression. Technically, this is the square of **StDev**.

- **VarP**: Returns the population variance of all non-null values of the specified expression. Technically, this is the square of **StDevP**.

Conditional Formatting

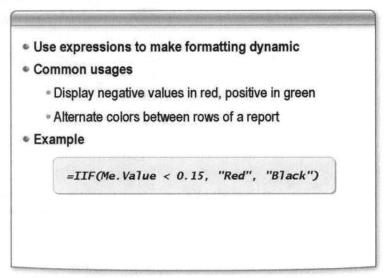

Use expressions to make formatting dynamic
- Common usages
  - Display negative values in red, positive in green
  - Alternate colors between rows of a report
- Example

```
=IIF(Me.Value < 0.15, "Red", "Black")
```

Introduction	When formatting reports, it is sometimes useful to highlight particular occurrences of data values or ranges of values. You can use conditional formatting to achieve this.
Dynamic formatting	Conditional formatting ties report formatting to the evaluation of an expression.
Common usages	Most appearance properties can include conditional formatting. Examples of scenarios where conditional formatting is useful include:

- *Dynamically setting the font or background color to highlight exceptions.* For example, a report can draw attention to sales people who have exceeded their target sales total by highlighting the font color of values in a report.

- *Changing the background color of alternating rows to make a long report easier to read.* Alternating row colors allow the report reader to visually align row values more easily.

Example   For example, to conditionally format the text box named **Margin**, you can use the following expression:

```
=IIF(ReportItems!Margin.Value <0.015, "Red", "Black")
```

If you need to copy the expression to a text box named **Margin_Total**, you would need to change the expression. The following expression allows you to copy the expression to any text box that requires the same logic:

```
=IIF(Me.Value <0.015, "Red", "Black")
```

Demonstration: Adding Calculated Values

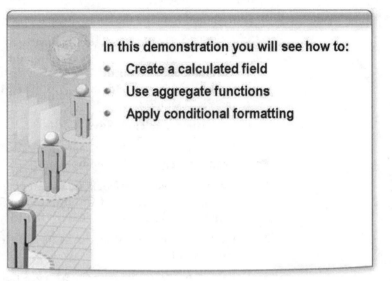

Introduction

In this demonstration, the instructor will add calculated values to a report. The instructor will create a calculated field, expressions that refer to text box values, expressions that aggregate at different scope levels, and expressions that reference a data set from outside the data region. The instructor will also add conditional formatting to the report.

Procedures

▶ **Open a saved project**

1. In **Visual Studio .NET 2003**, on the **File** menu, point to **Open**, and then click **Project**.

2. In the **Open Project** dialog box, navigate to the C:\Program Files\ Microsoft Learning\2030\Democode\Mod02\Demo03\Starter\Reseller Sales folder.

3. Double click the **Reseller Sales.sln** solution file.

4. In **Solution Explorer**, double-click the **Reseller Sales.rdl** report.

▶ **Create and add a margin calculated field**

1. Click the **Layout** tab.

2. In the **Fields** window, right-click a white area, and then click **Add**.

3. In the **Add New Field** dialog box, in the **Name** box, type **Margin**.

4. Click the **Calculated field** option, and then click the *fx* button.

5. In the **Edit Expression** dialog box, in the Fields pane, expand **Fields (DataDetail)**, click **SalesAmount**, and then click the **Append** button. The field is added to the Expression pane.

6. In the Expression pane, place the cursor after **=Fields!ListAmount.Value**, and then type a minus sign (-).

7. In the Fields pane, click the **DiscountAmount** field, and then click the **Append** button.

   You should now see the following expression in the Expression pane:

   ```
   = Fields!SalesAmount.Value - Fields!DiscountAmount.Value
   ```

8. Click **OK** to close the **Edit Expression** dialog box, and then click **OK** to close the **Add New Field** dialog box. The **Margin** calculated field is added to the **Field** window.

9. On the **File** menu, click **Save All**.

▶ **To add a margin to the report**

1. Click in the table, right-click the column handle for the **Order Quantity** field, and then click **Insert Column to the Right**. A new column appears with the same format as the **Order Quantity** column.

2. In the Fields window , drag the **Margin** field and drop it into the **Detail** row in the new column.

3. Repeat step 2 twice, placing the **Margin** field into the **table1_Category Footer** row and the **Table Footer** row in the new column.

4. Click the column handle for the **Margin** column. In the **Properties** window, in the **Format** property text box, type **C0**. The cell is formatted as currency with no decimal places.

▶ **Save and preview the report**

1. On the **File** menu, click **Save All**.

2. Click the **Preview** tab and examine the report.

▶ **Conditionally format rows with discounts greater than 5%**

1. Click the **Layout** tab.

2. Click the **Margin** cell in the **Detail** row.

3. In the **Properties** window, in the **Color** property drop-down list, click **Expression**.

4. In the **Edit Expression** dialog box, in the **Expression** box, delete the default expression and type:

   ```
   =IIF((Fields!DiscountAmount.Value/Fields!SalesAmount.Value)
   > 0.05,"Red","Black")
   ```

5. Click **OK**.

▶ **Save and preview the report**

1. On the **File** menu, click **Save All**.

2. Click the **Preview** tab. Notice that the **Margin** value appears in red for **Fitness Toy Store** on the first page of the report.

▶ **Sort products in descending order of sales amount**

1. Click the **Layout** tab.

2. Right-click the **Detail** row icon.

3. Select **Insert Group**.

4. In the **Grouping and Sorting Properties** dialog box, in the **Name** box, type **DetailSort**.

5. Under **Group on**, click the first row, and from the **Expression** drop-down list, click **=Fields!Reseller.Value**.

6. Click the **Sorting** tab. Under **Sort on**, click the first row, and from the **Expression** drop-down list, click **=Fields!SalesAmount.Value**. In the **Direction** column, click **Descending**, and then click **OK**.

▶ **Save and preview the report**

1. On the **File** menu, click **Save All**.

2. Click the **Preview** tab. Notice that the resellers are sorted by sales amount.

— Need to clear group header + group footer from Table Properties / Groups / Detail Sort

Review

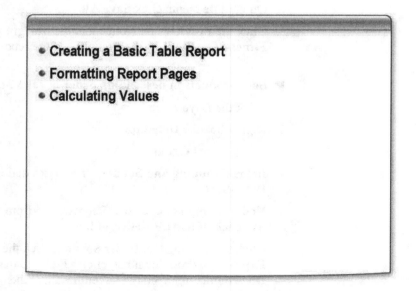

1. What is RDL?

2. What types of data regions can be used in a report?

3. What are the different types of headers and footers that can be used in a report?

4. What does the following code do?

```
Sum(Fields!SalesAmount.Value, "Category")
```

5. What are the five global object collections? Give three syntax examples of referring to the **Language** member of the **User** collection.

Lab 2: Designing a Simple Report

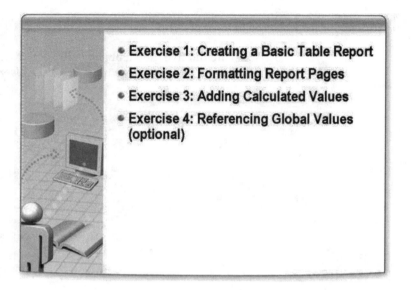

Objectives

In this lab, you will create the Adventure Works Product Profitability report. You will begin by creating a simple tabular report and then enhance it by adding formatting and summary totals.

After completing this lab, you will be able to:

- Create a basic table report.
- Add formatting to a report.
- Add calculated values to a report.

Prerequisites: None

Estimated time to complete this lab: 60 minutes

Exercise 1
Creating a Basic Table Report

In this exercise, you will create the Adventure Works Product Profitability report. To do this you will define a data source and data set, and then add groupings and basic formatting to the report table.

▶ **Create a new report named "Product Profitability"**

1. Click **Start**, point to **All Programs**, point to **Microsoft Visual Studio .NET 2003**, and then click **Microsoft Visual Studio .NET 2003**.

2. On the **File** menu, point to **New**, and then click **Project**.

3. In the **New Project** dialog box, in the Project Types pane, click the **Business Intelligence Projects** folder.

4. In the Templates pane, click **Report Project**.

5. Click **Browse** and navigate to the C:\Program Files\Microsoft Learning\2030\Labfiles\Lab02 folder, and then click **Open**.

6. In the **Name** text box, type **Product Profitability** and then click **OK**.

7. In **Solution Explorer**, right-click the **Reports** folder, point to **Add**, and then click **Add New Item**.

Tip If Solution Explorer is not visible, on the **View** menu, click **Solution Explorer**.

---

8. In the **Add New Item** dialog box, in the Templates pane, click **Report**. In the **Name** box, type **Product Profitability** and then click **Open**.

▶ **Create a shared data source**

1. In **Solution Explorer**, right-click the **Shared Data Sources** folder, and then click **Add New Data Source**.

2. In the **Data Link Properties** dialog box, on the **Connection** tab, in the **Select or enter a server name** text box, type **localhost**.

3. Under **Enter information to log on to the server**, ensure that the **Use Windows NT Integrated security** option is selected.

4. In the **Select the database on the server** drop-down list, click **AdventureWorksDW**.

5. Click **Test Connection**, and then click **OK** to close the **Microsoft Data Link** dialog box.

6. Click **OK** to close the **Data Link Properties** dialog box.

▶ **Add a data set**

1. In design view, in the **Dataset** drop-down list, click **<New Dataset...>**.

2. In the **Dataset** dialog box, type **DataDetail** in the **Name** text box on the **Query** tab.

Caution   Be sure that there are no spaces in the name of your data set.

---

3. In the **Data source** text box, verify that the data source is **AdventureWorksDW (shared)**.

4. In the **Query string** text box, type:

```
Select * from vProductProfitability Where Year = 2003 and
MonthNumberOfYear = 1
```

5. Click **OK**.

6. On the **Data** tab, click the **Run** button. A data set containing the query results is displayed.

7. On the **File** menu, click **Save All**.

▶ **Add a table data region**

1. Click the **Layout** tab.

2. In the **Toolbox**, double-click **Table**. A table is added to the report. Notice that it has placeholder rows for the table header, table detail, and table footer.

Tip By default, the **Toolbox** is located on the left side of the screen. If the Toolbox is not visible, on the **View** menu, click **Toolbox**.

▶ **Add fields to the detail row**

1. In the **Fields** window, drag the **Product** field and drop it into the first cell in the **Detail** row.

Tip By default, the **Fields** window is located on the left side of the screen. If the **Fields** window is not visible, on the **View** menu, click **Fields**.

---

2. Adjust the **Product** column to be approximately **2** inches (5 cm) wide.

3. In the **Fields** window, drag the **SalesAmount** field and drop it into the second cell in the **Detail** row.

4. Adjust the **Sales Amount** column to be approximately **2** inches (5 cm) wide.

5. In the **Fields** window, drag the **OrderQuantity** field and drop it into the third cell in the **Detail** row.

6. Adjust the **Order Quantity** column to be approximately **1.25** (3.5 cm) inches wide.

▶ **Add fields to the table footer**

1. In the **Fields** window, drag the **SalesAmount** field and drop it into the second cell in the table footer row. Note that when you add a numeric field to a header or footer row, Report Designer automatically adds a Sum function to aggregate the values.

2. In the **Fields** window, drag the **OrderQuantity** field and drop it into the third cell in the table footer row.

3. Click the first cell of the table footer row, type **Grand Total** and then press **Enter**.

▶ **Save and preview the report**

1. On the **File** menu, click **Save All**.

2. Click the **Preview** tab. Notice that the report shows a header for each column and detail values from the source data set.

▶ **Create the table1_Category group**

1. Click the **Layout** tab.

2. Click the table, right-click the row icon to the left of the **Detail** row (the second row), and then click **Insert Group**.

3. In the **Grouping and Sorting Properties** dialog box, set the **Name** to **table1_Category**.

Important   Group names are case sensitive.

---

4. Under **Group on**, click the first row, and from the **Expression** drop-down list, click =**Fields!Category.Value**, and then click **OK**.

5. In the **Fields** window, drag the **Category** field and drop in into the first cell in the **table1_Category Header** row, directly beneath the **Product** cell.

6. In the first cell in the **table1_Category Footer** row (directly above the **Grand Total** cell), type **Category Total** and then press **Enter**.

7. In the **Table Footer** row, CTRL+click the cells that contain the **SalesAmount** total and the **OrderQuantity** total, right-click, and then click **Copy**.

8. Right-click the second cell in the **table1_Category Footer** row (next to the **Category Total** cell), and then click **Paste**.

▶ **Create the table1_SubCategory group**

1. Right-click the row icon to the left of the **Detail** row and then click **Insert Group**.

2. In the **Name** box, type **table1_SubCategory**.

3. Under **Group on**, click the first row, and from the **Expression** drop-down list, click **=Fields!SubCategory.Value**.

4. On the **Sorting** tab, under **Sort on**, click the first row, and from the **Expression** drop-down list, click **=Fields!SubCategory.Value**, and then click **OK**.

5. In the **Fields** window, drag the **SubCategory** field and drop it into the first cell in the **table1_SubCategory Header** row.

6. In the first cell in the **table1_SubCategory Footer** row, type **SubCategory Total** and then press **Enter**.

7. In the **Table Footer** row, CTRL+click the cells that contain the **SalesAmount** total and the **OrderQuantity** total, right-click, and then click **Copy**.

8. Right-click the second cell in the **table1_SubCategory Footer** row (next to the **SubCategory Total** cell), and then click **Paste**.

▶ **Apply basic formatting to the table**

1. Click the column handle (the gray box above the column) for the **Sales Amount** column.

2. In the **Properties** window, in the **Format** property text box, type **C0** and then press **Enter**. The cells format is set to currency with no decimal places.

3. Click the column handle for the **Order Quantity** column.

4. In the **Properties** window, in the **Format** property text box, type **N0** and then press **Enter**. The cells format is set to numeric with no decimal places.

5. Click the **Detail** row icon to select the **Detail** row. On the **Report Formatting** toolbar, click the **Background Color** button, click the **Web** tab, click **WhiteSmoke**, and then click **OK**.

6. Click the **Table Header** row icon, and then press **CTRL** and click the **Table Footer** row icon. The header and footer rows are selected.

7. On the **Report Formatting** toolbar, perform the following tasks:

   • Click **12** in the **Font Size** drop-down list.

   • Click the **Bold** button to boldface the cells.

   • Click the **Background Color** button, click the **Web** tab, click **Black**, and then click **OK**.

   • Click the **Foreground Color** button, click the **Web** tab, click **White**, and then click **OK**.

8. Click the **table1_Category Header** row icon, and then press **CTRL** and click the **table1_Category Footer** row icon.

9. On the **Report Formatting** toolbar, perform the following tasks:

   - Click **12** in the **Font Size** drop-down list.

   - Click the **Bold** button to boldface the cells.

   - Click the **Background Color** button, click the **Web** tab, click **Gainsboro**, and then click **OK**.

9. Click the **table1_SubCategory Header** row icon, and then press **CTRL** and click the **table1_SubCategory Footer** row icon.

10. On the **Report Formatting** toolbar, perform the following tasks:

    - Click **11** in the **Font Size** drop-down list

    - Click the **Bold** button to bold the cells.

▶ **Indent row captions**

1. Click the first cell in the **Detail** row.

2. In the **Properties** window, expand the **Padding** property group.

3. In the padding **Left** property text box, type **22pt**

4. Click the first cell in the **table1_SubCategory Header** row, and then press **CTRL** and click the first cell in the **table1_SubCategory Footer** row.

5. In the **Properties** window, in the padding **Left** property text box, type **12pt**

▶ **Save and preview the report**

1. On the **File** menu, click **Save All**.

2. Click the **Preview** tab, and verify that you have the report subset as shown in the following illustration:

Product	Sales Amount	Order Quantity
Clothing		
Bib-Short		
Men's bib-short, L	$1,111	19
Men's bib-short, M	$3,685	63
Men's bib-short, S	$2,281	39
SubCategory Total	$7,078	121
Cap		
AWC logo cap	$478	85
SubCategory Total	$478	85
Gloves		
Full-finger Gloves, L	$4,229	176

Exercise 2
Formatting Report Pages

In this exercise, you will apply additional formatting to the report that you created in Exercise 1. You will add headers and footers, images, and page breaks.

▶ **Open a saved project**

Note   You can omit this step if you already have the Product Profitability report open from Exercise 1.

---

1. In **Visual Studio .NET 2003**, on the **File** menu, point to **Open**, and then click **Project**.

2. In the **Open Project** dialog box, double-click the **Product Profitability** report project you created to Exercise 1 or the solution file found in C:\Program Files\Microsoft Learning\2030\Labfiles\Lab02\Solution\ Product Profitability.

3. In **Solution Explorer**, double-click the **Product Profitability.rdl** report.

▶ **Add a page break at the end of each category group**

1. Click the **Layout** tab.

2. Click in the table, click the **table1_Category Footer** row icon to select the row, and right-click the group footer handle button.

3. Select **Edit Group**.

4. Select the **Page break at end** check box and then click **OK**.

Note   When you add a page break after a grouping level, the report will go to a new page at the end of each element of the group, including the last. If there is a table footer on the report, it will appear alone on the last page. Currently, it is not possible to have a page break after each group member without getting an orphan total at the end of the report.

► **Add a report header to the first page of the report**

1. Click in the table so that you see the row and column handles, and then click the handle in the top left corner to select the table item.

2. Drag the table down so that the top of the table is approximately **1.5** inches (4 cm) from the top of the report.

3. In the **Toolbox** window, click **Line**. Drag a horizontal line across the top of the report, aligned with the width of the table.

4. In the **Properties** window, change the **LineWidth** property of the line (**line1**) to a value of **12pt**.

5. In the **Toolbox** window, click **Textbox**. On the report grid, click just under the line in the upper left corner and drag the text box to size it **2.5in** (6 cm) wide and **1.25in** (4 cm) high. Reposition and resize the text box as needed.

Tip   You can use the **Size**, **Width**, and **Height** properties in the **Properties** window to adjust the size of the text box.

Once an item is selected in Layout view, you can use the arrow keys for large movements, or **CTRL** and arrow keys for fine movements.

---

6. Click inside the text box, type **AdventureWorks Product Profitability Report** and then press **Enter**.

Tip   You can force a new line by pressing **SHIFT+ENTER**.

---

7. On the Report Formatting toolbar, in the **Font Size** drop-down list, click **20**, and then click the **Bold** button to format the text box.

► **Add an image to the report**

1. In the **Toolbox** window, click **Image**. On the report grid, click to the right of the report title text box.

2. In the Image Wizard, on the **Welcome to the Image Wizard** page, click **Next**.

3. On the **Select the Image Source** page, click **Embedded**, and then click **Next**. Note that an embedded image cannot be shared with other reports in the project.

4. On the **Choose the Embedded Image** page, click the **New Image** button.

5. Navigate to **the C:\Program Files\Microsoft Learning\2030\ Labfiles\Lab02** folder, click **logopart.jpg**, and click **Open**.

6. Click the **Name** column, delete the existing text, type **Logo** and then click **Next**.

7. On the **Completing the Image Wizard** page, click **Finish**. The image is added to the report.

8. Stretch and align the image as required to match the height of the **Report Title** text box.

▶ **Save and preview the report**

1. On the **File** menu, click **Save All**.

2. Click the **Preview** tab. Notice that:

   - The report header and image appears on the first page only

   - Each category appears on its own page.

▶ **Add a repeating table header**

1. Click the **Layout** tab.

2. Click the Table Header row icon.

3. In Properties pane set the **RepeatHeaderOnNewPage** to **True**.

Note   Group headers and footers only appear, by default, at the beginning or ending of a group. Within the **Grouping and Sorting Properties** dialog box for a group, you can set an option to cause the header or footer to repeat on each new page.

---

4. Click the **Preview** tab, and notice that the product header appears in black on each report page.

▶ **Add a page header to the Report**

1. Click the **Layout** tab.

2. Right-click the margin to the left of the report body, and then click **Page Header**. Notice that a new section, labeled **Page Header**, appears at the top of the report.

3. In the **Toolbox** window, click **Textbox**.

4. Click inside the **Page Header**, and size the text box to **2** inches (5 cm) wide and **0.25** inches (0.5 cm) high.

5. Drag the text box to align it with the right edge of the line.

6. With the text box selected, in the **Properties** window, in the **Appearance** section, in the **TextAlign** property drop-down list, click **Right**.

7. Click inside the text box, type **Product Profitability Report** and then press **Enter**.

8. In the **Properties** window drop-down list, click **PageHeader**.

9. In the **PrintOnFirstPage** property drop-down list, set the value to **False**.

10. In the **PrintOnLastPage** property drop-down list, set the value to **True**.

11. Click the **Preview** tab. Notice that the page header is printed on every page except for the first page.

▶ **Add a page footer to the report**

1. Click the **Layout** tab.

2. Right-click the margin to the left of the report body, and then click **Page Footer**.

3. In the **Toolbox** window, click **Textbox**.

4. Click inside the **Page Footer**, and size the text box to **1.5** inches (4 cm) wide and **0.25** inches (0.5 cm) high.

5. Click inside the text box, and then type **Company Confidential**.

6. On the **Report Formatting** toolbar, click the **Italic** button.

7. In the **Properties** window drop-down list, click **PageFooter**.

8. Verify that the **PrintOnFirstPage** and **PrintOnLastPage** properties are set to **True**.

▶ **Save and preview the report**

1. On the **File** menu, click **Save All**.

2. Click the **Preview** tab, and verify that you have the report subset as shown in the following illustration:

Notice that each category is on a different page and that the table header and page footer are repeated on all pages of the report. The page header is also on all pages except the first page.

Exercise 3
Adding Calculated Values

In this exercise, you will add calculated values to your report. You will create a calculated field, expressions that refer to text box values, expressions that aggregate at different scope levels, and expressions that reference a data set from outside the data region. You will also use conditional formatting.

▶ **Open a saved project**

Note   You can omit this step if you already have the Product Profitability report open from Exercise 2.

---

1. In **Visual Studio .NET 2003**, on the **File** menu, point to **Open**, and then click **Project**.

2. In the **Open Project** dialog box, double-click the **Product Profitability** report project you created in Exercise 2 or the solution file found in the C:\Program Files\Microsoft Learning\2030\Labfiles\Lab02\Starter\ Product Profitability folder.

3. In **Solution Explorer**, double-click the **Product Profitability.rdl** report.

▶ **Create and add a margin calculated field**

1. Click the **Layout** tab.

2. In the **Fields** window, right-click a white area, and then click **Add**.

3. In the **Add New Field** dialog box, in the **Name** box, type **Margin**.

4. Click the **Calculated field** option, and then click the *fx* button.

5. In the **Edit Expression** dialog box, in the Fields pane, expand **Fields (DataDetail)**, click **SalesAmount**, and then click the **Append** button. The field is added to the Expression pane.

6. In the Expression pane, place the cursor after **=Fields!SalesAmount.Value**, and then type a minus sign (-).

7. In the Fields pane, click the **CostAmount** field, and then click the **Append** button.

   You should now see the following expression in the Expression pane:

   ```
   = Fields!SalesAmount.Value - Fields!CostAmount.Value
   ```

8. Click **OK** to close the **Edit Expression** dialog box, and then click **OK** to close the **Add New Field** dialog box. The **Margin** calculated field is added to the **Field** window.

9. On the **File** menu, click **Save All**.

▶ **To add a margin to the report**

1. Right-click the column handle for the **Order Quantity** field, and then click **Insert Column to the Right**. A new column appears with the same format as the **Order Quantity** column.

2. In the **Fields** window, drag the **Margin** field, and drop it into the **Detail** row in the new column.

3. In the **Fields** window, drag the **Margin** field, and drop it into the **table1_SubCategory Footer** row in the new column. Notice that the expression becomes a Sum expression.

4. Press **Enter** to select the entire expression in the last cell in the **table1_SubCategory Footer** row, and then press **CTRL+C** to copy it.

5. Click the last cell in the **table1_Category Footer** row. Then click the cell again to edit the empty formula. Press **CTRL+V** to paste the copied formula.

Note   Copying just the formula preserves the formatting in the destination cell.

---

6. Click the last cell in the **Table Footer** row. Then click the cell again to edit the empty formula. Press **CTRL+V** to paste the copied formula.

7. Click the column handle for the **Margin** column. In the **Properties** window, in the **Format** property text box, type **C0**. The cell is formatted as currency with no decimal places.

▶ **Save and preview the report**

1. On the **File** menu, click **Save All**.

2. Click the **Preview** tab, and verify that you have a report subset like the following illustration:

Product	Sales Amount	Order Quantity	Margin
Clothing			
Bib-Short			
Men's bib-short, L	$1,111	19	$406
Men's bib-short, M	$3,685	63	$1,346
Men's bib-short, S	$2,281	39	$834
SubCategory Total	**$7,078**	**121**	**$2,586**
Cap			
AWC logo cap	$478	85	$33
SubCategory Total	**$478**	**85**	**$33**

▶ **Add the Detail Margin % expression**

1. Click the **Layout** tab.

2. Right-click the handle at the top of the **Margin** column, and then click **Insert Column to the Right**.

3. In the last cell in the **Table Header** row, type **Margin %**.

4. Click the column handle for the **Margin %** column. In the **Properties** window, in the **Format** property text box, type **P1**.The cells are formatted as a percentage with one decimal place.

5. Right-click the **Detail** cell of the **Margin %** column, and then click **Expression**.

6. In the **Edit Expression** dialog box, in the **Expression** box, type:

```
=ReportItems!Margin.Value/ReportItems!SalesAmount.Value
```

7. Click **OK**.

8. To view the new column, click the **Preview** tab.

▶ **Add the Table Footer Margin % expression**

1. Click the **Layout** tab.

2. Click the **Sales Amount** cell in the **Table Footer** row. In the **Properties** window, in the **Name** property text box, replace the existing name with **SalesAmount_Total**.

3. Click the **Margin** cell in the **Table Footer** row. In the **Properties** window, in the **Name** property text box, replace the existing name with **Margin_Total**.

4. Right-click the **Margin %** cell in the **Table Footer** row, and then click **Expression**.

5. In the **Edit Expression** dialog box, in the **Expression** box, type :

```
=ReportItems!Margin_Total.Value /
ReportItems!SalesAmount_Total.Value
```

6. Click **OK**.

7. To view the added **Margin %** table footer, click the **Preview** tab, and then navigate to the end of the report.

▶ **Add the Category Margin % expression**

1. Click the **Layout** tab.

2. Click the **Sales Amount** cell in the **table1_Category Footer** row. In the **Properties** window, in the **Name** property text box, replace the existing name with **SalesAmount_Category**.

3. Click the **Margin** cell in the **table1_Category Footer** row. In the **Properties** window, in the **Name** property text box, replace the existing name with **Margin_Category**.

4. Right-click the **Margin %** cell in the **table1_Category Footer** row, and then click **Expression**.

5. In the **Edit Expression** dialog box, in the **Expression** box, type:

```
=ReportItems!Margin_Category.Value /
ReportItems!SalesAmount_Category.Value
```

6. Click **OK**.

7. Click the **Preview** tab. Notice that a margin percent exists for each category.

▶ **Add the SubCategory Margin % expression**

1. Click the **Layout** tab.

2. Click the **Sales Amount** cell in the **table1_SubCategory Footer** row. In the **Properties** window, in the **Name** property text box, replace the existing name with **SalesAmount_SubCategory**.

3. Click the **Margin** cell in the **table1_SubCategory Footer** row. In the **Properties** window, in the **Name** property text box, replace the existing name with **Margin_SubCategory**.

4. Right-click the **Margin %** cell in the **table1_SubCategory Footer** row, and then click **Expression**.

5. In the **Edit Expression** dialog box, in the **Expression** box, type:

```
=ReportItems!Margin_SubCategory.Value /
ReportItems!SalesAmount_SubCategory.Value
```

6. Click **OK**.

7. Click the **Preview** tab. Notice that a value for margin percent now exists at subcategory level.

► **Conditionally format rows with low margin percents**

1. Click the **Layout** tab.

2. In the **Detail** row, click the **Margin %** cell.

3. In the **Properties** window, in the **Color** property drop-down list, click **Expression**.

4. In the **Edit Expression** dialog box, in the **Expression** text box, delete the default expression and type:

```
=IIF(Me.Value<0.15, "Red", "Black")
```

> **Note** The *Me* keyword refers to the report item for which the expression is being calculated. For a text box named **MarginPercent**, the expression *Me.Value* is equivalent to *ReportItems!MarginPercent.Value*.

5. Click **OK**.

► **Copy conditional formatting to additional rows**

1. In the **Properties** window, in the **Color** property drop-down list, click the expression, and then press **CTRL+C** to copy the expression.

2. In the **table1_SubCategory Footer** row, click the **Margin %** cell.

3. In the **Properties** window, click the **Color** property, delete the existing value, and press **CTRL+V** to paste the expression.

4. Repeat steps 2 and 3 for the **Margin %** cell in the following rows:

   • **table1_Category Footer**

   • **Table Footer**

5. Ensure that the **Margin %** cell in the **Table Footer** row is selected. In the **Properties** window, in the **Color** property drop-down list, click **Expression**.

6. Modify the expression by replacing **"Black"** with **"White"**, and then click **OK**.

▶ **Save and preview the report**

1. On the **File** menu, click **Save All**.

2. Click the **Preview** tab, and verify that the margin percent for AWC logo cap and the Cap SubCategory Total are both **6.9%** and appear in red.

▶ **Sort products in descending order of sales amount**

1. Click the **Layout** tab.

2. Right-click the **Detail** row icon.

3. Select **Insert Group**.

4. In the **Grouping and Sorting Properties** dialog box, in the **Name** box, type **DetailSort**.

5. Under **Group on**, click the first row, and from the **Expression** drop-down list, click **=Fields!Product.Value**.

6. Click the **Sorting** tab. Under **Sort on**, click the first row, and from the **Expression** drop-down list, click **=Fields!SalesAmount.Value**. In the **Direction** column, click **Descending**, and then click **OK**.

▶ **Save and preview the report**

1. On the **File** menu, click **Save All**.

2. Click the **Preview** tab, and verify that you have the report subset as shown in the following illustration:

Product	Sales Amount	Order Quantity	Margin	Margin %
Clothing				
Bib-Short				
Men's bib-short, M	$3,685	63	$1,346	36.5 %
Men's bib-short, S	$2,281	39	$834	36.5 %
Men's bib-short, L	$1,111	19	$406	36.5 %
SubCategory Total	**$7,078**	**121**	**$2,586**	**36.5 %**
Cap				
AWC logo cap	$478	85	$33	6.9 %
SubCategory Total	**$478**	**85**	**$33**	**6.9 %**

AdventureWorks Product Profitability Report

Notice that the products are listed in descending order based on sales amount.

▶ **Show cumulative sales amount within subcategory**

1. Click the **Layout** tab.

2. Right-click the handle at the top of the **Sales Amount** column, and click **Insert Column to the Right**.

3. In the new cell in the **Table Header** row, type **Cumulative**.

4. In the **Detail** row, right-click the **Cumulative** cell, and then click **Expression**.

5. In the **Edit Expression** dialog box, in the Expression pane, type

```
=RunningValue(Fields!SalesAmount.Value, Sum,
"table1_SubCategory")
```

6. Click **OK**. Note that this expression calculates a running total of the sales amount, resetting each time the value of the **table1_SubCategory** level changes.

▶ **Save and preview the report**

1. On the **File** menu, click **Save All**.

2. Click the **Preview** tab, and verify that you have the report subset as shown in the following illustration:

Notice the **Cumulative** value increases within each subcategory until it matches the total for the subcategory.

▶ **Convert the cumulative value to a percentage**

1. Click the **Layout** tab.

2. In the **Detail** row, right-click the **Cumulative** cell, and then click **Expression**.

3. In the **Edit Expression** dialog box, in the Expression pane, change the expression to:

```
=RunningValue(Fields!SalesAmount.Value, Sum,
"table1_SubCategory") /
ReportItems!SalesAmount_SubCategory.Value
```

4. Click **OK**. Note that this expression calculates the cumulative percentage of the subcategory for each product.

5. In the **Properties** window, in the **Format** property text box, type **P1**.

6. Change the label in the **Table Header** row to **Cumulative %**.

▶ **Save and preview the report**

1. On the **File** menu, click **Save All**.

2. Click the **Preview** tab, and verify that you have the report subset as shown in the following illustration:

Notice that the cumulative percentages accumulate to 100% for each subcategory and then restart with each new subcategory.

Exercise 4
Referencing Global Values (Optional)

In this optional exercise, you will use global values within the report. You will refer to the globally held report name (rather than hard coding the name within the report) and the date held within the data region.

▶ **Modify the report title text box to reference a global variable**

1. Click the **Layout** tab.

2. In the **Page Header**, right-click the text box containing the **Product Profitability Report** report title, and then click **Expression**.

3. In the **Edit Expression** dialog box, in the Fields pane, expand **Globals**, click **ReportName**, and then click the **Replace** button.

4. In the Expression pane, place the cursor after = **Globals!ReportName**, and then type + " **Report"**.

   You should now see the following expression in the Expression pane:

   ```
   = Globals!ReportName + " Report"
   ```

5. Click **OK** to close the **Edit Expression** dialog box.

6. Right-click the text box containing the **AdventureWorks Product Profitability Report** report title, and then click **Expression**.

7. In the **Edit Expression** dialog box, in the Expression pane, delete the existing value, type =**"AdventureWorks "** + . In the Fields pane, expand **Globals**, click **ReportName**, click the **Append** button, and then type + " **Report"** at the end of the expression.

   You should now see the following expression in the **Expression** pane:

   ```
   ="AdventureWorks " + Globals!ReportName + " Report"
   ```

8. Click **OK** to close the **Edit Expression** dialog box. Any subsequent updates to the report name in Solution Explorer will be automatically updated in the report and page headers.

▶ **Refer to data set values from outside the data region**

1. Drag the top of border of the report logo down about **0.25** inches.

2. In the **Toolbox** window, click **Textbox**. Above the report logo, create a text box and size it to the same width as the logo and approximately **0.25** inches (1 cm) high.

3. Click inside the text box, and then type =**First(Fields!Month.Value, "DataDetail") + " " + First(Fields!Year.Value, "DataDetail")**.

4. In the **Report Formatting** toolbar, in the **Font Size** drop-down list, click **12**, click the **Bold** button, and then click the **Align Right** button.

▶ **Save and preview the report**

1. On the **File** menu, click **Save All**.

2. Verify that you have the report subset as shown in the following illustration:

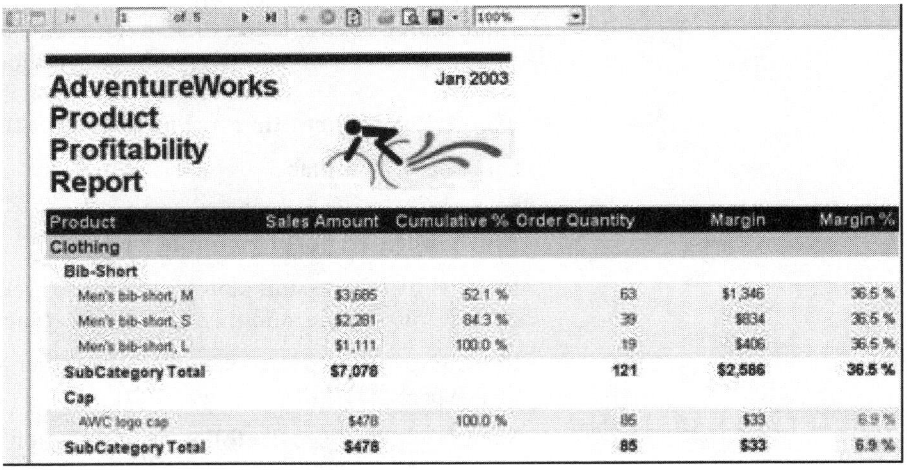

Notice that "AdventureWorks Product Profitability Report" appears as the report title. Also, notice that "Jan 2003" is displayed in the new text box. Because of the **WHERE** clause in the data set SQL query, all the rows retrieve values from January 2003. The text box can choose the values from the first row of the data set, because all the rows contain the same Month and Year values.

3. Click the **Next Page** button. Notice that the report name, **Product Profitability Report**, is displayed in the page header.

Microsoft®

Module 3: Enhancing Basic Reports

Contents

Overview

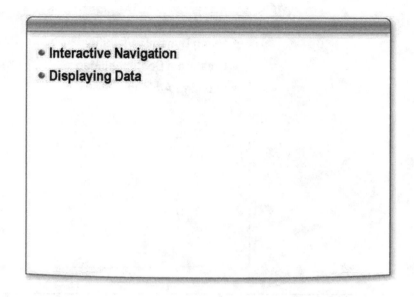

- Interactive Navigation
- Displaying Data

Introduction

When developing a report, you should think about how information will be presented to the report user and how the user will browse the information. This module introduces navigational controls and some types of data regions and discusses how to use them to enhance a basic report.

Navigational controls such as document maps and actions can be used to create a report contents page. They can also be used to add links within a report and between reports.

Data regions such as matrix, list, and chart, provide alternatives to tables for structuring data in a report.

Objectives

After completing this module, you will be able to:

- Create interactive navigation using report links.
- Display data using data regions.

Lesson: Interactive Navigation

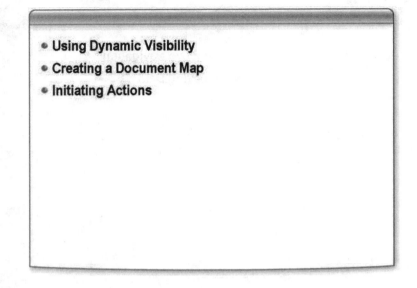

- Using Dynamic Visibility
- Creating a Document Map
- Initiating Actions

Introduction

This lesson introduces dynamic visibility and the creation of custom actions. *Dynamic visibility* allows report data to be shown in summary of detail views under the control of the user. *Actions* provide a mechanism for adding interactive functionality to a report.

Lesson objectives

After completing this lesson, you will be able to:

- Allow the user to navigate to an appropriate level of detail.
- Create a document map.
- Create links and custom report actions.

Using Dynamic Visibility

- **Use show/hide to provide drill-down interactivity**
  - Allows users to navigate from summarized data to detailed data
  - Implemented by toggling the visibility of the detail, row group, or column group
- **Only supported by rendering extensions that support interactivity, such as HTML**

Introduction

By using dynamic visibility, you can create a report that enables the user to show or hide the detail it contains. Report items can be hidden based on the contents of other report items. Any report item can be hidden, including groups, columns, or rows in a table or matrix.

Drill-down reports

Hidden report items can be used to enable the user to toggle between summary and detail views ("drilling down"). By following these steps in Report Designer, you can create this drill-down effect:

1. Select the group, column, or row to hide.

2. Set its hidden state to **True**.

3. Set the toggle item to the name of a text box in a containing group.

When the report is rendered, the user can click the text box to expand and collapse the detail data.

Rendering interactive controls

In some situations, you may want to hide items in a report once it is rendered. Depending on the rendering format chosen, hidden items may or may not be shown in the report. For example, when rendering reports, Hypertext Markup Language (HTML) will render show-and-hide toggles on report items and respect hidden items, whereas Extensible Markup Language (XML) will render all report items, regardless of whether they are hidden.

Demonstration: Using Dynamic Visibility

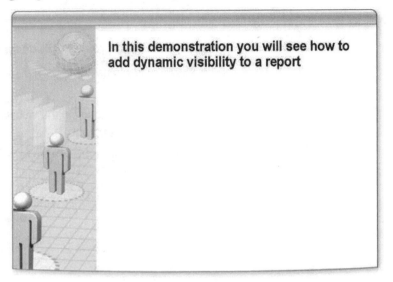

In this demonstration you will see how to add dynamic visibility to a report

Introduction

The Product Profitability report shows total sales amount and order quantity by product, as well as summarized totals by product category. In this demonstration, you will see how to use dynamic visibility to allow users to hide and reveal product detail within the Product Profitability report.

Procedures

▶ **Open a saved solution**

1. Click **Start**, point to **All Programs**, point to **Microsoft® Visual Studio® .NET 2003**, and then click **Microsoft Visual Studio .NET 2003**.

2. On the **File** menu, click **Open Solution**.

3. In the **Open Solution** dialog box, navigate to the C:\Program Files\Microsoft Learning\2030\Democode\Mod03\Demo01\Starter folder, click **Report Authoring Demo.sln**, and then click **Open**.

4. In **Solution Explorer**, expand the **Report Authoring Demo** project, expand **Reports**, and then double-click **Product Profitability.rdl**.

▶ **Preview the report**

1. Click the **Preview** tab. Notice that the report is broken down into product, product category, product subcategory, and product details. Summary data is provided at each category level.

2. Click the **Layout** tab.

▶ **Hide the Product Detail and table1_SubCategory Footer rows**

1. Click the table data region, and then click the icon to the left of the **Detail** row.

2. In the **Properties** window, expand the **Visibility** property, and in the **Hidden** property drop-down list, click **True**.

3. Click the icon to the left of the **table1_SubCategory Footer** row, and then in the **Properties** window, within the **Visibility** property, in the **Hidden** property drop-down list, click **True**.

▶ **Save and preview the report**

1. On the **File** menu, click **Save All**.

2. Click the **Preview** tab. Notice that the detailed product rows and subcategory footers are now hidden.

3. Click the **Layout** tab.

▶ **Toggle the visibility of the hidden rows**

1. Click the icon to the left of the **Detail** row.

2. In the **Properties** window, within the **Visibility** property, in the **ToggleItem** property drop-down list, click **SubCategory**.

3. Click the icon to the left of the **table1_SubCategory Footer** row.

4. In the **Properties** window, within the **Visibility** property, in the **ToggleItem** property drop-down list, click **SubCategory**.

▶ **Save and preview the report**

1. On the **File** menu, click **Save All**.

2. Click the **Preview** tab.

3. Click the plus sign next to **Gloves** to view the products for this subcategory. (You might need to click a bit to the left of the plus sign.) Notice that the product detail and subcategory footer rows are shown.

4. Click the **Layout** tab.

▶ **Show SubCategory totals when the detail is hidden**

1. In the **table1_SubCategory Footer** row, click the **SalesAmount** total cell, press **SHIFT** and click the **Margin %** total cell, right-click, and then click **Copy**.

2. In the **table1_SubCategory Header** row, right-click the **Sales Amount** cell, and then click **Paste**.

3. With the pasted cells still selected, in the **Properties** window, within the **Visibility** property, in the **ToggleItem** property drop-down list, click **SubCategory**.

Important   Make sure to keep the **Hidden** property = **False**. Toggling visibility will *hide* the values in the fields.

▶ **Save and preview the report**

1. On the **File** menu, click **Save All**.

2. Click the **Preview** tab.

3. Click the plus sign next to **Gloves** to view the products for this subcategory. Notice that the data next to **Gloves** in the **table1_SubCategory Header** row is now hidden when you drill down.

4. On the **File** menu, click **Close Solution**.

Creating a Document Map

- **Provides report navigation support**
- **Requires rendering mechanism that can support document maps**
  - HTML
  - PDF
- **Specified by adding Document Map labels to report items**

Introduction

Reports can contain large amounts of data that can be difficult to display effectively to a user. Users will not use a report if they find it impossible to work with. To improve this situation, you can create a document map.

Provides report navigation

A *document map* appears as a table of contents for the report and provides links to particular areas of the report.

To create a document map, add a Document Map label to a grouping level. When you render the report, the document map is automatically generated.

Document Map rendering

When you view an HTML, Microsoft Excel, or Portable Document Format (PDF) report, a document map is displayed along the side of the report. Clicking an item in the document map refreshes the report and displays the area of the report that corresponds to the clicked item. Document maps are rendered for different formats as follows:

- HTML: The document map appears as a panel on the left side of the document.
- PDF: The document map is generated as a set of bookmarks.
- Most other outputs, including TIFF files and printed documents, ignore the document map.

Document Map labels

All report items contain a Document Map label property. If any report items have a Document Map label, a document map is automatically generated when a user views the report in HTML Viewer or Adobe Acrobat Reader. Data regions and independent report items can appear in a document map.

Initiating Actions

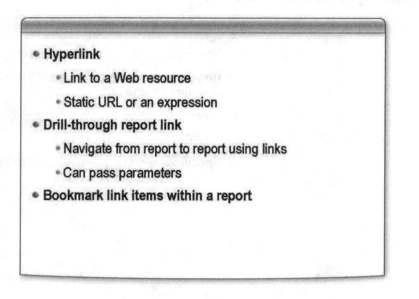

- **Hyperlink**
  - Link to a Web resource
  - Static URL or an expression
- **Drill-through report link**
  - Navigate from report to report using links
  - Can pass parameters
- **Bookmark link items within a report**

Introduction

You can add links to a report to help users navigate to particular areas of a report, to other resources located on the report server, or to resources located elsewhere that are identified by a valid URL.

Hyperlinks

Hyperlinks can be added to a report's text boxes and images to allow the user to jump to a particular URL. A hyperlink can link to a static URL resource or an expression that evaluates to a URL. To create dynamic hyperlinks, URLs can be stored in a database and rendered in a data region.

Drill-through

Drill-through report links allow reports to be linked together. Where a parameter is specified, the target report may be filtered using the passed parameter. Drill-through reports commonly contain details about an item that is contained in an original, separate summary report.

For example, product numbers contained in a sales summary report can be linked to a product report, allowing the user to "drill through" to product information from the summary report.

Any report that is stored on the report server can be a drill-through report. You can only add drill-through links to text boxes and images.

Bookmarks

A *bookmark link* is a link that a user clicks to move to another area or page in a report. Setting up a bookmark link is a two-step process:

1. Add a bookmark to a report item. This should be the destination report item. All report item types may be bookmarked.

2. Add a bookmark link to the report item you want the user to click to jump to the bookmark created in step 1. Bookmarked links can only jump to text boxes and images.

As with all interactive features, the behavior of links is dependent on the rendering engine. HTML supports all three link types.

Demonstration: Initiating Actions

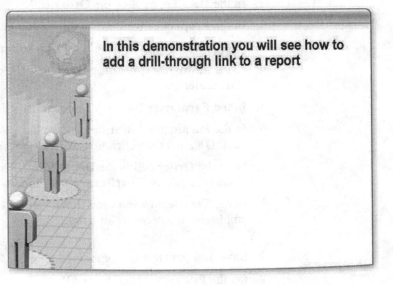

In this demonstration you will see how to add a drill-through link to a report

Introduction

The Order Details report uses a table to display order detail information. Adventure Works uses this report to verify the status of orders, troubleshoot order complaints, and answer questions from resellers. To troubleshoot reseller inquiries, they would like to be able to jump to product detail information.

In this demonstration, you will see how to add an action in the Order Details report to jump to the Product Details report.

Procedures

▶ **Open a saved solution**

1. Click **Start**, point to **All Programs**, point to **Microsoft Visual Studio .NET 2003**, and then click **Microsoft Visual Studio .NET 2003**.

2. On the **File** menu, click **Open Solution**.

3. In the **Open Solution** dialog box, navigate to the C:\Program Files\Microsoft Learning\2030\Democode\Mod03\Demo02\Starter folder.

4. Click **Action.sln**, and then click **Open**.

5. In **Solution Explorer**, expand the **Action** project, and then expand **Reports**.

▶ **Preview the report**

1. Double-click **Order Details.rdl**.

2. Click the **Preview** tab. Notice that the report displays order information, but provides only limited information regarding product details.

3. Click the **Layout** tab.

▶ **Add an action to jump to a report**

1. In the **Detail** row, click the **Order** cell.

2. In the **Properties** window, in the **Action** property box, click the ellipsis.

3. In the **Action** dialog box, click **Jump to report**.

4. In the **Jump to report** drop-down list, click **Product Detail**, and then click **Parameters**.

5. In the **Parameter Name** drop-down list, click **Product**.

6. In the **Parameter Value** drop-down list, click **=Fields!Product.Value**, click **OK**, and then click **OK** to close the **Action** dialog box.

7. With the **Order** cell in the **Detail** row still selected, in the **Properties** window, click the **TextDecoration** property.

8. In the **TextDecoration** drop-down list, click **Underline**. This will emphasize the presence of a link.

▶ **Save and preview the report**

1. On the **File** menu, click **Save All**.

2. Click the **Preview** tab.

3. Click the product named **Road-650 Black, 60**. The Product Detail report is displayed filtered, using the product number as a parameter.

4. On the **File** menu, click **Close Solution**.

Lesson: Displaying Data

- ● Data Regions
- ● Table
- ● Chart
- ● List
- ● Matrix
- ● Working with Data Regions
- ● Subreport

Introduction

Remember that a data region is an area on a report that contains data from a data source that is repeated. The types of data regions are table, chart, list, and matrix. In this lesson, you will learn the main differences between the data region types. You will also learn how to add a data region to a report.

Lesson objectives

After completing this lesson, you will be able to:

- Describe the data regions available within Report Designer.
- Create a table data region.
- Create a chart data region.
- Create a list data region.
- Create a matrix data region.
- Choose data regions for a particular report.
- Create a subreport.

Data Regions

Data Region	Container Type	Grouping
Report Body (or Rectangle)*	Free-form	Non-repeating
List	Free-form	Single grouping level, detail or grouped
Table	Fixed	Multiple grouping levels on rows axis
Matrix	Fixed	Multiple grouping levels on rows and columns
Chart	N/A	Single grouping level, dynamically created

Introduction

A data region is a report item that displays repeating data. The choice of data region type is dependent on the structure of the underlying data set and the way in which data is to be displayed in the report.

The following list defines the data regions that are discussed in this lesson:

- List data regions are *free-form container data regions*, which means that they can contain multiple items, freely arranged.

- Table and Matrix data regions are *fixed container data regions*, which means that a single cell of a table or matrix can contain only a single report item.

- Chart data regions graphically represent data series. These data regions are not containers and therefore do not contain report items.

Groupings

Data regions group data in the following ways:

- A list has a single grouping level.

- A table can have multiple grouping levels, but only on the rows axis.

- A matrix can have multiple grouping levels on both the rows and columns axes.

- A chart has a single grouping level that is dynamically created.

The five types of data regions are discussed in more detail in the following topics.

Table

Fixed container type
- Each cell contains one report item

Multiple grouping levels
- Variable data in rows
- Fixed columns

Formatting columns
- Padding
- Merge cells
- Rectangle in cell

Product Profitability for May, 2003

	Sales	% Of Total	Margin %	Avg Sale
Tights				
Women's tights, L	$10,187	48.15 %	36.54 %	$192
Women's tights, S	$8,876	41.95 %	36.22 %	$222
Women's tights, M	$2,096	9.91 %	36.54 %	$131
	$21,160	**25.52 %**	**36.43 %**	**$182**
Gloves	$19,123	23.07 %	35.72 %	$102
Bib-Short	$18,588	22.42 %	36.51 %	$230
Jersey	$13,824	16.43 %	6.71 %	$121
Shorts	$9,046	10.91 %	36.54 %	$144
Cap	$1,362	1.64 %	6.32 %	$28
Clothing	**$82,903**		**29.96 %**	**$141**

Introduction

The Table data region displays data from a single data set in a fixed, tabular structure. A table is an effective way to display data that has a fixed set of columns with recurring detail rows. Rows can be grouped at multiple levels if required.

Fixed container type

The Table data region contains other report items in a fixed manner—that is, each cell of the table can contain only one report item. This makes it easy to align columns of numbers and labels. Each cell in a table contains a text box by default. You can type any expression into any cell, or you can change the report item within the cell to another item.

Multiple grouping levels

The Table data region allows you to add multiple levels of grouping, but for rows only. The definition of values on rows changes based on the current contents of the data set.

Formatting columns

You can use the following formatting techniques to alter the appearance of tables:

- Modify padding: Adjusts the space between the edge of a cell and its contents

- Merge cells: Combines two or more adjacent cells into one cell

- Insert a rectangle report item into a cell and then insert free-form report items into the rectangle.

Chart

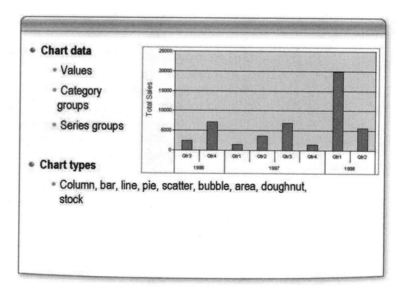

Introduction

The Chart data region is used to display a graphical representation of data in a report. You can add different types of charts to a data region, and you can specify values as well as category and series groups. Charts can include different colors, symbols, and 3D effects.

Chart data

Data for charts in Reporting Services is organized into three areas:

- Values

  A chart must include at least one data value series. Values determine the size of the chart element for each category group.

  Value series are static. To display a single chart element for each category group, define a single value series and no series groups, To display a chart element for each value series, define multiple values. If there are multiple value series, the chart legend displays the name of each value series.

  If you want to group data by category, you must use an aggregate expression for the value expressions in the chart.

- Category Groups

  Category groups are used to group data. Categories provide the labels for chart elements. For example, in a column chart (described below), a category label is displayed on the X-axis for each set of columns.

  You can nest category groups. When you define multiple category groups, each category is nested within another category.

- Series Groups

  You can optionally use series groups to add an additional dimension of data to a report. Using a series group produces one chart element for each value in the group. When combined with categories, this can result in a large number of chart elements.

Chart types

Reporting Services supports the following chart types:

- Column

  A column chart displays vertical columns grouped by category. Column height indicates value. Category labels are displayed on the X-axis.

- Bar

  A bar chart displays sets of horizontal bars grouped by category. Bar length indicates value. Category labels are displayed on the X-axis.

- Line

  A line chart displays values as a set of points connected by a line. Category labels are displayed on the X-axis.

- Pie and Doughnut

  A pie chart and a doughnut chart each display value data as percentages of the whole. Categories are represented by individual slices.

- Scatter

  A scatter chart displays series as a set of points. Categories are represented by different points in the chart.

- Bubble

  A bubble chart displays series as a set of symbols. Values are represented by the position of the symbol in the chart space and the size of the symbol. Categories are represented by different symbols in the chart.

- Area

  An area chart displays series as a set of points connected by a line, with an area filled in below the line. Values are represented by the height of the point as measured by the Y-axis. Category labels are displayed on the X-axis.

- Stock

  A stock chart displays series as a set of lines with markers for high, low, close, and open values. Values are represented by the height of the marker as measured by the Y-axis. Category labels are displayed on the X-axis.

List

Introduction

Table data regions do not always provide the necessary functionality for your report design. However, creating a List data region provides an alternative.

Free-form container

A List data region is a free-form container that permits the placement of report items anywhere within the list. The list repeats for each group or row in the underlying data set. A list can be used for free-form reports or in conjunction with other data regions.

The List data region provides more flexibility than other kinds of data regions, such as the Table data region. However, the report author has to position each report item required in the list, and lists therefore take more effort to format correctly.

Using Report Designer, you can define lists that contain any number of report items. A list can be nested within another list to provide multiple groupings of data.

Single grouping level

In a list, you can display detail data—with one instance of the list rectangle for each row of the detail data set, or a grouping level—with one instance of the list rectangle for each unique combination of values for the grouping. Unlike a table, a list allows only a single grouping. If you want to display multiple grouping levels, nest one list inside another.

Matrix

- **Also known as CrossTab report**
- **Fixed container**
  - Each cell contains one report item
- **Multiple grouping levels (both rows and columns)**
  - Cells repeat both horizontally and vertically
  - Supports dynamic rows and columns

		2002	2003	2004
France	Ranjit Varkey Chudukatil	$1,028,497	$2,818,588	$1,658,518
Germany	Rachel Valdez		$1,225,913	$1,015,291
United Kingdom	José Saraiva	$925,012	$2,261,597	$1,491,541

Introduction

The Matrix data region displays data as a series of columns and rows. Matrices are also known as *pivot tables* and *crosstabs*. As opposed to tables, columns in a matrix can be dynamic. Using Report Designer, you can define matrices that contain static and dynamic rows and columns.

Fixed container

In addition to creating automatic rows and columns based on data set values, you can also add static rows or columns using the Matrix data region. Static columns are similar to the fixed columns of a table report. Static rows or columns make it possible to add more than one aggregation for a single numeric field. For example, you can add an aggregation to calculate the standard deviation of sales amount, as well an aggregation to calculate the sum of sales amount. Alternatively, you can also use static rows or columns to add different numeric fields—for example, sales amount and order quantity.

Multiple grouping levels

In a matrix, there is no detail level. Even at the lowest level, you create a grouping level and use an aggregate function. The aggregate function you specify for the most detailed data is automatically used for all higher levels.

By default, a matrix shows value only for the lowest visible level. To show totals for a higher level, you must add a subtotal. Subtotals are added one level at a time, on both rows and columns.

When you add a subtotal to a level, the label for that level displays a green triangle in the top right corner of the cell. Click the green triangle to select the subtotal in the **Properties** window. With the subtotal selected, you can format the subtotal cell and decide whether the subtotal should come above or below the detail values.

Working with Data Regions

- • Repeating data regions
- • Empty data regions
- • Rendering dependencies

Introduction

When working with data regions, consideration should be given to the nesting and rendering of data regions in a final report.

Repeating data regions

Data regions can be nested to allow the display of the same data region multiple times in a report. For example, a sales order data report may repeat a single sales order table once for each employee.

Nested data regions must use the same underlying data set. If you wish to create nested groupings but with different data sets, you must use a subreport.

Empty data regions

A data region is only rendered if it contains data. If no data is returned, a text box containing the value of the **NoRows** property is displayed. **NoRows** can be set using Report Designer.

Rendering dependencies

In some rendering formats—for example, HTML—the position of other report items can change to allow for expansion of a data region. Rectangles can be used to fix the position of a data region.

Subreport

- **A report included inside the body of the main report**
  - Is stored on report server
  - Can be repeated within a data region in main report
  - Only the body of the subreport is included
  - Subreport data source can differ from data source in main report
- **Consider using data regions instead**

Introduction

Sometimes the detail of a report's data region is so complex that a better option than using the previously described data region types is using a subreport.

Report included within a report

A *subreport* is used to display a child report inside the body of a parent report. Consider the following facts about subreports:

- The report that the subreport displays is stored on a report server, usually in the same folder as the parent report.
- You can configure the parent report to pass parameters to the subreport.
- A subreport can be repeated within data regions, using a parameter to filter data in each instance of the subreport.

Consider using data regions

In some cases, using data regions is preferable to using subreports. Reports with data regions often perform better than reports that include subreports. When you run a report that contains a subreport, the report server has to process each of the two reports. If the report contains data regions instead, the report server processes only one report.

Use the following guidelines to decide between data regions and subreports:

- Use data regions when you need to nest groups of data from the same data source within a single data region.
- Use subreports if you need to:
  - Nest groups of data from different data sources within a single data region.
  - Reuse a subreport in multiple parent reports.
  - Display a standalone report inside of another report.

Review

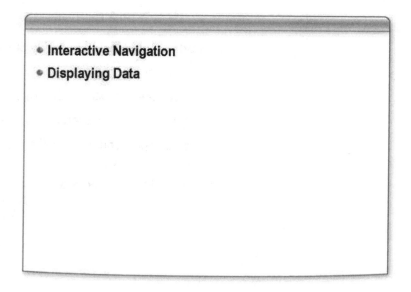

- Interactive Navigation
- Displaying Data

1. How does dynamic visibility improve report readability?

2. What types of links can be added to a report?

3. In what kind of situation would you use a subreport?

Lab 3: Enhancing a Simple Report

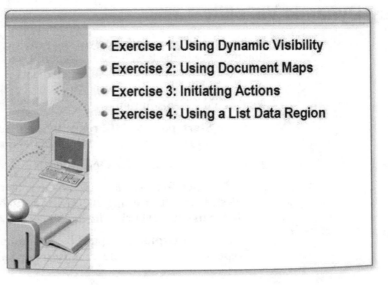

Objectives

In this lab, you will enhance the Adventure Works Reseller Sales report to include the interactive features covered in this module.

After completing this lab, you will be able to:

■ Use dynamic visibility to show and hide detail in a report.

■ Use a document map to provide quick navigation to report items within a report.

■ Use a drill-through report link to link a summary report to a detail report

■ Use the List data region.

Prerequisites: None Estimated time to complete this lab: 45 minutes

Exercise 1
Using Dynamic Visibility

In this exercise, you will use dynamic visibility to enable the hide/show functionality in the Reseller Sales report. Users will then be able to easily navigate from summary data to detailed data.

▶ **Open a saved solution**

1. Click **Start**, point to **All Programs**, point to **Microsoft Visual Studio .NET 2003**, and then click **Microsoft Visual Studio .NET 2003**.

2. On the **File** menu, click **Open Solution**.

3. In the **Open Solution** dialog box, navigate to the C:\Program Files\Microsoft Learning\2030\Labfiles\Lab03\Exercise01\Starter folder, click **AdventureWorks.sln**, and then click **Open**.

4. In **Solution Explorer**, expand the **Customer Sales** project, expand **Reports**, and then double-click **Reseller Sales.rdl**.

▶ **Preview the report**

1. Click the **Preview** tab to view the report.

   Notice that the report contains detail and summarized values for resellers, subcategories, and categories, including both header and footer summaries for subcategories and categories.

2. Click the **Layout** tab.

▶ **Hide the Reseller Detail and table1_State Footer rows**

1. Click the table data region, and then click the icon to the left of the **Detail** row.

2. In the **Properties** window, expand the **Visibility** property, and in the **Hidden** property drop-down list, click **True**.

3. In the table data region, click the icon to the left of the **table1_SubCategory Footer** row.

4. In the **Properties**.window, under the **Visibility** property, in the **Hidden** property drop-down list, click **True**.

▶ **Save and preview the report**

1. On the **File** menu, click **Save All**.

2. Click the **Preview** tab. Notice that the detailed reseller rows and state footers are now hidden.

3. Click the **Layout** tab.

▶ **Toggle the visibility of the hidden rows**

1. In the table data region, click the icon to the left of the **Detail** row.

2. In the **Properties** window, under the **Visibility** property, in the **ToggleItem** property drop-down list, click **State**.

3. In the table data region, click the icon to the left of the **table1_SubCategory Footer** row.

4. In the **Properties** window, under the **Visibility** property, in the **ToggleItem** property drop-down list, click **State**.

▶ **Save and preview the report**

1. On the **File** menu, click **Save All**.

2. Click the **Preview** tab.

3. Click the plus sign next to **Connecticut** to view the resellers for this state. Notice that the plus sign allows you to drill down and view the detailed reseller and state total footer rows.

4. Click the **Layout** tab.

▶ **Show state totals when the detail is hidden**

1. In the **table1_SubCategory Footer** row, click the **SalesAmount** total cell, and then press **SHIFT** and click the **Margin %** total cell. Right-click the selected row, and then click **Copy**.

2. In the **table1_SubCategory Header** row, right-click the **SalesAmount** cell, and then click **Paste**.

3. With the pasted cells still selected, in the **Properties** window, expand the **Visibility** property, in the **ToggleItem** property drop-down list, click **State**.

Important Make sure to keep the **Hidden** property set to **False**. Toggling visibility will hide the data values from the fields.

▶ **Save and preview the report**

1. On the **File** menu, click **Save All**.

2. Click the **Preview** tab.

3. Click the plus sign next to **Texas** to view the resellers for this state. Notice that the data next to Texas in the **table1_State Header** row is now hidden when you drill down.

4. On the **File** menu, click **Close Solution**.

Exercise 2
Using Document Maps

The Product Catalog report contains a detailed listing of over 350 Adventure Works products. In this exercise, you will create a document map to provide a navigation mechanism for users of this lengthy report.

▶ **Open a saved solution**

1. Click **Start**, point to **All Programs**, point to **Microsoft Visual Studio .NET 2003**, and then click **Microsoft Visual Studio .NET 2003**.

2. On the **File** menu, click **Open Solution**.

3. In the **Open Solution** dialog box, navigate to the C:\Program Files\Microsoft Learning\2030\Labfiles\Lab03\Exercise02\Starter folder.

4. Click **Document Map.sln**, and then click **Open**.

5. In **Solution Explorer**, expand the **Document Map** project, and then expand **Reports**.

▶ **Preview the report**

1. Double-click **Product Catalog.rdl**.

2. Click the **Preview** tab. (The document map might not appear for several seconds after the report appears.)

3. On the left side of the report, in the **Document Map** window, expand **Product Catalog**, and then click **Clothing** to navigate to the clothing products.

4. Click the **Layout** tab.

▶ **Add a label to the group in SubCategoryList**

1. In the **Properties** window drop-down list, click **SubCategoryList**.

2. In the **Properties** window, in the **Grouping** property, click the ellipsis.

3. In the **Detail Groupings** dialog box, in the **Document map label** drop-down list, click **=Fields!ProdSubCat.Value**, and then click **OK**. By adding a label to the group in the list, you are adding this report item to the document map.

▶ **Add a label to the group in ModelList**

1. In the **Properties** window drop-down list, click **ModelList**.

2. In the **Properties** window, in the **Grouping/Sorting** property, click the ellipsis.

3. In the **Grouping and Sorting Properties** dialog box, in the **Document map label** drop-down list, click **=Fields!ProdModel.Value**, and then click **OK**.

▶ **Save and preview the report**

1. On the **File** menu, click **Save All**.

2. Click the **Preview** tab.

3. On the left side of the report, in the **Document Map** window, expand **Product Catalog**, expand **Clothing**, expand **Jersey**, and then click **Short-sleeve classic jersey**. Notice that subcategory and model groups are now contained in the document map and that the matching report item is displayed in the report. (You might need to scroll through the report to see the matching report item.)

Note The document map can be hidden by pressing the document map button directly above it.

---

4. On the **File** menu, click **Close Solution**.

Exercise 3
Initiating Actions

The Order Details report uses a table to display order detail information. Adventure Works uses this report to verify the status of orders and to troubleshoot order complaints and answer questions from resellers. To troubleshoot reseller inquiries, they would like to be able to jump to the product detail information.

In this exercise, you will add an action in the Order Details report to jump to the Product Detail report.

▶ **Open a saved solution**

1. Click **Start**, point to **All Programs**, point to **Microsoft Visual Studio .NET 2003**, and then click **Microsoft Visual Studio .NET 2003**.

2. On the **File** menu, click **Open Solution**.

3. In the **Open Solution** dialog box, navigate to the C:\Program Files\Microsoft Learning\2030\Labfiles\Lab03\Exercise03\Starter folder.

4. Click **Action.sln** and then click **Open**.

5. In **Solution Explorer**, expand the **Action** project, and then expand **Reports**.

▶ **Preview the report**

1. Double-click **Order Details.rdl**.

2. Click the **Preview** tab. Notice that the report contains a series of orders for a single customer.

3. Click the **Layout** tab.

▶ **Add an action to jump to report**

1. In the **Detail** row of the table, click the **Order** column.

2. In the **Properties** window, in the **Action** property, click the ellipsis.

3. In the **Action** dialog box, click **Jump to report**.

4. In the **Jump to report** drop-down list, click **Product Detail**, and then click **Parameters**.

5. In the **Parameter Name** drop-down list, click **Product**.

6. In the **Parameter Value** drop-down list, click **=Fields!Product.Value**, click **OK**, and then click **OK** to close the **Action** dialog box.

7. With the **Order** cell still selected, in the **Properties** window, in the **TextDecoration** drop-down list, click **Underline**. This will help to emphasize the report link.

▶ **Save and preview the report**

1. On the **File** menu, click **Save All**.

2. Click the **Preview** tab. Click the product named **Road-650 Black, 60** in the report to jump to the Product Detail report. Notice that the report is filtered by product number.

3. On the **File** menu, click **Close Solution**.

Exercise 4
Using a List Data Region

In this exercise, you will create a basic product sales report by using the List data region. Lists require more development effort from the report author but provide a greater level of flexibility when compared to tables.

▶ **Open a saved solution and report**

1. Click **Start**, point to **All Programs**, point to **Microsoft Visual Studio .NET 2003**, and then click **Microsoft Visual Studio .NET 2003**.

2. On the **File** menu, click **Open Solution**.

3. In the **Open Solution** dialog box, navigate to the C:\Program Files\Microsoft Learning\2030\Labfiles\Lab03\Exercise04\Starter folder.

4. Click **Data Regions.sln**, and then click **Open**.

5. In **Solution Explorer**, expand the project, and then expand **Reports**.

▶ **Preview the report**

1. Double-click **Table Product Profitability.rdl**.

2. Click the **Preview** tab. Notice that the report includes a table with a table header and footer, a category header and footer, and a subcategory header. The report contains no detail rows.

3. Close the report.

▶ **Copy the report**

1. In **Solution Explorer**, right-click **Table Product Profitability.rdl**, and then click **Copy**.

2. Press **CTRL+V** to paste a copy of the report.

3. Right-click the copy of the report, and then click **Rename**.

4. Type **List Product Profitability.rdl** and then press **Enter**.

5. Double-click **List Product Profitability.rdl**.

▶ **Expand the height of the report**

1. Click the **Body** header bar to select the body of the report.

2. In the **Properties** window, expand the **Size** property group, and in the **Height** property text box, replace the existing value with **3** inches (7.5 cm).

▶ **Add the Category list**

1. In the **Toolbox** window, click **List**.

2. Drag a list data region beneath the existing table. Ensure that the list is the same width as the table and approximately **0.75** inches (2 cm) high.

3. Position the list **0.5** inches (1 cm) below the existing table.

▶ **Add grouping and sorting to the Category list**

1. Right-click the list data region and select **Properties**. Under the Data Set name listbox, choose **DataDetail**, click the **Edit details group** button.

2. In the **Details Grouping** dialog box, in the **Name** text box, type **list1_Category**.

3. In the Group on pane, click the first row, and from the **Expression** drop-down list, click **=Fields!Category.Value**, and then click **OK**.

4. On the **Sorting** tab, in the Sort on pane, click the first row, and from the **Expression** drop-down list, click **=Fields!Category.Value**, and then click **OK**.

Note   With a Table data region, you can right-click a row handle to add a new grouping level. With a List data region, there is no option for adding a new grouping level.

▶ **Add fields to the Category list**

1. In the **Fields** window, drag the **Category** field, and then drop it inside the top left corner of the list.

2. Drag the right side of the **Category** text box until the text box is approximately **2** inches (5 cm) wide. Resize and reposition as needed to move the text box to the upper left corner of the list.

Tip   Use the table above the list as a guide when you are resizing text boxes in the list.

---

3. Copy the **Category** text box by holding down the **CTRL** key as you drag and drop the text box underneath the **Category** text box.

4. Leave about **0.5** inches (1 cm) of space between the text boxes inside the list. Later in this exercise, you will place a control in the space between the text boxes.

5. Click inside the copied text box, and replace the existing value with **Category Total**.

6. In the **Fields** window, drag the **SalesAmount** field and drop it to the right of **Category Total** inside the list. Resize the **SalesAmount** text box so that it is approximately **1.25** inches (3 cm) wide.

7. With the **SalesAmount** text box still selected, in the **Properties** window, in the **Format** property, type **C0** to format the numbers as currency with 0 decimal places.

8. In the **Fields** window, drag an **OrderQuantity** field and drop it to the right of the **SalesAmount** field inside the list. Resize the **OrderQuantity** text box so that it is approximately **1.25** inches (3 cm) wide.

9. With the **OrderQuantity** text box still selected, in the **Properties** window, in the **Format** property, type **N0** to format as numbers with 0 decimal places.

10. Click all four text boxes while holding down **CTRL**. On the Report Formatting toolbar, click the **Bold** button.

▶ **Add SubCategory list**

1. In the **Toolbox** window, click **List**.

2. Click and drag a rectangle inside the existing **Category** list between the existing text boxes. Resize the list to be the same width as the containing list and approximately **0.25** inches (0.5 cm) high.

▶ **Add grouping and sorting to the SubCategory list**

1. Right-click the list data region and select **Properties**. Under the Data Set name listbox, choose **DataDetail** and click the **Edit details group** button.

2. In the Details Grouping dialog box, in the **Name** text box, type **list2_SubCategory**.

3. In the Group on pane, click the first row, and from the Expression drop-down list, click **=Fields!SubCategory.Value**, and then click **OK**.

4. On the **Sorting** tab, in the Sort on pane, click the first row, and from the **Expression** drop-down list, click =Fields!SubCategory.Value, and then click **OK**.

▶ **Add fields to the SubCategory list**

1. In the **Fields** window, drag the **SubCategory** field and drop it into the **SubCategory** list. Drag the text box **0.25** inches (0.5 cm) from the left edge inside the **SubCategory** list, and resize the text box to approximately **1.75** inches (4.5 cm) wide.

2. In the **Category** list, click the **SalesAmount** and **OrderQuantity** text boxes while holding down **CTRL**.

3. Copy the selected text boxes by holding down the **CTRL** key as you drag the text boxes into the **SubCategory** list to the right of the **SubCategory** text box.

4. With the two new **SalesAmount** and **OrderQuantity** text boxes selected in the **SubCategory** list, on the **Report Formatting** toolbar, click the **Bold** button to turn off boldfacing.

5. Horizontally align the **SalesAmount** and **OrderQuantity** text boxes.

▶ **Add header and footer rows**

1. In the **Category** list, click the **Category Total, SalesAmount,** and **OrderQuantity** text boxes while holding down **CTRL**.

2. Copy the selected text boxes by holding down the **CTRL** key as you drag the text boxes just under the **Category** list.

3. In the **Category** list, click the **Category Total, SalesAmount,** and **OrderQuantity** text boxes while holding down **CTRL**.

4. Copy the selected text boxes by holding down the **CTRL** key as you drag the text boxes just above the **Category** list.

5. Click all six new header and footer text boxes while holding down **CTRL**.

6. With the six new text boxes selected outside the lists, on the **Report Formatting** toolbar, perform the following tasks:

   - Click **12** in the **Font Size** drop-down list

   - Click the **Background Color** button, click the **Web** tab, click **Black**, and then click **OK**.

   - Click the **Foreground Color** button, click the **Web** tab, click **White**, and then click **OK**.

7. In the **Category Total** footer text box, replace the text with **Grand Total**.

8. In the **Category Total** header text box, replace the text with **Product**.

9. In the **SalesAmount** header text box, replace the text with **Sales Amount**.

10. In the **OrderQuantity** header text box, replace the text with **Order Quantity**.

▶ **Save and preview the report**

1. On the **File** menu, click **Save All**.

2. Click the **Preview** tab. Notice that the table and the list data now look the same.

Tip   If you see repetitions of a header or footer element, you might have inadvertently moved a text box into one of the lists. To check whether a text box is in a list, choose the list's name from the drop-down list in the **Properties** window to make the list's boundary visible.

---

3. Click the **Layout** tab.

► **Delete the table version of the report**

1. Click the table, right-click, and then click **Delete** to delete the table version of the report.

2. Press **CTRL+A** to select the remainder in the report, and then click and drag the list to the top of the report.

► **Save and preview the report**

1. On the **File** menu, click **Save All**.

2. Click the **Preview** tab to preview the report.

3. Close the solution.

Module 4: Manipulating Data Sets

Contents

Overview

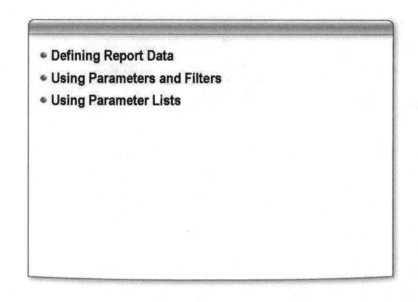

- Defining Report Data
- Using Parameters and Filters
- Using Parameter Lists

Introduction

Report data retrieved from a data source is held in a data set and is often displayed through the use of a data region. In this module, data sets are explored to a greater depth—the use of alternative data sources and interacting with a data set through the use of parameters are both discussed. You will learn how to dynamically modify the data set underlying a data region, allowing parameters to be sent to the underlying query. You will also learn best practices for dealing with static and dynamic parameter lists when interacting with queries and stored procedures.

Objectives

After completing this module, you will be able to:

- Describe the features of a data set.
- Use parameters to restrict query results.
- Use parameter lists with a report.

Lesson: Defining Report Data

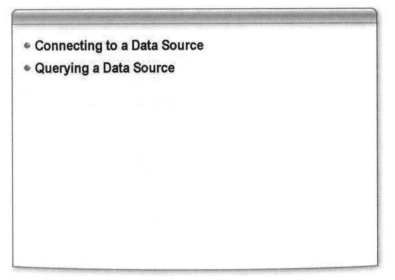

- Connecting to a Data Source
- Querying a Data Source

Introduction

During the process of creating a new report, the report author is able to define the source of data held within the report. A data source holds information about the underlying data connection. Data sources can be report specific, or shared across reports. Data queries can be used to return information from a data source into a data set. Data sets in turn can be used by data regions to display data in a report.

Lesson objectives

After completing this lesson, you will be able to:

- Connect to a data source.
- Query a data source using a data set.

Connecting to a Data Source

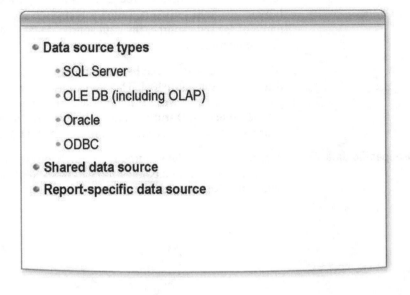

- **Data source types**
  - SQL Server
  - OLE DB (including OLAP)
  - Oracle
  - ODBC
- **Shared data source**
- **Report-specific data source**

Introduction

A data source contains information about the data connection used within a report. The report definition holds this connection information, including the data source type, the connection string, and the credentials used to access the data source.

Data source types

The following types of data sources are supported by Reporting Services: Microsoft® SQL Server™; OLE DB, including the Online Analytical Processing (OLAP) provider; Oracle; and open database connectivity (ODBC).

Data sources do not contain any query information, just details about the connection itself. Data sources can be report specific or specified as a shared resource that is able to be shared between multiple reports.

Credentials for accessing a data source should not be stored in the connection string, but rather stored using the login information in the **Credentials** tab within Report Designer.

The connection string associated with the data source contains the server name, provider, and initial database catalog. For example, to attach to an OLAP server using OLE DB on the local machine, use the following:

```
Provider=MSOLAP.2;Data Source=localhost;Initial
Catalog=AdventureWorks
```

OLAP is chiefly concerned with reading and aggregating large groups of related data. OLAP analyzes relationships and identifies patterns and trends within the set of data. It is typically employed for very large sets of data, and yet must provide fast response times. Microsoft SQL Server Analysis Services contains a powerful OLAP engine. You can create very effective Reporting Services reports by using OLAP as a data source.

Note To access an Oracle data source, Oracle client tools must be installed on the Report Designer machine and the report server.

Shared data source

A shared data source can be saved to a report server and accessed by multiple reports. A shared data source is saved in a separate Extensible Markup Language (XML) document in a folder on the report server and contains the name of the data source, the data source ID, and other information specific to the connection.

A shared data source can be published from within Report Designer at the same time a report is published. The data source is created only once, when it is first published. To overwrite a shared data source each time the project is published, set the **OverwrteDataSources** property of the project to **True**. Shared data sources provide a convenient, centrally managed mechanism for accessing data.

Report-specific data source

A report-specific data source is available only in the report in which it is defined. Note that the connection can be used as the data source for multiple data sets within the report.

Querying a Data Source

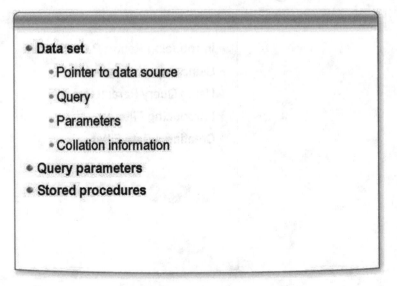

- **Data set**
  - Pointer to data source
  - Query
  - Parameters
  - Collation information
- **Query parameters**
- **Stored procedures**

Introduction

In order to work with a data source, you should be familiar with three different areas: the data set, query parameters, and stored procedures.

Data set

A data set contains the query information used by data regions within a report. It contains the pointer to a data source, the query, any parameters that are used alongside the query, and information for grouping and collating the data. The query stored in the data set varies depending on the type of data source being accessed.

When using a SQL Server data source, data can be retrieved through the use of a SQL query, a stored procedure, or a table name. Additional properties allow the data set to be configured, such as **CaseSensitivity** and parameters to be passed to the query.

Data sets can be easily constructed using Report Designer. Queries can be created manually using SQL or created automatically through the graphical query designer.

Query parameters

Within a data set, parameters can be declared so that that the same query can be run multiple times using differing parameters. Query parameters can be linked to report parameters, allowing the parameter values to be chosen by the report user at report runtime. You will see examples of this later in the module.

Stored procedures

To use stored procedures, the command type for the data set must be set to **StoredProcedure** and the name of the stored procedure must be supplied. Only single data sets may be returned from the stored procedure. Values often are passed to the stored procedure using a parameter list. Default parameter values can be defined if required.

Lesson: Using Parameters and Filters

- **Introducing Report Parameters**
- **Using Report Parameters**
- **Using Query Parameters**
- **Introducing Filters**
- **Creating a Data Filter**

Introduction

Simple SQL queries and stored procedures are not always sufficient when building data sets for a report. In many cases, queries and stored procedures require the passing of a list of parameter values at report runtime. By linking query parameters to report parameters, the user can vary the value of the report parameters at runtime, thereby changing the data contained within the report.

Lesson objectives

In this lesson, you will learn how to use parameters effectively in a report. After completing this lesson, you will be able to:

- Describe why report parameters are used.
- Use report parameters.
- Use query parameters.
- Describe the use of filters.
- Create a data filter.

Introducing Report Parameters

- **Restrict or filter data**
  - Incorporate into a data set as a query parameter
  - Use in conjunction with a filter
  - Pass from report to report
  - Create dynamic parameter lists
  - Restrict by Windows user account
- **Use as a report variable**
  - Dynamically change report format
  - Calculate data within the report

Introduction

Using report parameters allows users to manipulate the data contained in the report at runtime. Report parameters provide a greater level of flexibility. For example, they allow the display of different values to different users or time-date dependent data, such as sales for a particular month—all from a single report. Using report parameters can reduce the number of individual reports required by the user.

Report parameters are configured at design time, whereas the parameter values can be chosen at the time the report is run, entered using a mechanism such as a text box or a drop-down list. If a report has a non-optional parameter, the report will not run until the parameter is satisfied. If a default value is supplied for the non-optional parameter, then the user does not have to supply a value at runtime.

Restrict or filter data

Perhaps the most common use of a report parameter is to restrict or filter the data in a report. You can use a report parameter in the following ways:

- To provide a value to a SQL parameter in a query that creates the data set for the report.

  This is useful when requiring a user to type in an account number or PIN in order to see a report containing their account details.

- To control a filter that limits rows after they are retrieved into the data set.

  This can be useful when focusing on different regions within a sales report. The user can quickly switch from one region to another, without creating a large report.

- To navigate from one report to another, either as a subreport or as a jump to a report from an action.

- To control the data set that feeds the possible values of another report parameter, effectively creating dynamic parameter lists.

- To restrict the data or filter the report based on the Windows user account running the report.

Use as a report variable

In addition to using a report parameter to filter a data set, you can also use a report parameter for other purposes in the report. You can use a parameter value in additional ways:

- To calculate the appearance of text boxes or other report items, by using a parameter value in expressions.

  This could be used to switch the report from one color scheme to another when the report is included on different Web pages.

Using Report Parameters

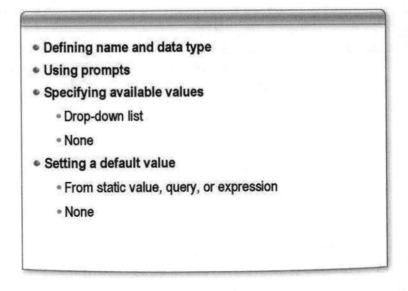

- Defining name and data type
- Using prompts
- Specifying available values
  - Drop-down list
  - None
- Setting a default value
  - From static value, query, or expression
  - None

Introduction	When you use report parameters, you must consider various aspects of the parameters. Some of these aspects will only affect the report author and some will affect the end user.
Defining name and data type	Each parameter added to a report must be given a unique name within the scope of the report. Also, each parameter must be associated with a data type (the default is **string**). Parameters can be configured to allow null (a value that has not been specified) and blank values.
Using prompts	When a parameterized report is run in a browser, the parameter is displayed in a text box in a pane at the top of the report. A prompt may be set for the parameter so that a label will be displayed next to the parameter in the rendered report.

When using a date or numeric data types, the parameter prompt will format the parameter value by using a default format that you cannot control. For example, numeric data types do not include thousand separators, and a **DataTime** data type always displays a time, even when you only need the date portion.
You may want to use a string data type for the parameter in order to have more control over the parameter format.

If the report user enters an invalid value for a date or numeric parameter, the parameter value is set to null, if that is an option for the parameter. Otherwise, it is set to blank.

Report parameters may also be passed as part of a report's URL or as part of a scheduled execution of a report.

Specifying available values

When the parameter value is an option in a list of values, a drop-down list can be displayed within the report. The data values contained in the list can be created as a static list at design time or can be created dynamically through the use of a data set.

Setting a default value

Parameters can be assigned a default value based on a static value, a query, or an expression. A default value is used when the report user does not specify a value for a parameter.

Using Query Parameters

- Query parameters and report parameters can be linked

SQL query parameter	Parameters collection
SELECT * FROM Sales	Parameters!Office.Value
WHERE Office = @Office AND UserID = @UserID	User!UserID (built-in parameter variable)

Introduction

When using query parameters, there are two types of parameters to consider; the SQL query parameter and the report parameter. A query parameter restricts the data contained in the data set in order to restrict the information displayed to the user. The report parameter is the link to the query parameter.

SQL query parameter

Query parameters can be created as part of the SQL query in a data set. When a query is constructed that contains a query parameter, Report Designer automatically creates a corresponding report parameter. This allows the parameter to be entered by the user when they view the report. To add a SQL parameter to a query, use the @ symbol followed by the parameter name. A data set containing a query is typically recreated every time the parameter changes.

Parameters collection

Query parameters are stored in the **Parameters** collection within the report. You can reference them using the following syntax:

```
Parameters!ParameterName.Value
```

For example, if a query uses a parameter called **@Office**, a parameter will be available in the report called **Parameters!Office.Value**.

User!UserID is a special global variable used in Reporting Services to identify the current Windows user. It can restrict the source query of a report or restrict the report data. In either scenario, you typically create a series of mapping tables that define the relationships between Windows users and the data that they are allowed to see.

For example, in a sales performance report, you might include the table that maintains permissions in your source query. This table maps the current Windows user to the sales data that he or she can see. To restrict the query based on the user, you join the user column from the permissions table to the **User!UserID** global variable.

Linking query and report parameters

When you add a SQL parameter to a query, Report Designer automatically creates a corresponding report parameter (if one with the same name does not already exist) and then maps the query parameter to the report parameter.

Note that when a query parameter is removed or renamed, the corresponding report parameter must be manually updated. If you need to manually modify or create a mapping between a query parameter and a report parameter, select the data set in the **Data** view, click the **Edit Selected Dataset** button, and select the **Parameters** tab.

Demonstration: Using Parameters in a Report

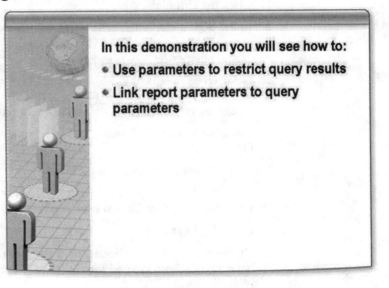

Introduction

The Employee Product Sales report displays the sales performance of all employees, listing product sales figures against the months of 2003. The report information is displayed using a Matrix data region.

In this demonstration, the instructor will add parameters to allow the user to specify employees to be displayed in the report.

Procedures

▶ **Launch the report design environment**

1. Click **Start**, point to **All Programs**, point to **Microsoft Visual Studio®** **.NET 2003**, and then click **Microsoft Visual Studio .NET 2003**.

2. On the **File** menu, click **Open Solution**.

3. In the **Open Solution** dialog box, navigate to **the C:\Program Files\Microsoft Learning\2030\Democode\Mod04\Demo01\Starter** folder.

4. Click **Sales Force Performance.sln**, and then click **Open**.

5. In **Solution Explorer**, expand the **Sales Force Performance** project, expand **Reports**, and then double-click **Employee Product Sales.rdl**.

▶ **Preview the report**

• Click the **Preview** tab. Notice that the report shows sales information by employee, month, and product for the year 2003.

▶ **Modify the data set query**

1. Click the **Data** tab.

2. In the SQL pane, replace the **WHERE** clause in the SQL statement so that it appears as follows:

```
WHERE  (DimTime.CalendarYear = @Year) AND
(DimSalesTerritory.SalesTerritoryGroup = @Group)
```

Note that **@Year** and **@Group** are query parameters.

3. Click the **Verify SQL** button to verify that the query is valid, and then click **OK**.

4. On the **File** menu, click **Save All**.

▶ **Edit the Year and Group report parameters**

1. Click the **Layout** tab.

2. On the **Report** menu, click **Report Parameters**. Notice that the parameters have already been created for you.

3. Perform the following steps to edit the **Year** parameter:

   • In the Parameters pane, click the **Year** parameter.

   • Clear the **Allow null value** check box. Notice that the **Available values** option is set to **Non-queried**.

   • For the **Default values** option, click **Non-queried**.

   • In the **Default values** text box, type **2003**.

   Tip   Note that the **Year** parameter could be set by using an expression such as **=Year(Now)**.

   ---

4. Perform the following steps to edit the **Group** parameter:

   • In the Parameters pane, click the **Group** parameter.

   • Clear the **Allow null value** check box.

   • For the **Default values** option, click **Non-queried**.

   • In the **Default values** text box, type **Europe**.

5. Click **OK** to close the **Report Parameters** dialog box.

6. In **textbox1**, located at the top of the report body, enter the following code to display a report title based on the parameter values supplied by the user:

```
=Parameters!Group.Value & " " & Parameters!Year.Value & " "
& Globals!ReportName
```

▶ **Save and preview the report**

1. On the **File** menu, click **Save All**.

2. Click the **Preview** tab. Notice that the default parameter values are used to restrict the data returned from the data set query.

3. In the **Group** text box, type **North America** and then click the **View Report** button. The data set is requeried.

4. Click the **Layout** tab.

5. On the **File** menu, click **Close Solution**.

6. If prompted, click **Yes** to save the changes.

Introducing Filters

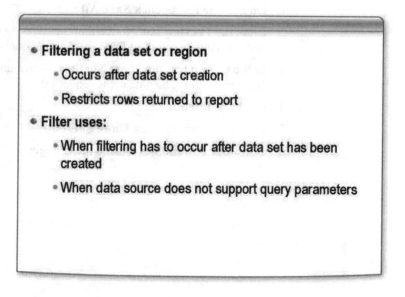

- Filtering a data set or region
  - Occurs after data set creation
  - Restricts rows returned to report
- Filter uses:
  - When filtering has to occur after data set has been created
  - When data source does not support query parameters

Introduction

Query parameters restrict the data that a report displays. An alternative approach to restricting certain data is to use a technique called *filtering*.

Filtering a data set or region

A filter can be added to a data set or a data region to filter data displayed in a report. Filters play a similar role to query parameters in that they both restrict the data being returned to the report. The key difference however is in timing. With a query parameter, the row elimination occurs as the original data set is created. With a filter, the row elimination occurs after the data set is created, but before the data region is rendered. In some cases, this can result in more responsive refreshing when switching from one report parameter to another.

Filtering uses

You should use data filters in scenarios where filtering has to take place after the data set has been created, or where the underlying data source does not support query parameters.

Creating a Data Filter

- **Compare an expression to a value**

Expression	Operator	Value
=Fields!Category.Value	=	=Parameters!Category.Value

- **Apply filters in different locations**
  - Data set
  - Data region
  - Grouping

Introduction

You create data filters for a report item within Report Designer. The **Dataset** dialog box includes a **Filters** tab where you can specify multiple filters for a single report.

Comparing an expression to a value

In order to filter your data, you must compare an expression against a value. The **Filters** tab requires three pieces of information:

- An expression (fields are often used)
- An operator
- A value to compare against (report parameters are often used)

Filter locations

A filter can be added not only to a data set, but also to a data region (such as a matrix) or a grouping level. For example, a single data set can supply data to a number of data regions in a single report. By using data filters, a different filter can be applied to each data region as required.

To apply filters to these different locations, access the **Filters** tab within the appropriate dialog box for each data region or grouping level.

Demonstration: Using Data Filters

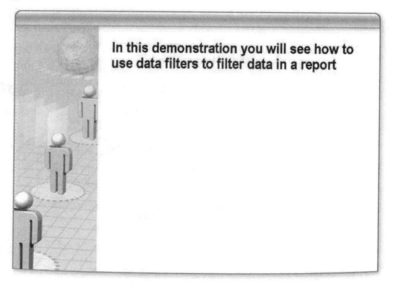

In this demonstration you will see how to use data filters to filter data in a report

Introduction

In this demonstration, the instructor will add a data filter to the Matrix data region to allow the data to be filtered by product for the Employee Product Sales report. Note that the filtering will be very restrictive in that only a single product can be displayed at any one time.

Procedures

▶ **Launch the report design environment**

1. Click **Start**, point to **All Programs**, point to **Microsoft Visual Studio .NET 2003**, and then click **Microsoft Visual Studio .NET 2003**.

2. On the **File** menu, click **Open Solution**.

3. In the **Open Solution** dialog box, navigate to the C:\Program Files\Microsoft Learning\2030\Democode\Mod04\Demo02\Starter folder.

7. Click **Sales Force Performance.sln**, and then click **Open**.

8. In **Solution Explorer**, expand the **Sales Force Performance** project, expand **Reports**, and then double-click **Employee Product Sales.rdl**.

▶ **Preview the report**

• Click the **Preview** tab. Notice that this is the solution report from the first demonstration.

▶ **Add a data set for the ProductCategory parameter**

1. Click the **Data** tab.

2. In the **Dataset** drop-down list, click **<New Dataset...>**.

3. In the **Dataset** dialog box, on the **Query** tab, in the **Name** text box, type **ProductCategory**.

4. In the **Query String** text box, type the following SQL statement and then click **OK**:

```
SELECT DISTINCT ProductCategoryName AS Category
FROM DimProductCategory
```

5. Click the **Verify SQL** button to verify that the query is valid, and then click **OK**.

▶ **Create the ProductCategory parameter**

1. Click the **Layout** tab.

2. On the **Report** menu, click **Report Parameters**.

3. In the **Report Parameters** dialog box, click the **Add** button to create a new parameter.

4. Perform the following steps to edit the **Category** parameter:

   - In the **Name** box, type **ProductCategory**.
   - In the **Prompt** box, type **Product Catagory**.
   - Clear the **Allow null value** check box.
   - For the **Available values** option, click **From query**.
   - In the **Dataset** drop-down list, click **ProductCategory**.
   - In the **Value field** drop-down list, click **Category**.
   - In the **Label field** drop-down list, click **Category**.
   - For the **Default values** option, click **Non-queried**.
   - In the **Default values** text box, type **Component**.

5. Click **OK** to close the **Report Parameters** dialog box.

▶ **Add a filter to the matrix data region**

1. Click inside the matrix data region.

2. Right-click the gray box in the upper left corner of the matrix to select the matrix, and then click **Properties**.

3. In the **Matrix Properties** dialog box, click the **Filters** tab.

4. In the **Expression** drop-down list, click **=Fields!ProductCategoryName.Value**.

5. In the **Operator** drop-down list, verify that = appears.

6. In the **Value** drop-down list, click **Expression**.

7. In the **Edit Expression** dialog box, in the Fields pane, expand **Parameters**, click **ProductCategory**, and then click the **Replace** button to add it to the Expression pane.

8. Verify that the resulting expression is:

```
= Parameters!ProductCategory.Value
```

9. Click **OK** to close the **Edit Expression** dialog box, and then click **OK** again to close the **Matrix Properties** dialog box.

▶ **Save and preview the report**

1. On the **File** menu, click **Save All**.

2. Click the **Preview** tab.

3. In the **Product Category** drop-down list, click **Bike**, and then click **View Report**. Note that the report is being filtered without requerying the underlying data set.

4. On the **File** menu, click **Close Solution**.

Lesson: Using Parameter Lists

- **Using Parameters with a Stored Procedure**
- **Dynamic Parameter Lists**
- **Adding "All Items" to a Parameter List**
- **Simulating a Multi-Select Parameter List**

Introduction
When using parameters within a report, it is a common requirement that at runtime the user must be able to assign each parameter value from a list of possible values.

Lesson objectives
In this lesson, you will learn how to use parameter lists in a report. After completing this lesson, you will be able to:

- Pass parameters to a stored procedure.
- Create a dynamic parameter list.
- Allow the user to display all items in a data set.
- Simulate the effect of a multi-select parameter list.

Using Parameters with a Stored Procedure

- **Generating a data set:**
  - Specify **StoredProcedure** as command type
  - Use Generic Query Designer in data tab
  - Pass input parameters to stored procedure
  - Only works with stored procedures that return a single data set
- **Benefits of stored procedures:**
  - Hide details of data access
  - Extended logic
  - Security
  - Reuse

Introduction

Although creating a data filter within a data set achieves the required goal of filtering data, it may not be the optimal solution. As an alternative, you can use a stored procedure (under certain conditions) to do the filtering.

Generating a data set

To use a stored procedure, you must set the command type for the data set to **StoredProcedure** and specify the name of the stored procedure.

When you access a stored procedure, you use the Generic Query Designer version of the Data view. This prevents Report Designer from attempting to parse and interpret the SQL statement. If you want to switch from a text-based query to a stored procedure, click the **Generic Query Designer** toolbar button, and then click **StoredProcedure** in the **Command type** drop-down list.

Reporting Services supports input parameters to a stored procedure. All input parameters are automatically detected and made available as report parameters or other values.

Reporting Services only supports stored procedures that return a single data set.

Benefits

Using stored procedures provides you with the following benefits:

- Details of the source query for data access are hidden, which gives you flexibility in creating the source for a data set.

- Extended logic allows you to take advantage of procedural logic or other techniques that are not possible in a standard query or view.

- Security configuration options using standard SQL Server security are provided.

- The logic within a stored procedure can be reused much more simply than the logic in a hard-coded query.

Demonstration: Using Stored Procedures

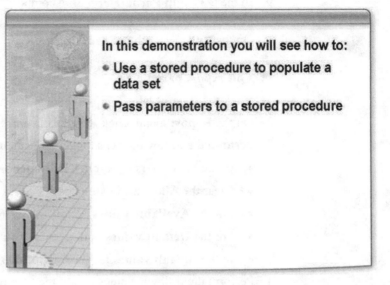

In this demonstration you will see how to:

- Use a stored procedure to populate a data set
- Pass parameters to a stored procedure

Introduction

A stored procedure can be used by a data set to supply data to a report. Parameters used by stored procedures can be linked to report parameters.

In this demonstration, you will see how to use a stored procedure named **sp_ActualVsQuota** to supply the data for a report. Also, you will see how to set up two input parameters to control the data set, **CalendarYear** and **Group**.

Procedures

▶ **Open a saved project and report**

1. Click **Start**, point to **All Programs**, point to **Microsoft Visual Studio .NET 2003**, and then click **Microsoft Visual Studio .NET 2003**.

2. On the **File** menu, click **Open Solution**.

3. In the **Open Solution** dialog box, navigate to the C:\Program Files\Microsoft Learning\2030\Democode\Mod04\Demo03\Starter folder.

5. Click **Stored Procedure.sln** and then click **Open**.

6. In **Solution Explorer**, double-click **Actual Vs Quota.rdl**.

▶ **Create a stored procedure data set**

1. Click the **Data** tab.

2. In the **Dataset** drop-down list, click **<New Dataset...>**.

3. In the **Dataset** dialog box, on the **Query** tab, in the **Name** text box, type **Detail**.

4. In the **Data source** drop-down list, click **AdventureWorksDW (shared)**.

5. In the **Command type** drop-down list, click **StoredProcedure**, and then click **OK**.

7. In the **Stored Procedure** drop-down list, click **sp_ActualVsQuota**, and then click the **Run** button to view the results of the stored procedure.

8. In the **@CalendarYear Parameter Value** combo box, type **2003**.

9. In the **@Group Parameter Value** combo box, type **Europe**, and then click **OK**.

10. On the **File** menu, click **Save All**.

▶ **Edit report parameters**

1. Click the **Layout** tab.

2. On the **Report** menu, click **Report Parameters**.

3. Perform the following steps to edit the **CalendarYear** parameter:

   • In the Parameters pane, click the **CalendarYear** parameter.

   • Clear the **Allow null value** check box.

   • For the **Available values** option, click **Non-queried**.

   • For the **Default values** option, click **Non-queried**.

   • In the **Default values** text box, type **2003**.

4. Perform the following steps to edit the **Group** parameter:

   • In the Parameters pane, click the **Group** parameter.

   • Clear the **Allow null value** check box.

   • For the **Available values** option, click **Non-queried**.

   • For the **Default values** option, click **Non-queried**.

   • In the **Default values** text box, type **North America**.

5. Click **OK** to close the **Report Parameters** dialog box.

▶ **Save and preview the report**

1. On the **File** menu, click **Save All**.

2. Click the **Preview** tab.

3. In the **Group** parameter text box, type **Europe**, and then press **Enter**.

   The report preview should change to display the Europe sales performance information.

4. On the **File** menu, click **Close Solution**.

Dynamic Parameter Lists

- Parameter list uses a data set
- Add first parameter to query for second parameter's data set

    SELECT Region FROM DimGeography
    WHERE CountryID = Parameters!Country.Value

- Put parameters in sequential order in list

Introduction

A dynamic parameter list is simply a list of values for one parameter that changes dynamically based on the value you select for a different parameter. This dependency between parameters is also known as *cascading parameters*.

Parameter list uses a data set

You can create a dynamic parameter list when the source for the list is a SQL query. Simply add a query parameter to the data set query for the report parameter, and then link that query parameter to its own parameter.

For example, when creating a report, a parameter named **Country** is specified and displayed to the user in a text box. A second parameter named **Region** is added to the report using a drop-down list. The **Region** query uses the value of the **Country** parameter in its query to filter the data contained in its drop-down list. The query for the **Region** drop-down list appears as follows:

```
SELECT Region FROM DimGeography
WHERE CountryID = Parameters!Country.Value
```

Sequential order

It is important to order the parameters so that the dependent parameter comes after the parameter upon which it is dependent. Otherwise, the dependent parameter will attempt to evaluate its list of values before the parameter that it is dependent upon is set. This would produce at best an incorrect value and at worst an error.

Adding "All Items" to a Parameter List

- **Problem**
  - Parameter lists are often used to filter data regions
  - Filtering can leave the user unable to display all of the data contained in a data region
- **Solution**
  - For parameter list, create UNION query to add single item with constant
    ```
    SELECT Key, Name FROM DimProduct
    UNION
    SELECT -1, 'All Items'
    ```
  - For main data set, add OR condition for "All Items" parameter

Introduction

Parameter lists can sometimes cause problems for the end user because the report may not be able to display an unfiltered version of the data. In this case, you must manually implement a way to achieve this requirement.

Problem

A parameter list allows you to select a single item for a parameter. Typically, the list of values for a parameter comes from the distinct values of a database field. Consequently, the default list does not have an option for "All Items."

Solution

You can add an "All Items" option to a parameter list by following this two-step process:

1. Change the parameter list query to include an appropriately named item—for example, "All Items"— along with a key value that will not be present in the actual database values. You can add this item by using a **UNION** operator along with a constant, single-row query.

2. Change the SQL query that includes the linked query parameter to include an **OR** option to test for the "All Items" key.

Simulating a Multi-Select Parameter List

- **Parameter lists do not allow multi-select**
- **Options for multi-select:**
  - Allow text input for user to type list of values
  - For numeric values, embed string into IN clause
    ```
    ="SELECT * FROM vProductProfitability
      WHERE MonthNumber IN (" +
      Parameters!Month.Value + ")"
    ```
  - For string values, send string to user-defined function (UDF) to parse into table that can be joined

Introduction

In some situations, you may want the user to select multiple items for report parameters. For example, a report may need to be displayed based on multiple months rather than a single month.

Parameters lists do not allow multi-select

When designing a report, it is common to supply a list of parameter values from which the user can select. By default, the user can only choose a single item from a parameter list. There is no built-in way to make the list a multi-select style list.

Options for multi-select

One way to get the effect of a multi-select parameter is to allow the user to type in a list. You can achieve this in the following ways:

- Change the value of the parameter to a string, and let the user type in a list of values.

- If the parameter values are numbers, change the query to an expression that incorporates the list into an **IN** clause. To do this, you must switch to the Generic Query Designer and then convert the query to a string expression that concatenates the parameter with the rest of the query. The following example shows how to achieve this:

```
="SELECT * FROM vProductProfitability
   WHERE MonthNumber IN (" +
   Parameters!Month.Value + ")"
```

- If the parameter values are strings, you may want to avoid requiring the user to type in quotation marks. In this case, create a user-defined function (UDF) that can split the multi-select parameter string into an inline table that you can use in an **IN** clause, or that can be joined with the main view.

Caution   When you create a query as a string expression, you must first create and execute the expression as a standard query to allow Report Designer to identify the fields in the resulting data set. Then you can convert the expression to a string so that you can concatenate elements.

Demonstration: Using Parameter Lists

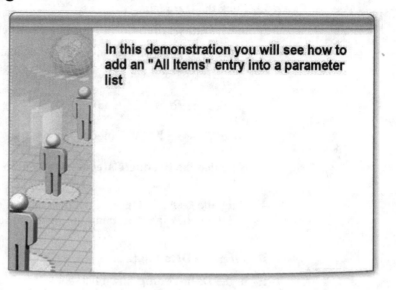

In this demonstration you will see how to add an "All Items" entry into a parameter list

Introduction

In this demonstration, the instructor will add a new category named **All Categories** to the product report parameter in the Employee Product Sales report so that all products can be displayed.

Procedures

▶ **Launch the report design environment**

1. Click **Start**, point to **All Programs**, point to **Microsoft Visual Studio .NET 2003**, and then click **Microsoft Visual Studio .NET 2003**.

2. On the **File** menu, click **Open Solution**.

3. In the **Open Solution** dialog box, navigate to the C:\Program Files\Microsoft Learning\2030\Democode\Mod04\Demo04\Starter folder.

3. Click **Sales Force Performance.sln**, and then click **Open**.

4. In **Solution Explorer**, expand the **Sales Force Performance** project, expand **Reports**, and then double-click **Employee Product Sales.rdl**.

▶ **Remove the filter from the matrix data region**

1. Click the data region, right click the gray box in the top left corner, and then click **Properties**.

2. On the **Filters** tab, click the first column of the first row, and then click the **Delete** button (the button looks like a cross icon). The expression is deleted.

3. Click **OK**.

▶ **Add All Categories to the ProductCategory data set**

1. Click the **Data** tab.

2. In the **Dataset** drop-down list, click **ProductCategory**.

3. In the SQL pane, change the query to appear as below:

```
SELECT DISTINCT ProductCategoryKey AS CategoryKey,
                ProductCategoryName AS Category
FROM DimProductCategory
UNION
SELECT - 1, 'All Categories'
```

Note that the **ProductCategoryKey** is used to uniquely define a product category.

4. Click the **Generic Query Designer** button, click **Yes** at the warning prompt, and then click the **Run** button to see the results of the query.

▶ **Alter the Detail data set**

1. In the **Dataset** drop-down list, click **Detail**.

2. In the SQL pane, change the **WHERE** clause to appear as follows:

```
WHERE  (DimTime.CalendarYear = @Year) AND
       (DimSalesTerritory.SalesTerritoryGroup = @Group) AND
       (DimProductCategory.ProductCategoryKey =
       @ProductCategory OR @ProductCategory = - 1)
```

Note again that the **ProductCategoryKey** is used to uniquely define a product category. The key will be matched up against the **ProductCategory** report parameter.

3. Click the **Generic Query Designer** button, click **Yes** if you see a warning, and then click the **Run** button to see the results of the query.

4. In the **Define Query Parameters** dialog box, type in the following values:

Name	Value
@Year	2003
@Group	Europe
@ProductCategory	-1

5. Click **OK**. Notice that data is now displayed for all categories.

▶ **Edit the ProductCategory report parameter**

1. Click the **Layout** tab.
2. On the **Report** menu, click **Report Parameters**.
3. In the Parameters pane, click **ProductCategory**.
4. In the **Properties** group, change the **Data type** to **Integer**.
5. In the **Value field** drop-down list, select **CategoryKey.**
6. In the **Default values** text box, type **-1** and then click **OK**.

▶ **Save and preview the report**

1. On the **File** menu, click **Save All**.
2. Click the **Preview** tab.
3. In the **Product Category** parameter drop-down list, click **Accessory**, and then click **View Report**.
4. On the **File** menu, click **Close Solution**.

Review

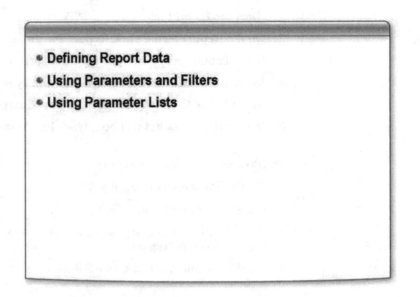

- Defining Report Data
- Using Parameters and Filters
- Using Parameter Lists

1. What is the difference between a data source and a data set and how are they used?

2. What is the difference between a query parameter and a report parameter?

3. What is a filter?

4. How are parameter lists used?

Lab 4: Manipulating Data Sets

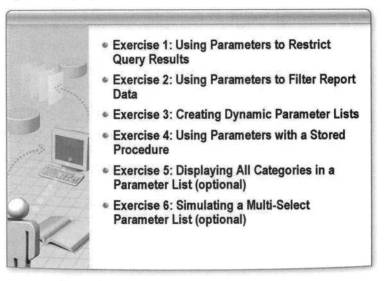

- Exercise 1: Using Parameters to Restrict Query Results
- Exercise 2: Using Parameters to Filter Report Data
- Exercise 3: Creating Dynamic Parameter Lists
- Exercise 4: Using Parameters with a Stored Procedure
- Exercise 5: Displaying All Categories in a Parameter List (optional)
- Exercise 6: Simulating a Multi-Select Parameter List (optional)

In this lab, you will use both query and report parameters to filter data in a report. You will then enhance the user interface of the report, allowing users to select multiple items from a parameter list and display information matching all items in the parameter list.

Objectives

After completing this lab, you will be able to:

- Use parameters to restrict query results.
- Use parameters to filter report data.
- Create a dynamic parameter list.
- Pass parameters to a stored procedure.
- Display data matching all categories in a parameter list.
- Allow the user to choose multiple items from a parameter list.

Estimated time to complete this lab: 60 minutes

Exercise 1
Using Parameters to Restrict Query Results

In this exercise, you will use parameters to restrict the results displayed in a report.

Scenario

The Product Profitability report uses a table to display total sales performance by product and summarized totals by product subcategory and category. To restrict data in the report by month and by product category, you will create parameters.

To view the data for a month and year, you will create hard-coded parameters to filter the report. You will also create a query-based parameter for product categories to restrict the data in the report. You will create parameters in the Product Profitability report using the following steps and criteria.

▶ **Launch the report design environment**

1. Click **Start**, point to **All Programs**, point to **Microsoft Visual Studio .NET 2003**, and then click **Microsoft Visual Studio .NET 2003**.

2. On the **File** menu, click **Open Solution**.

3. In the **Open Solution** dialog box, navigate to the C:\Program Files\Microsoft Learning\2030\Labfiles\Lab04\Exercise01\Starter folder.

4. Click **Data Manipulation.sln**, and then click **Open**.

5. In **Solution Explorer**, expand the **Data Manipulation** project, expand **Reports**, and then double-click **Product Profitability.rdl**.

▶ **Preview the report**

- Click the **Preview** tab. Notice that the report is hard-coded to display data for January 2003. The user cannot change the date used in the report.

▶ **Modify the data set query**

1. Click the **Data** tab.

2. In the SQL pane, replace the numeric constants for **Year** and **Month** with the parameters **@Year** and **@Month**. You should now have the following SQL statement in the SQL pane:

```
SELECT    *
FROM      vProductProfitability
WHERE     (Year = @Year) AND (MonthNumberOfYear = @Month)
```

3. Click the **Verify SQL** button to verify that the query is valid, and then click **OK**.

4. On the **File** menu, click **Save All**.

▶ **Edit the Year and Month parameters**

1. Click the **Layout** tab.

2. On the **Report** menu, click **Report Parameters**. Notice that the **Month** and **Year** report parameters have been automatically created.

3. Perform the following steps to edit the **Year** parameter:

   • In the Parameters pane, click the **Year** parameter.

   • Clear the **Allow null value** check box. Notice that the **Available values** option is set to **Non-queried**.

   • For the **Default values** option, click **Non-queried**.

   • In the **Default values** text box, type **2003**.

   Tip   If you want the default value of the **Year** parameter to be dynamically based upon the current year, use the expression **=Year(Now)**.

   ---

4. Perform the following steps to edit the **Month** parameter:

   • In the Parameters pane, click the **Month** parameter.

   • Clear the **Allow null value** check box.

   • In the **Available values** table, type in the following values:

Label	Value
Jan	1
Feb	2
Mar	3
Apr	4
May	5
Jun	6

   • For the **Default values** option, click **Non-queried**.

   • In the **Default values** text box, type **1**.

   Tip   If you want the default value of the **Month** parameter to be dynamically based upon the current month, use the expression **=Month(Now)**.

   ---

5. Click **OK** to close the **Report Parameters** dialog box.

► **Save and preview the report**

1. On the **File** menu, click **Save All**.

2. Click the **Preview** tab. Notice that a **Year** text box and a **Month** drop-down list appear at the top of the report.

3. In the **Month** drop-down list, click **Jun**, and then click the **View Report** button.

4. Click the **Layout** tab.

5. On the **File** menu, click **Close Solution**.

Exercise 2
Using Parameters to Filter Report Data

In this exercise, you will use parameters to filter the report data rather than filtering the actual data source, as in the previous exercise.

▶ **Open a saved project and report**

1. Click **Start**, point to **All Programs**, point to **Microsoft Visual Studio .NET 2003**, and then click **Microsoft Visual Studio .NET 2003**.

2. On the **File** menu, click **Open Solution**.

3. In the **Open Solution** dialog box, navigate to the C:\Program Files\Microsoft Learning\2030\Labfiles\Lab04\Exercise02\Starter folder.

4. Click **Data Manipulation.sln**, and then click **Open**.

5. In **Solution Explorer**, double-click **Product Profitability.rdl**.

▶ **Add a data set for the Category parameter**

1. Click the **Data** tab.

2. In the **Dataset** drop-down list, click **<New Dataset...>**.

3. In the **Dataset** dialog box, on the **Query** tab, in the **Name** text box, type **Category**.

4. In the **Data source** drop-down list, verify that the data source is **AdventureWorksDW**, and then click **OK**.

5. In the SQL pane, type the following SQL statement:

```
SELECT DISTINCT ProductCategoryName AS Category
FROM DimProductCategory
```

6. Click the **Verify SQL** button to verify that the query is valid, and then click **OK**.

▶ **Create the Category parameter**

1. Click the **Layout** tab.

2. On the **Report** menu, click **Report Parameters**.

3. In the **Report Parameters** dialog box, click the **Add** button to create a new parameter.

4. Perform the following steps to add the **Category** parameter:

   - In the **Name** box, type **Category**.

   - In the **Prompt** box, type **Category**.

   - Clear the **Allow null value** check box.

   - For the **Available values** option, click **From query**.

   - In the **Dataset** drop-down list, click **Category**.

   - In the **Value field** drop-down list, click **Category**.

   - In the **Label field** drop-down list, click **Category**.

   - For the **Default values** option, click **Non-queried**.

   - In the **Default values** text box, type **Component**.

   - Click **OK** to close the **Report Parameters** dialog box.

▶ **Add a filter to the table data region**

1. Click inside the table data region.

2. Right-click the gray box in the upper left corner of the table to select the table, and then click **Properties**.

3. In the **Table Properties** dialog box, click the **Filters** tab.

4. Click the first **Expression** cell, and then in the **Expression** drop-down list, click **=Fields!Category.Value**.

5. In the **Operator** drop-down list, verify that = appears.

6. In the **Value** drop-down list, click **<Expression>**.

7. In the **Edit Expression** dialog box, in the Fields pane, expand **Parameters**, click **Category**, and then click the **Replace** button to add it to the Expression pane.

8. Verify that the resulting expression is:

```
= Parameters!Category.Value
```

9. Click **OK** to close the **Edit Expression** dialog box, and then click **OK** again to close the **Table Properties** dialog box.

▶ **Remove the Category group page break**

1. Click inside the table data region.

2. Right-click the **table1_Category Footer** row icon to select the row, and select **Edit Group**.

3. Deselect the **Page break at end** check box, and then click **OK**.

▶ **Save and preview the report**

1. On the **File** menu, click **Save All**.

2. Click the **Preview** tab. Notice the new **Category** parameter.

3. In the **Category** drop-down list, select **Bike,** and then click **View Report**.

4. Click the **Layout** tab.

▶ **Create a Category parameter text box**

1. In the page header above the report graphic, hold down **CTRL** and click **textbox15**. Drag the text box into the space above the graphic.

2. Right-click the new text box, and then click **Expression**.

3. In the **Edit Expression** dialog box, in the Fields pane, expand **Parameters,** click **Category,** and then click the **Replace** button to replace the existing value and add the parameter to the Expression pane.

4. Verify that the resulting expression is:

```
= Parameters!Category.Value
```

5. Click **OK** to close the **Edit Expression** dialog box.

▶ **Save and preview the report**

1. On the **File** menu, click **Save All**.

2. Click the **Preview** tab. Notice that the current value of the **Category** parameter is displayed above the graphic.

3. In the **Month** drop-down list, click **Mar**. In the **Category** drop-down list, click **Bike,** and then click the **View Report** button.

4. On the **File** menu, click **Close Solution**.

Exercise 3
Creating Dynamic Parameter Lists

In this exercise, you will create a dynamic parameter list to filter the report based on the **BusinessType** value of the reseller.

Scenario

The Order Details report uses a table to display order detail information. Report parameters are used to restrict data in the report between a start date and end date and by reseller.

▶ **Open a saved project and report**

1. Click **Start**, point to **All Programs**, point to **Microsoft Visual Studio .NET 2003**, and then click **Microsoft Visual Studio .NET 2003**.

2. On the **File** menu, click **Open Solution**.

3. In the **Open Solution** dialog box, navigate to the C:\Program Files\Microsoft Learning\2030\Labfiles\Lab04\Exercise03\Starter folder.

4. Click **Dynamic Parameters.sln**, and then click **Open**.

5. In **Solution Explorer**, expand the **Dynamic Parameters** project, expand **Reports**, and then double-click **Order Details.rdl**.

▶ **Preview the report**

- Click the **Preview** tab. Notice that the **StartDate**, **EndDate**, and **Reseller** parameters are used to restrict data in the report. The default value for the **Reseller** parameter is **Retreat Inn**.

▶ **Add a data set for the BusinessType parameter**

1. Click the **Data** tab.

2. In the **Dataset** drop-down list, click **<New Dataset...>**.

3. In the **Dataset** dialog box, on the **Query** tab, in the **Name** text box, type **BusinessType**.

4. In the **Data source** drop-down list, verify that the data source is **DataSet1**, and then click **OK**.

5. Right-click in the white area at the top of the data view in the Diagram pane, and then click **Add Table**.

6. In the **Add Table** dialog box, click the **Views** tab, click the **vOrderDetails** view, click **Add**, and then click **Close**.

7. In the **vOrderDetails** table view, scroll down, and then select the **BusinessType** check box.

8. In the SQL pane, after **SELECT**, type **DISTINCT**.

   The following SQL statement should be displayed in the SQL pane:

   ```
   SELECT DISTINCT BusinessType
   FROM vOrderDetails
   ```

9. Click the **Verify SQL** button to verify that the query is valid, and then click **OK**.

▶ **Modify the Reseller data set query**

1. In the **Dataset** drop-down list, click **Reseller**.

2. In the Diagram pane, in the **vOrderDetails** table view, scroll down and then select the **BusinessType** check box.

3. In the SQL pane, add the following to the end of the **WHERE** clause in the SQL statement:

```
AND (BusinessType = @BusinessType)
```

The following SQL statement should be displayed in the SQL pane:

```
SELECT DISTINCT Reseller, BusinessType
FROM          vOrderDetails
WHERE        (OrderDate <= @EndDate) AND (OrderDate >=
@StartDate) AND (BusinessType = @BusinessType)
```

4. Click the **Verify SQL** button to verify that the query is valid, and then click **OK**.

▶ **Modify the Detail data set query**

1. In the **Dataset** drop-down list, click **Detail**.

2. In the SQL pane, add the following to the end of the **WHERE** clause in the SQL statement:

```
AND (BusinessType = @BusinessType)
```

The following SQL statement should be displayed in the SQL pane:

```
SELECT    *
FROM      vOrderDetails
WHERE     (Name = @Reseller) AND (OrderDate >= @StartDate)
          AND (OrderDate <= @EndDate)
          AND (BusinessType = @BusinessType)
```

3. Click the **Verify SQL** button to verify that the query is valid, and then click **OK**.

4. On the **File** menu, click **Save All**.

▶ **Create the BusinessType parameter**

1. Click the **Layout** tab.

2. On the **Report** menu, click **Report Parameters**. Notice that the **BusinessType** parameter has been created automatically.

3. Perform the following steps to edit the **BusinessType** parameter:

   - In the Parameters pane, click the **BusinessType** parameter.

   - Click the up arrow button to move **BusinessType** above **Reseller**.

   - Clear the **Allow null value** check box.

   - For the **Available values** option, click **From query**.

   - In the **Dataset** drop-down list, click **BusinessType**.

   - In the **Value field** drop-down list, click **BusinessType**.

   - In the **Label field** drop-down list, click **BusinessType**.

   - For the **Default values** option, click **Non-queried**.

   - In the **Default values** text box, type **Value-added**.

Important Make sure to type the default value exactly as follows to retrieve values for this business type: **Value-added**.

---

4. Click **OK** to close the **Report Parameters** dialog box.

▶ **Save and preview the report**

1. On the **File** menu, click **Save All**.

2. Click the **Preview** tab, and then in the **BusinessType** drop-down list, click **Warehouse**. Notice that the **Reseller** parameter is a dynamic parameter list dependent on the **BusinessType** parameter.

3. In the **Reseller** drop-down list, click **Active Life Toys**, and then click the **View Report** button.

4. On the **File** menu, click **Close Solution**.

Exercise 4
Using Parameters with a Stored Procedure

In this exercise, you will use a stored procedure named **sp_ActualVsQuota** to supply the data for a report. You will set up two input parameters to control the data set, **CalendarYear** and **Group**.

▶ **Open a saved project and report**

1. Click **Start**, point to **All Programs**, point to **Microsoft Visual Studio .NET 2003**, and then click **Microsoft Visual Studio .NET 2003**.

2. On the **File** menu, click **Open Solution**.

3. In the **Open Solution** dialog box, navigate to the C:\Program Files\Microsoft Learning\2030\Labfiles\Lab04\Exercise04\Starter folder.

4. Click t**Stored Procedure.sln**, and then click **Open**.

5. In **Solution Explorer**, double-click the **Actual Vs Quota.rdl** report.

▶ **Create a stored procedure data set**

1. Click the **Data** tab.

2. In the **Dataset** drop-down list, click **<New Dataset...>**.

3. In the **Dataset** dialog box, on the **Query** tab, in the **Name** text box, type **Detail**.

4. In the **Data source** drop-down list, click **AdventureWorksDW (shared)**.

5. In the **Command type** drop-down list, click **StoredProcedure** and then click **OK**.

6. In the **Stored procedure** drop-down list, click **sp_ActualVsQuota**, and then click the **Run** button to open the **Define Query Parameters** dialog box.

7. In the **@CalendarYear** Parameter Value text box, type **2003**.

8. In the **@Group** Parameter Value text box, type **Europe** and then click **OK**.

9. On the **File** menu, click **Save All**.

▶ **Edit report parameters**

1. Click the **Layout** tab.

2. On the **Report** menu, click **Report Parameters**.

3. Perform the following steps to edit the **CalendarYear** parameter:

   - In the Parameters pane, click the **CalendarYear** parameter.

   - Clear the **Allow null value** check box.

   - For the **Available values** option, click **Non-queried**.

   - For the **Default values** option, click **Non-queried**.

   - In the **Default values** text box, type **2003**.

4. Perform the following steps to edit the **Group** parameter:

   - In the Parameters pane, click the **Group** parameter.

   - Clear the **Allow null value** check box.

   - For the **Available values** option, click **Non-queried**.

   - For the **Default values** option, click **Non-queried**.

   - In the **Default values** text box, type **North America**.

5. Click **OK** to close the **Report Parameters** dialog box.

▶ **Save and preview the report**

1. On the **File** menu, click **Save All**.

2. Click the **Preview** tab.

3. In the **Group** parameter text box, type **Europe** and then press **Enter**.

4. On the **File** menu, click **Close Solution**.

Exercise 5
Displaying All Categories in a Parameter List (optional)

In this exercise, you will allow the user the option of selecting all of the categories from the parameter list.

▶ **Open a saved project and report**

1. Click **Start**, point to **All Programs**, point to **Microsoft Visual Studio .NET 2003**, and then click **Microsoft Visual Studio .NET 2003**.

2. On the **File** menu, click **Open Solution**.

3. In the **Open Solution** dialog box, navigate to the C:\Program Files\Microsoft Learning\2030\Labfiles\Lab04\Exercise05\Starter folder.

4. Click **All Items.sln**, and then click **Open**.

▶ **Preview the report**

1. Double-click **All Items Product Profitability.rdl**.

2. Click the **Preview** tab. Notice that the report contains the **Category** parameter, which has a default value of **Accessory** and a drop-down list from which you can select.

3. In the **Category** parameter drop-down list, click **Bike**, and then click **View Report**. Notice that there is no way to display all categories in the same report.

▶ **Add all categories to the Category data set**

1. Click the **Data** tab.

2. In the **Dataset** drop-down list, click **Category**.

3. In the SQL pane, add the following to the end of the SQL statement:

```
UNION SELECT -1, 'All Categories'
```

4. Click the background of the Report Designer pane, and when warned that the query cannot be displayed graphically, click **Yes** to preserve your changes.

   You should have the following SQL statement in the SQL pane:

```
SELECT DISTINCT ProductCategoryKey AS CategoryKey,
                ProductCategoryName AS Category
FROM   DimProductCategory
UNION
SELECT -1, 'All Categories'
```

5. On the **Data** tab, click the **Generic Query Designer** button, and then click the **Run** button to see the results of the query. Notice that the All Categories entry has been added to the query with a key value of -1.

▶ **Update the DataDetail data set query**

1. In the **Dataset** drop-down list, click **DataDetail**.

2. In the Grid pane, in the **Criteria** column, at the end of the = **@Category** statement, type **OR @Category = -1** and then press **Enter**.

   The following SQL statement should be displayed in the SQL pane:

   ```
   SELECT    *
   FROM      vProductProfitability
   WHERE     (Year = 2003) AND
             (MonthNumberOfYear IN (1, 2, 3)) AND
             (CategoryKey = @Category OR @Category = -1)
   ```

3. Click the **Verify SQL** button to verify that the query is valid, and then click **OK**.

▶ **Save and preview the report**

1. On the **File** menu, click **Save All**.

2. Click the **Preview** tab.

3. In the **Category** parameter drop-down list, click **All Categories**, click **View Report**, and then verify that all categories are displayed in the report.

4. On the **File** menu, click **Close Solution**.

Exercise 6
Simulating a Multi-Select Parameter List (optional)

In this exercise, you will simulate a multi-select parameter list.

The problem with string manipulation for multiple selections is that if you use text items in a list, the user must type quotation marks around each element. You will use a user-defined function named **SplitList** to parse the parameter list and use the parameters to restrict the results of a SQL statement.

▶ **Open a saved project and report**

1. Click **Start**, point to **All Programs**, point to **Microsoft Visual Studio .NET 2003**, and then click **Microsoft Visual Studio .NET 2003**.

2. On the **File** menu, point to **Open**, and then click **Project**.

3. In the **Open Project** dialog box, navigate to the C:\Program Files\ Microsoft Learning\2030\Labfiles\Lab04\Exercise06\Starter folder.

4. Double-click **Multi-Select Parameter.rptproj**.

▶ **Preview the report**

1. Double-click **Muli-Select Product Profitability.rdl**.

2. Click the **Preview** tab. Notice that the report contains the **Month** parameter.

3. In the **Month** parameter text box, type **2** and then click **View Report**. The Profitability report displays sales figures for all products for the month of February 2003.

4. In the **Month** parameter text box, type **2,3** and then click **View Report**.

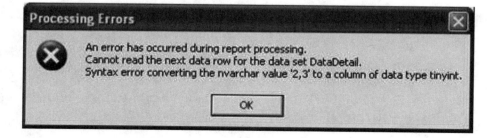

Notice that you receive an error. You cannot type multiple selections in the parameter text box.

5. Click **OK**.

▶ **Convert data set query to a string**

1. Click the **Data** tab.

2. Click the **Generic Query Designer** button.

3. In the SQL pane, replace the existing code with the following:

```
="SELECT * FROM  vProductProfitability
WHERE (Year = 2003) AND
(MonthNumberOfYear IN (" + Parameters!Month.Value + "))"
```

Note   Enter this code on a single line.

▶ **Save and preview the report**

1. On the **File** menu, click **Save All**.

2. Click the **Preview** tab.

3. In the **Month** parameter text box, type **1,2,3** and then click **View Report**. Notice that the corresponding months are displayed in the report.

▶ **Use a UDF to parse a parameter list**

1. In **Solution Explorer**, double-click **UDF Product Profitability.rdl**.

2. Click the **Data** tab.

3. In the SQL statement, delete the following code:

```
AND (MonthNumberOfYear IN (@Month))
```

4. In the Diagram pane, right-click the background, and then click **Add Table**.

5. In the **Add Table** dialog box, click the **Functions** tab, click **SplitList**, click **Add**, and then click **Close**.

6. In the Diagram pane, in the **vProductProfitability** table, scroll down and drag the **Month** field to the **ListItem** field in the **SplitList** function. This will create an inner join between **vProductProfitability.Month** and **SplitList.ListItem**.

7. In the SQL statement, replace **SplitList(,)** with **SplitList(',', @Month)**.

   The first argument to the function is the list separation character (a comma). The second argument is the string to split; the user will type a value for this report parameter—for example, **Jan,Feb,Mar**.

   The following SQL statement should be displayed in the SQL pane:

```
SELECT *
FROM    vProductProfitability
INNER JOIN SplitList(',', @Month) SplitList
ON      vProductProfitability.Month = SplitList.ListItem
WHERE   (vProductProfitability.Year = 2003)
```

▶ **Save and preview the report**

1. On the **File** menu, click **Save All**.

2. Click the **Preview** tab.

3. In the **Month** parameter text box, type **Jan, Feb, Mar** and then click **View Report**. The Profitability report shows all products for the months January, February, and March.

Microsoft®

Module 5: Managing Content

Contents

Overview

- **Publishing Content**
- **Executing Reports**
- **Creating Cached Instances**
- **Creating Snapshots and Report History**
- **Creating Subscriptions**

Introduction

After you have designed your reports, you need to be able to publish them to a report server so that users can access them. In this module, you will learn how to manage content stored in the report server database.

Objectives

After completing this module, you will be able to:

- Publish content to a report server.
- Execute reports on demand.
- Created cached instances of reports.
- Create snapshot reports and report history.
- Deliver reports using subscriptions.

Lesson: Publishing Content

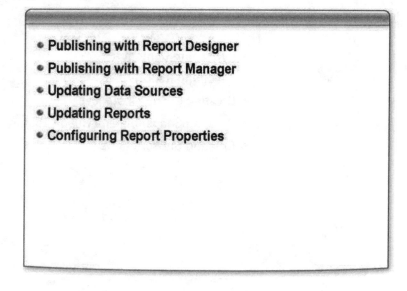

- Publishing with Report Designer
- Publishing with Report Manager
- Updating Data Sources
- Updating Reports
- Configuring Report Properties

Introduction

Publishing is the process of storing items (reports or data sources) in the report server database so that users can later retrieve them.

In this lesson, you will learn how to publish reports to a report server using Report Designer and Report Manager. You will also learn how to organize your reports and to update both data sources and reports after their initial publication.

Lesson objectives

After completing this lesson, you will be able to:

- Publish a report using Report Designer.
- Publish a report using Report Manager.
- Update a data source.
- Update a report.
- Configure report properties.

Publishing with Report Designer

- **Options for deployment:**
  - Single file deployment - report or data source
  - Project deployment - all elements of a project
  - Solution deployment - all projects in a solution
- **Project deployment options:**
  - Publish reports to a specific folder location
  - Specify the project's target folder

Introduction

The Report Designer tool provided in Microsoft® Visual Studio® .NET 2003 allows you to design your reports and data sources. It also has the ability to deploy reports and data sources to Report Server. This is an intuitive approach—after you have finished designing your item, you can deploy it immediately.

Options for deployment

Report Designer provides the following options for deployment:

- Single file deployment: Deploys only a single file, such as a report or data source, to the Report Server database
- Project deployment: Deploys all of the data sources, reports, and any other custom content in the project to the Report Server database
- Solution deployment: Deploys all of the projects within the solution to the Report Server database

To deploy an item, right-click it in **Solution Explorer** and then click the **Deploy** context menu.

Project deployment options

You can configure project deployment options by opening the report project **Property Pages** dialog box and clicking **Properties** on the **Project** menu.

You can configure the following project deployment options:

- **TargetFolder**: The folder where items are deployed. You can select any folder or subfolder defined in the Report Server database, or you can specify a new folder for creation at the time of deployment.
- **TargetServerURL**: The URL of the report server that will host your items.

Publishing with Report Manager

- Upload files
- Create additional folders
- Move content between folders
- Enable My Reports folder

Introduction

Report Manager enables you to perform various deployment tasks using your Internet browser. This feature allows users who do not have Report Designer installed to deploy reports. It also provides flexibility for managing existing reports.

Upload files

Using Report Manager, you can upload individual files to the report server, such as reports, data sources, and resources, to a maximum limit of 4,096 KB per item.

To upload a file, open Report Manager and click **Upload File**. The browser then displays a page that allows you to enter all necessary information.

Create additional folders

Report Manager folders provide mechanisms to organize content based on whatever groups are appropriate for your application.

To create a folder, open Report Manager and click **New Folder**. The browser then displays a page similar to the Upload File page to allow you to add the folder information with a description.

Move content between folders

Report Manager allows you to move content between folders after you have uploaded the content to the report server.

To move content, you must first display the properties of the report in Report Manager and click **Move**. The browser then displays a page that allows you to move the report.

Enable My Reports folder

A report administrator can enable **My Reports** folders to provide end users (one folder for each user) with a location to store and customize their favorite reports without affecting other users. Administrators can enable this feature in the **Site Settings** area of Report Manager.

Note   You can also write scripts that deploy multiple reports, data sources, or resources using the rs.exe utility. You will learn about this utility in Module 7, "Programming Reporting Services," in Course 2030, *Creating Reporting Solutions Using Microsoft SQL Server 2000 Reporting Services.*

Updating Data Sources

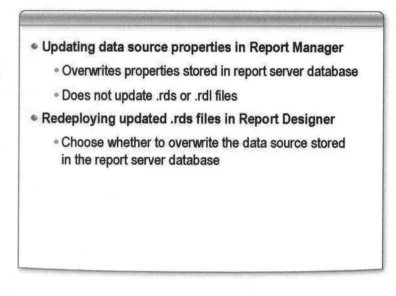

Introduction

During the life cycle of your Microsoft SQL Server™ 2000 Reporting Services implementation, you will probably need to update data source properties. For example, if you move the reporting solution from a development environment to a production environment, you will need to change the data source's server and database properties.

Updating data source properties

You can use Report Manager to update data sources and overwrite properties stored in the report server database. However, these updates will not update any .rds files (shared data source files) or .rdl files (data source files embedded in the report definition).

Report Manager allows you to update the following properties:

- Name
- Connection type
- Connection string
- Connection credentials

Reploying .rds files

You can use Report Designer to redeploy updated .rds files to the report server. The same data source properties can be updated as when using Report Manager.

When you republish a data source file, you can choose whether you want to overwrite the data source properties stored in the report server database. To overwrite the stored version, set the **OverwriteDataSources** option to **True** in the report project **Property Pages** dialog box.

Updating Reports

- **Consequences of modifying and republishing reports:**
  - Replaces report definitions stored in report server database
  - Does not overwrite parameter property changes made in Report Manager
  - Does not change execution, history, security, or subscription properties
- **Use either Report Designer or Report Manager**

Introduction

Just as you will need to update data sources during the lifecycle of your implementation, you will also need to update the reports themselves. Updating a report requires you to change the .rdl file and then republish it.

Modifying and republishing reports

Updating and republishing reports has the following consequences:

- Replaces the report definition stored in the report server database
- Does not overwrite any parameter changes that have been made in Report Manager

  Any Report Manager changes to the default value or a parameter prompt will be maintained, even if you have changed them in the report itself.

- Does not update execution, history, security, or subscription properties

  This consequence is advantageous, since you will most likely want to keep existing settings when simply updating the report's definition.

Republishing options

You can use either Report Designer or Report Manager to republish a report by following the same approach used for first time deployment.

Configuring Report Properties

Property	Options
Data Sources	• Can be shared or custom • Specify database login credentials • Store credentials in report server database
Execution	• Designate report execution frequency • Create execution schedules (shared and custom) • Determine report persistence
History	• Determine how report history is retained
Parameters	• Enable/disable parameter interactivity • Identify default value
Subscriptions	• Select report delivery, for example email or file share
Security	• Control how users interact with content

Introduction

You often need to make configuration changes to reports when you deploy them in order to control the report output. Configuration properties provide control over issues such as security, report delivery, and execution performance. Report Manager allows you to configure these properties.

Configurable properties

Configurable properties for deployed reports include:

- Data Sources: Enables you to specify how a report's queries connect to their respective data sources. Depending on your execution scenario, you can specify that login credentials should be stored in the report server database or that the user must log on when viewing the report. You can also specify whether the report should use a shared data source or a data source that is specific to a particular report.

- Execution: Enables you to specify the report execution frequency based on either a timeout value or a schedule. Choosing to cache a report in the report server database can improve performance for queries that take a long time to execute. You will learn more about execution and report caching later in this module.

- History: Enables you to schedule report snapshots and add them to the report history. You can also set limits on the number of report snapshots that are stored in report history for future viewing.

- Parameters: Enables you to control how users interact with each report parameter by enabling or disabling the parameter prompt and assigning a specific default value. For more information about report parameters, see Module 4, "Manipulating Data Sets," in Course 2030, *Creating Reporting Solutions Using Microsoft SQL Server 2000 Reporting Services.*

- Subscriptions: Enables you to define how report users view reports. In a push delivery scenario, users and administrators can create subscriptions that automate report execution and route rendered reports using e-mail or file shares. You will learn more about subscriptions later in this module.

- Security: Enables you to control end-user access to specific reports or folders and to control which data an end user can view within a specific report. You will learn more about security in Module 6, "Administering Reporting Services Components," in Course 2030, *Creating Reporting Solutions Using Microsoft SQL Server 2000 Reporting Services*.

Demonstration: Publishing Reports

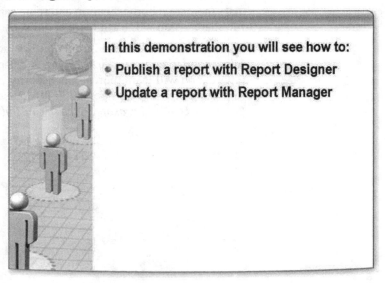

In this demonstration you will see how to:
- Publish a report with Report Designer
- Update a report with Report Manager

Introduction

In this demonstration, you will see how to publish some example reports using Report Designer and Report Manager.

Procedures

▶ **Open the Module 5 Reports solution**

1. Click **Start**, point to **All Programs**, point to **Microsoft Visual Studio .NET 2003**, and then click **Microsoft Visual Studio .NET 2003**.

2. On the **File** menu, click **Open Solution**.

3. In the **Open Solution** dialog box, navigate to the C:\Program Files\Microsoft Learning\2030\Democode\Mod05 folder containing the demonstration files. Click **Module 5 Reports.sln** and then click **Open**.

4. In **Solution Explorer**, double-click **AdventureWorks.rds**.

5. In the **Shared Data Source** dialog box, click the **Credentials** tab.

6. Select the **Use a specific user name and password** check box.

7. In the **User name** text box, type **ReportExecution** and click **OK**.

8. In the **Password** text box, type **P@ssw0rd** and click **OK**.

9. In **Solution Explorer**, right-click the **Module 5 Reports** project, and then click **Properties**.

10. In the **Module 5 Reports Property Pages** dialog box, under **Deployment**, verify that the **TargetFolder** and **TargetServerURL** are set to **Module 5 Reports** and **http://localhost/ReportServer** respectively, and then click **OK**.

▶ **Deploy the Module 5 Reports solution**

1. In **Solution Explorer**, right-click the solution, and then click **Deploy Solution**.

2. In the **Output** window, confirm that the project was successfully deployed without warnings.

3. Keep **Report Designer** open.

▶ **Browse the published reports**

1. Open **Internet Explorer**. If **Report Manager** isn't your default home page, then from **Favorites**, click **Report Manager Home**. When the home page is displayed, browse to the new folder.

2. Click the **Module 5 Reports** folder link.

3. Click the **Order Details** report link and browse the report.

4. Click the **Module 5 Reports** link on the top left side of the page.

5. Click **Upload File**.

6. Click **Browse**, navigate to the C:\Program Files\Microsoft Learning\2030\Democode\Mod05 folder, click **Product Catalog.rdl**, and click **Open**.

7. Select the **Overwrite item if it exists** check box and click **OK**.

   The report has now been updated manually.

Important   Keep the Report Manager open for the next demonstration.

Lesson: Executing Reports

- Execution Process Flow
- Executing Reports On-Demand
- Session Caching
- Using Linked Reports

Introduction

Executing reports is the most common task end users will perform on a regular basis. To ensure that your reports system performs well and that it can handle your expected user loads, you must understand how Reporting Services executes reports and how you can gain the best performance from the system.

In this lesson, you will learn how to execute reports. You will learn about the process flow for report execution and how to execute reports on demand, improve performance with session caching, and utilize linked reports.

Lesson objectives

After completing this lesson, you will be able to:

- Describe the process of report execution.
- Describe how an on-demand report is executed.
- Describe how session caching works.
- Create a linked report.

Execution Process Flow

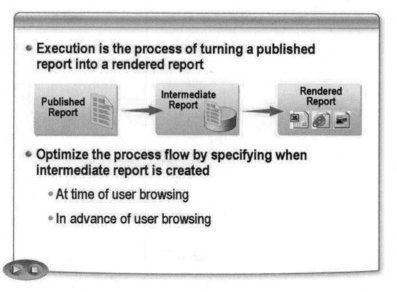

- Execution is the process of turning a published report into a rendered report

Published Report → Intermediate Report → Rendered Report

- Optimize the process flow by specifying when intermediate report is created
  - At time of user browsing
  - In advance of user browsing

Introduction

Execution is the process of turning a published report into a rendered report. Understanding this process is vital to ensuring that reports run efficiently even when your report system is under heavy load.

Process flow

At the time of report execution, a published report undergoes data retrieval and processing. During this phase, the report server combines the layout definition with the report's source data to produce an intermediate format of the report. To deliver the report to end users in a usable format, the Report Server sends the intermediate report to a rendering extension, which interprets it into a rendered report.

Optimizing the execution process

You can optimize the execution process flow by specifying when process steps should occur. In Report Manager, you can manipulate settings to specify whether steps occur at the time of user browsing or in advance of user browsing. On-demand execution provides reports upon browsing, while cached instances and snapshot reports can be created ahead of time. The following topics examine these different options.

Executing Reports On-Demand

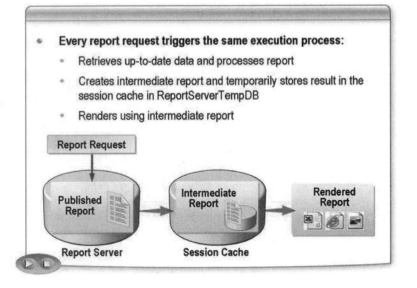

Introduction	The default execution process for all reports is known as *on-demand execution*. Following this execution process, a report executes when the user browses it, providing the user with the most up-to-date data.
Execution process	The report server follows the same process for each user who opens a report using on-demand execution. If ten users open the report, ten queries are issued to the source database.

For an on-demand report, the user request triggers the following execution process:

1. The report server queries the source database to retrieve data and processes the data according to the report definition.

2. The report server creates an intermediate format of the report and stores a temporary copy in the session cache. The session cache is located in the ReportServerTempDB database

3. The report server sends the intermediate report to a rendering extension with rendering format instructions and then forwards the rendered report to the end user.

On-demand execution is the default report behavior. It often applies to the following execution scenarios:

- Reports that have dynamic source data, such as an order status report that requires up-to-the-minute data from the online transaction processing (OLTP) database.

  Note that you will need to assess the performance impact of this report on your OLTP database.

- Infrequently accessed reports, such as an error tracking report that is only executed once every couple of weeks.

  Precreating reports that are accessed infrequently wastes resources, since the reports must be stored in the report server database. In this scenario, it is more efficient to retrieve the data only when requested.

Session Caching

- **Session management**
  - Maintains state between client and server over HTTP
  - Groups together HTTP requests from the same session
- **Reports in session cache**
  - Added to session cache upon browsing
  - Persisted in ReportServerTempdb
  - Require refresh to display report or data changes

Introduction

Session caching improves report execution performance for individual users without requiring any special configuration settings. On-demand reports automatically take advantage of this execution feature. However, a user still needs to manually refresh an on-demand report to see any data changes that have taken place during the time since the report was placed in the session cache.

Session management

Sessions maintain the state between the client and server over HTTP. The user-specific information relevant to a particular client session is known as the *session state*. Session management enables the grouping together of HTTP requests from the same session to form a conversation.

Reports in session cache

When you browse a report, the report is added to the session cache that is stored in the ReportServerTempDB. Each report has a default expiration time of ten minutes, after which the session will be automatically terminated and the report removed from storage.

While a report is stored in session state, the underlying report can change without affecting the report being viewed by the user. Report Manager provides a **Refresh Report** button so that users can manually refresh the report they are viewing to display any changes.

Using Linked Reports

- **Allow reuse of base report data source and report definition**
- **Alter linked report properties:**
  - **Execution**
  - **Parameters**
  - **Subscriptions**
  - **Security**
- **Created in Report Manager**

Introduction

Linked reports are an easy and flexible way to customize report output for end users without the need to design new reports with Report Designer.

Alter linked report properties

The main advantage that linked reports provide is the ability to alter the base report properties without affecting any other reports. Report properties that you can modify include:

- Execution
- Parameters
- Subscriptions
- Security

For example, you can use linked reports to create product category views of the Product Profitability report. In this scenario, you create one linked report for each product category. For each linked report, you assign a distinct default value for the category parameter.

Created with Report Manager

To create a linked report using Report Manager, follow these procedures:

1. Open the existing report that you wish to use as the base report in Report Manager.
2. Open the base report's **General** properties page.
3. Click **Create Linked Report**.
4. Enter a new report's name and description. Optionally, you can change the new report's location by clicking **Change Location** and the new location.
5. Click **OK** to save the new report.

Lesson: Creating Cached Instances

- Executing Cached Instances
- Using Query Parameters with Cached Instances
- Using Filters with Cached Instances
- Configuring Cached Instances

Introduction

Session caching only improves performance for *individual* users. In order to create better performance for *multiple* users, you need to use cached instances. In this lesson, you will learn how to enhance the performance of on-demand reports with cached instances.

Lesson objectives

After completing this lesson, you will be able to:

- Describe the processing steps when executing a cached report.
- Describe the use of query parameters on a cached instance.
- Describe the use of filters on a cached instance.
- Configure a cached instance of a report.

Executing Cached Instances

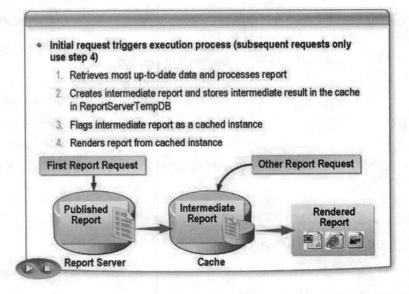

- Initial request triggers execution process (subsequent requests only use step 4)
  1. Retrieves most up-to-date data and processes report
  2. Creates intermediate report and stores intermediate result in the cache in ReportServerTempDB
  3. Flags intermediate report as a cached instance
  4. Renders report from cached instance

First Report Request   Other Report Request

Published Report → Intermediate Report → Rendered Report

Report Server   Cache

Introduction

To enhance the performance of report execution for multiple users, you can enable caching of a report and create a *cached instance*. This simple configuration change provides increased performance when compared to on-demand execution.

Execution process

Instance caching uses the following execution process:

1. When the first user requests a report, the report server retrieves the most up-to-date data and processes the report.

2. The report server creates an intermediate report and stores it in the cache in the ReportServerTempDB. Unlike on-demand session caching, this report can stay in the cache for a specified number of minutes or until a particular scheduled time.

3. The report server flags the intermediate report as a cached instance.

4. The report server renders the report from the cached instance.

Subsequent requests for the report from all users are processed using the cached instance until the cached instance expires; this greatly increases the performance of the report.

Using Query Parameters with Cached Instances

- Query parameters are applied when the cached instance is created
- Changing report parameter values creates a new cached instance if one does not already exist
  - Multiple cached instances can exist for the same report based on different parameters
  - Can result in many copies stored in the cache

Introduction

Cached instances require report storage in the report server cache. If a report uses query parameters, multiple instances of the report may need to be cached. However, this can still provide a performance improvement when compared to on-demand execution.

Query parameters are applied when instance created

A report's query parameters are applied when a cached instance is created. Therefore, the data stored in the cached instance is a restricted data set and only contains the data matching the supplied parameters.

Changing report parameters creates a new instance

When a user specifies different parameter values for a report, a new cached instance is created if one does not already exist that exactly matches the newly supplied parameters.

At any time, a cached instance can exist for every combination of parameter values. For example, if you have a sales report with a sales office parameter, you can have a cached instance for each sales office.

Use caution when creating cached instances involving query parameters, as this may result in a large number of instances being stored in the report server cache. An alternative to creating multiple cached instances is to filter a single cached instance as described in the following topic.

Using Filters with Cached Instances

- **Filters are applied to the cached instance during each viewing**
- **Filters use current report parameter values**
- **Changing report parameter values:**
  - Does not create a new cached instance
  - Filters the cached instance

Introduction

In order to avoid caching multiple copies of a report based on their query parameters, you can apply filters to a linked report. This option provides some of the performance benefits of caching and also reduces the number of cached instances.

Filters are applied when viewed

Unlike query parameters, filters are applied to the cached instance each time the linked report is viewed. The report server uses the same cached instance of the report for each new request even if the parameters are different.

Filters use current parameters

Filters use the current report parameter values defined by the user. The filtered cached instance is not available to other users, so it is recreated dynamically for each user who requests it.

Changing report parameters

When a user specifies different report parameter values, instead of creating a new cached instance, the existing cached instance is filtered.

Because filters are applied after a cached instance is created and because the filtered instance is not available to other users, filters do not receive as many performance benefits from cached instances as query parameters. However, this technique can prevent the cache from becoming bloated with multiple versions of the same report.

Configuring Cached Instances

> * **Cached instances are temporary and must expire**
>   * Defined interval
>   * Report-specific schedule
>   * Shared schedule
>   * Forced expiration
> * **No limit to the number of cached instances**
> * **Expirations are implemented using SQL Server Agent**
> * **Cached instances must have stored data source credentials**

Introduction

In order to take advantage of instance caching, you must manually configure reports using Report Manager. Otherwise, reports will be executed using the on-demand technique by default.

Cached instances are temporary

All cached instances are temporary and must expire at a certain point in time to allow for data refresh. You can control how the cache expires by choosing from the following list of options available in Report Manager:

- At a defined interval: Allow a cached instance to expire after a specific number of minutes from the time of its creation—for example, 30 minutes after creation.

- Report-specific schedule: Apply an expiration schedule that pertains to a particular report. For example, you can set up a schedule to clear a single report cache once every day of the week.

- Shared schedule: Apply a common expiration schedule to be used across multiple reports. For example, you can set up a shared schedule to clear multiple reports in the cache once per week.

- Forced expiration: Report Server may force expiration of cached instanced under certain conditions. These conditions include:

  - Modification of the report definition

  - Modification of the data source credentials

  - Deletion of the report from the server

  - Modification of execution options

Cache instance limits　　You can have a cached instance for every combination of parameter values that are associated with query parameters. There is no hard-coded limit on the number of cached instances allowed.

Expirations　　Expirations are implemented using SQL Server Agent jobs. For this reason, you must ensure that SQL Server Agent is running.

Storing credentials　　To create a cached instance, you must configure the data source settings to use login credentials stored in the report server database. Report Manager will display an error if you attempt to create a cached instance without this setting. You can choose to use Microsoft Windows® or SQL Server authentication.

Demonstration: Creating Cached Instances

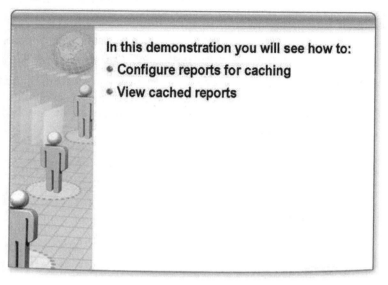

In this demonstration you will see how to:
* Configure reports for caching
* View cached reports

Introduction

In this demonstration, you will see how to configure cache settings for the Order Details report.

Procedures

▶ **Configure and test caching for the Order Details report**

1. In **Report Manager**, click the **Home** link on the upper right-hand side of the screen.

2. Click the **Module 5 Reports** folder link.

3. On the right-hand side of the screen, click the **Show Details** button to view the details of each of the links.

4. Under the **Edit** column header, click the **Properties** button next to the **Order Details** report.

5. On the left-hand side of the screen, click the **Execution** link.

6. Select **Cache a temporary copy of the report. Expire copy of report after a number of minutes**, change the value to **1** minute, and click **Apply**.

7. Click the **View** tab, and browse to the end of the report where the execution time is displayed. Note the time.

8. Click the **Refresh Report** button in the upper right-hand side of the page to show that the execution time does not update until one minute has expired.

Important   Keep Report Manager open for the next demonstration.

Lesson: Creating Snapshots and Report History

- Executing Snapshot Reports
- Using Query Parameters with Snapshots
- Using Filters with Snapshots
- Configuring Snapshots
- Using Report History
- Configuring Report History

Introduction

Instance caching only retrieves report data when the first user browses to the report. You may wish to remove the slight delay experienced by the first user by preemptively creating the report using a snapshot. In this lesson, you will learn how to create snapshots and how to add snapshots to report history for future reference.

Lesson objectives

After completing this lesson, you will be able to:

- Describe how a snapshot report is executed.
- Use query parameters on a snapshot report.
- Use filters on a snapshot report.
- Configure a snapshot report.
- Describe the purpose of report history.
- Configure report history.

Executing Snapshot Reports

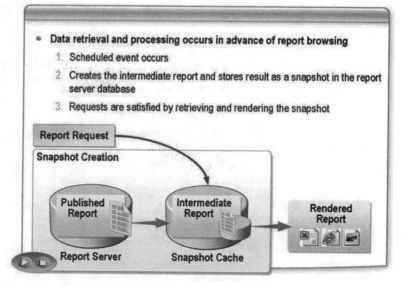

- Data retrieval and processing occurs in advance of report browsing
  1. Scheduled event occurs
  2. Creates the intermediate report and stores result as a snapshot in the report server database
  3. Requests are satisfied by retrieving and rendering the snapshot

Report Request

Snapshot Creation

Published Report   →   Intermediate Report   →   Rendered Report

Report Server   Snapshot Cache

Introduction

Snapshot reports precreate reports to maximize performance of your reporting system. This is particularly useful for reports that take a long time to generate.

Execution process

Unlike on-demand reports, snapshots undergo data retrieval and processing in advance of report browsing. Snapshot reports execute the following process:

1. A scheduled event occurs.

2. The intermediate report is generated and the result is then stored as a snapshot in the report server database. Note that this is a different database location than for cached instances.

3. Report requests are satisfied by retrieving and rendering the stored snapshot.

Snapshots reports often apply to the following execution scenarios:

- Capturing report data at a specific point in time.

  For example, the batch window for executing the on-hand inventory report is between 3:00 A.M. and 4:00 A.M. each workday. In this scenario, you can schedule a snapshot to be created at 3:00 A.M..

- Multiple people need access to the same data.

  For example, to make sure that everyone has the same finance data, you set up the company's financial statements as report snapshots that execute at specific intervals.

■ Prevention of arbitrary report execution.

For example, when the customer invoice report queries the OLTP database during business hours, it slows down system performance. To prevent unnecessary data load on your OLTP database as well as inconsistent result sets, you execute the report as a snapshot every evening.

■ Reports using queries that take a long time to run.

For example, you configure the lengthy year-to-date commission sales report to execute every week on Sunday evening so that it is available to users on Monday morning.

Using Query Parameters with Snapshots

- Query parameters are applied when the snapshot is created
- Query parameters use report parameter default values
- Report parameter values cannot be changed at time of browsing

Introduction

Cached instances of reports support the use of query parameters. However, snapshot reports cannot make use of query parameters due to the execution process of the snapshot.

Application of query parameters

Query parameters are applied at the time a snapshot is created. This means that the snapshot contains a restricted data set.

Query parameters use default values

The query parameters used to create a snapshot are assigned the parameters' default values, which have been defined in Report Manager.

If you want a snapshot for multiple values of a parameter, then keep in mind that you can use linked reports, each with a different default value.

Report parameters values cannot change

A user cannot change report parameter values when viewing a snapshot report, so only the restricted data set can be viewed. Using snapshots with query parameters freezes the data at a point in time. This behavior may or may not be appropriate for your situation depending on what flexibility you want to grant to users.

For example, if you want your company's sales performance report to show data only for a specific month, specify default query parameters for the month and year and create a snapshot report. Each user will see the same view of the report until the snapshot is altered.

Using Filters with Snapshots

- **Filters are applied to the snapshot during browsing**
- **Filters use current report parameter values**
- **Changing report parameter values:**
    - **Does not create a new snapshot**
    - **Filters the current snapshot**

Introduction

Again, when using snapshop reports, query parameters do not provide any flexibility because users cannot change the parameter values. However, users can apply filters to snapshots to achieve this extra level of functionality.

Filters applied during browsing

The report server applies filters to a snapshot during browsing. The performance improvements of snapshots still exist because data retrieval only occurs when producing the snapshot.

Filters use report parameter values

Filters use the current report parameter values specified by the user so that the report only displays the information required by each user. You will often use filters with linked reports.

Changing report parameter values filters snapshot

Changing the report parameter values does not create a new snapshot. Instead, it filters the current snapshot.

For example, you want your company's sales performance report to execute for a specific month but you also want end users to be able to change which sales office they are viewing. In this scenario, you might use query parameters for month and year and apply a filter for sales office. The snapshot freezes the data for the particular month and year and filters the sales office dynamically for whatever value the end user specifies.

Each user's sales office view comes from the same snapshot; however, the snapshot is filtered by the sales office that they specified.

Configuring Snapshots

- **A snapshot must be explicitly executed**
  - Manually
  - Report-specific schedule
  - Shared schedule
- **Each new snapshot replaces the current snapshot**
- **Scheduled snapshots are implemented using SQL Server Agent**
- **Snapshots require stored data source credentials**

Introduction

As with instance caching, you must manually configure snapshot reports using Report Manager. Otherwise, reports will use on-demand execution by default.

Snapshots require explicit execution

All snapshots require explicit execution before they become visible to end users. You can control this execution by choosing from the following list of options available in Report Manager:

- Manually: Create a snapshot manually with the **New Snapshot** button when viewing the history of a report. Use this option when you want to store a snapshot for future viewing even if new replacement snapshots are created.

  Alternatively, you can create a snapshot without adding it to the report history by selecting the **Create a snapshot of the report when the apply button is selected** check box on the **Execution** property page of a report.

- Report-specific schedule: Apply a schedule for a particular report. You configure this schedule on the **Execution** property page of the report.

- Shared schedule: Apply a common schedule that can be used across multiple reports. You configure this schedule by creating a shared schedule on the **Shared Schedules** page in Report Manager and linking to it on the **Execution** property page of the report.

Only one snapshot exists

The report server will only allow one snapshot at a time for a particular report and each new snapshot replaces the previous one unless specified otherwise.

Scheduling

Scheduled snapshots are implemented using SQL Server Agent jobs. For this reason, you must ensure that SQL Server Agent is running.

Storing credentials

Like cached instances, snapshots require data source credentials to be stored in the report server database.

Using Report History

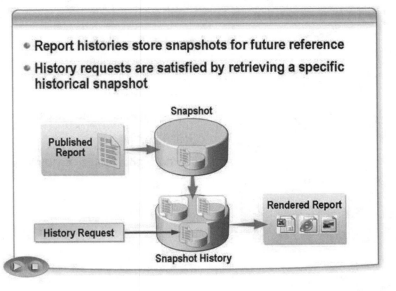

- Report histories store snapshots for future reference
- History requests are satisfied by retrieving a specific historical snapshot

Introduction

By default, a new snapshot automatically replaces the previous snapshot, so the report server database only keeps one version. However, you may want to be able to retrieve older versions of a snapshot for various reasons. You can achieve this with report history.

Stores snapshots for future reference

Report history is a collection of snapshots that have been stored in the report server database for future reference. Report history enables you to keep a record of all snapshot reports that are generated.

There are a variety of ways to create report history. One of the most common is to add a snapshot to report history on creation of the snapshot.

History requests retrieve specific snapshots

End users or processes can specifically request a report history instance. In these situations, the report history requests are satisfied using report history snapshots.

Configuring Report History

- **Report history options:**
  - Store all snapshots
  - Manually add snapshots
  - Use a schedule to add snapshots
  - Limit report history
- **Producing report history requires stored credentials**

Introduction

Report history is not maintained by default for any report. You must manually configure this feature using Report Manager. Report Manager provides various options when configuring report history.

Report history options

When you configure report history, you have the following options:

- Store all snapshots for a particular report in report history.

  In this scenario, whenever a snapshot is created, it is copied to report history automatically.

- Manually add snapshots on an as-needed basis.

  Here, only snapshots that you have chosen manually are added. This may be useful when a particular set of data will be of interest in the future, but you cannot predict exactly when that time will be; in other words, it does not fit a defined schedule.

- Use a schedule to add snapshots to report history.

  If a report you schedule does not have a snapshot, then report history scheduling will first create a snapshot and then add it to report history. If the snapshot already exists, then report history scheduling will use the current snapshot and add it to report history. To implement the scheduled creation of report history, you use SQL Server Agent jobs.

- Limit the number of snapshots stored in report history.

  You can set a limit on snapshots for a specific report by using the History property page of a report. Alternatively, you can set a limit globally across all reports using the **Site Settings** page in Report Manager.

  Note that you can also keep an unlimited number of snapshots stored in report history—this is the default option.

Storing credentials

Like snapshots and cached instances, producing report history requires a report to have stored credentials.

Demonstration: Creating Snapshots and Report History

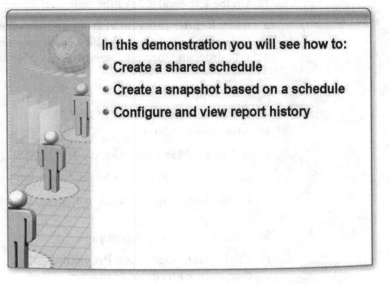

In this demonstration you will see how to:
- Create a shared schedule
- Create a snapshot based on a schedule
- Configure and view report history

Introduction

In this demonstration, you will see how to create a snapshot that executes early on Monday morning before any employees arrive for work. You will also see how to use report history.

Procedures

▶ **Create a shared schedule**

1. In **Report Manager**, on the upper right-hand side of the screen, click the **Site Settings** link.

2. At the bottom on the screen, under **Other**, click the **Manage shared schedules** link.

3. Click the **New Schedule** button.

4. In the **Schedule Name** text box, type **Monday Morning**.

5. Under **Scheduled Details**, click **Week**.

6. Under **Weekly Schedule**, to configure the **Start Time**, type **06:00** and click **OK**.

▶ **Store snapshots in report history**

1. In **Report Manager**, on the upper right-hand side of the screen, click the **Home** link.

2. Click the **Module 5 Reports** folder link.

3. Under the **Edit** column header, click the **Properties** button next to the **Order Details** report.

4. On the left-hand side of the screen, click the **History** link.

5. Select the **Store all report execution snapshots in history** check box.

6. Click **Apply**.

► **Configure the report execution**

1. On the left-hand side of the screen, click the **Execution** link.

2. Click **Render this report from an execution snapshot**, select the **Use the following schedule to create execution snapshots** check box, click **Shared schedule**, and then click the **Monday Morning** schedule in the drop-down list.

3. Click **Apply**.

► **View report history**

1. In **Report Manager**, click the **History** tab.

2. Click the new snapshot link, and view the snapshot output.

3. On the **File** menu, click **Close** to close the snapshot.

► **View SQL Server Agent job**

1. Click **Start**, point to **All Programs**, point to **Microsoft SQL Server**, and then click **Enterprise Manager**.

2. Under **Console Root**, expand **Microsoft SQL Servers**, expand **SQL Server Group**, and then expand the **(local)** server.

3. In the tree-view, expand **Management**, expand **SQL Server Agent**, and then click **Jobs**.

4. In the right pane, in the job list, double-click the job that has a **Next Run Date** of **06:00:00** on the first day of the next week. (You might need to adjust the width of the column headers to see this information.)

5. Click the **Steps** tab, and then double-click the step to open the **Edit Job Step** dialog box.

6. View the **Command** script, click **Cancel**, and then click **Cancel**.

7. On the **File** menu, click **Exit**.

Lesson: Creating Report Subscriptions

- **What Are Subscriptions?**
- **Creating Standard Subscriptions**
- **Creating Data-Driven Subscriptions**
- **Using Linked Reports**

Introduction

Reports often need to be distributed automatically, either on a prescribed schedule or an a once-only occurrence, so that users do not have to manually request reports. Subscriptions provide this ability through extensible delivery mechanisms such as e-mail and file shares. In this lesson, you will learn how to use subscriptions to distribute reports to end users using both these delivery mechanisms. You will also learn the differences between standard and data-driven subscriptions.

Lesson objectives

After completing this lesson, you will be able to:

- Describe the purpose of subscriptions.
- Create a standard subscription.
- Create a data-driven subscription.

What Are Subscriptions?

- **Mechanisms to execute and deliver rendered reports**
- **Two types of subscriptions:**
  - Standard – end-user driven
  - Data-driven – administrator driven
- **Default delivery extensions:**
  - E-mail (SMTP)
  - File share

Introduction

Some users will be satisfied by manually viewing reports only when they feel they need to. Other users may prefer or require automated notification that they should view a report.

Mechanism of delivery

Subscriptions are mechanisms to execute and deliver rendered reports to end users at regular or irregular intervals.

Subscription types

There are two types of subscriptions: standard and data driven. Users typically create standard subscriptions, while administrators typically create data-driven subscriptions. You will learn more about these two types of subscriptions in the following topics.

Delivery extensions

Reporting Services supplies a set of default delivery extensions, including:

- E-mail delivery: Enables you to send rendered reports, report hyperlinks, or notifications to end users through automated e-mail. This form of delivery requires the e-mail server to be a remote or local Simple Mail Transfer Protocol (SMTP) server located on the same network as the report server.

- File delivery: Enables you to deliver rendered reports to file shares.

Note You can add to this list of delivery options by creating your own custom delivery extensions.

Creating Standard Subscriptions

- Standard subscription features in Reporting Services:
  - Deliver one rendered report to one destination
  - Can be defined by an end-user or administrator
- Configuration options:
  - Delivery method
  - Delivery information
  - Render format
  - Processing conditions
  - Parameters

Introduction

Standard subscriptions are simple to create and do not require any level of expertise in how reports are created. Both administrators and users can create standard subscriptions using Report Manager.

Standard subscription features

A standard subscription delivers one rendered report to one destination, such as an e-mail address (or addresses) or a single file share.

Both end users and administrators can define standard subscriptions by specifying the required delivery method and delivery options.

Configuration options

To set up a standard subscription, you must specify the following configuration options:

- Delivery method: E-mail or file share delivery

- Delivery information: For e-mail delivery, this includes the e-mail address or addresses, subject line, and so on. For file share delivery, this includes the share location and file name.

- Render format: This is the output format of the report. Options include Microsoft Excel, TIFF, Extensible Markup Language (XML), and more. For e-mail delivery, you can specify whether to include a hyperlink in addition to or in place of the rendered report. You can also choose not to render the report or link in an e-mail but simply provide notification.

- Processing conditions: This is the processing schedule of the subscription. For a subscription based on a snapshot, you can execute the subscription upon update of the snapshot. For non-snapshot reports, you can create a schedule or use a shared schedule.

- Parameters: Theses are the parameter values that the report will use when being rendered.

Creating Data-Driven Subscriptions

- **Data-driven subscription features in Reporting Services:**
  - Deliver many rendered reports to many destinations using dynamic values from a database table
  - Each delivery can be customized within the table
- **Configuration steps:**
  1. Create and populate a subscriber table
  2. Ensure that credentials are stored with the report
  3. Choose a delivery method
  4. Create a connection to the subscriber table
  5. Define a query to retrieve subscribers
  6. Set the subscription properties as for a standard subscription

Introduction

Creating a data-driven subscription is much more complex than creating a standard subscription. As such, only administrators normally create this type of subscription. Data-driven subscriptions are created using Report Manager and use a similar sequence to standard subscriptions.

Data-driven subscription features

A data-driven subscription delivers a report in many rendered formats to many destinations. For example, you can use a data-driven subscription to e-mail a sales performance report to a list of users in a custom format for each user.

To make a data-driven subscription dynamic, the report server uses delivery settings stored in a database table. This stored information can include the following:

- Dynamic list of destinations: Specify destinations, such as e-mail recipients or file share folders.

- Report rendering format: Assign a different rendering format for each destination.

- Parameter values: Assign a different parameter value for each destination.

Configuration steps

When creating a data-driven subscription, you must follow these steps:

1. Using Enterprise Manager or Query Analyzer, create a Subscribers table in a database and populate it with subscriber information.

2. Using Report Manager, ensure that connection credentials are stored with the report on the report server.

3. Create a new data-driven subscription and choose your delivery method.

4. Configure a connection to the database containing the Subscribers table.

5. Create a query to retrieve the subscriber information from the Subscribers table.

6. Set the subscription properties using the same options as for a standard subscription.

Note Data-driven subscriptions require Reporting Services Enterprise Edition.

Demonstration: Creating Standard Subscriptions

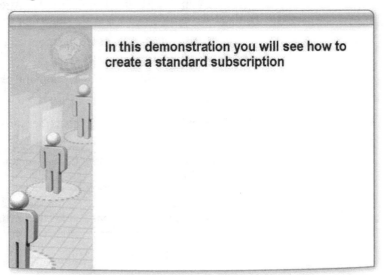

In this demonstration you will see how to create a standard subscription

Introduction

In this demonstration, you will see how to create a standard subscription that delivers a report to a shared network folder.

Procedures

▶ **Create a new standard subscription**

1. In **Report Manager**, on the upper right-hand side of the screen, click the **Home** link.

2. Click the **Module 5 Reports** folder link, and then click the **Properties** button next to the **Product Catalog** report.

   If the **Properties** button is not visible, click the **Show Details** button.

3. Click the **Subscriptions** tab, and then click **New Subscription** to view the subscription options.

   Note   Note that this report uses database credentials stored in the server. This is a requirement for subscriptions.

4. In the **Delivered by** drop-down list, click **Report Server File Share**.

5. Verify that the **Add a file extension when the file is created** check box is selected.

6. In the **Path** text box, type **\\COMPUTERNAME\workspace**.

   Important   Replace **COMPUTERNAME** with your machine name. Do not type **localhost**.

7. In the **Render Format** drop-down list, select **Acrobat (PDF) file**.

8. Leave the **Credentials used to access the file share** options alone for the moment.

9. Under **Run the subscription**, select the **When the scheduled report run is complete** check box, and then click **Select Schedule**.

10. Click **Once**, set the **Start time** to be two minutes later than the current time, and then click **OK**.

11. Under **Credentials used to access the file share**, in the **User Name** text box, type **SalesAnalyst**.

12. In the **Password** text box, type **P@ssw0rd** and click **OK**.

13. Click **OK**.

▶ **View the standard subscription output**

1. Right-click **Start**, and then click **Explore** to open **Windows Explorer**.

2. In the **Address** bar, type **\\COMPUTERNAME\workspace**.

    At the execution time that you specified above, the file should appear. Note that the file may take several minutes to appear.

3. Double-click **Product Catalog.pdf** to open it in Adobe Acrobat Reader.

4. View the **PDF** output, and then on the **File** menu, click **Exit**.

5. Close **Windows Explorer**.

Review

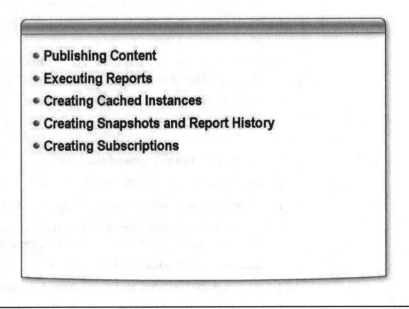

- Publishing Content
- Executing Reports
- Creating Cached Instances
- Creating Snapshots and Report History
- Creating Subscriptions

1. Describe the steps required to publish reports using Report Designer.

2. How does session caching work when executing a report?

3. What is the purpose of cached instances?

4. Why would you want to use a snapshot report instead of a cached instance?

5. Describe the difference between standard and data-driven subscriptions.

Lab 5: Managing Content

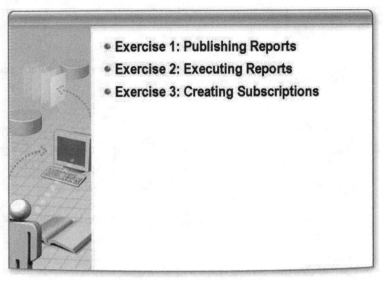

- Exercise 1: Publishing Reports
- Exercise 2: Executing Reports
- Exercise 3: Creating Subscriptions

Objectives

After completing this lab, you will be able to:

- Publish and view reports.
- Execute reports using session caching, cached instances, and snapshots.
- Deliver reports using standard subscriptions and data-driven subscriptions.

Estimated time to complete this lab: 75 minutes

Exercise 1
Publishing Reports

In this exercise, you will publish Adventure Works reports. You will view the reports using Report Manager and then modify one of the reports for redeployment. Finally, you will ensure that your redeployed report executes as expected.

▶ **Open the Adventure Works solution**

1. Click **Start**, point to **All Programs**, point to **Microsoft Visual Studio .NET 2003**, and then click **Microsoft Visual Studio .NET 2003**.

2. On the **File** menu, click **Open Solution**.

3. In the **Open Solution** dialog box, navigate to the C:\Program Files\Microsoft Learning\2030\Labfiles\Lab05\Starter\AdventureWorks folder containing the demonstration files. Click **AdventureWorks.sln**, and then click **Open**.

4. In **Solution Explorer**, browse the three projects the make up the Adventure Works solution and note the following:

   • The **Product Sales** project has three reports that use two shared data sources.

   • The **Territory Sales** project has three reports that use report-specific data sources.

   • The **Reseller Sales** project has three reports that use report-specific data sources.

Tip If the Solution Explorer pane is not visible, on the **View** menu, click **Solution Explorer**.

▶ **Deploy the Adventure Works solution**

1. In **Solution Explorer**, right-click the **Product Sales** project, and then click **Properties**. In the **Product Sales Property Pages** dialog box, under **Deployment**, in the **TargetServerURL** text box, type **http://localhost/ReportServer** and then click **OK**.

2. In **Solution Explorer**, right-click the solution, and then click **Deploy Solution**.

3. In the **Output** window, confirm that all three projects were successfully deployed without warnings.

4. Keep **Report Designer** open.

► **Browse the published reports**

1. Open **Internet Explorer**. If **Report Manager** is not your default home page, then from **Favorites**, click **Report Manager Home**.

   Notice that there is one new folder for each project in the Adventure Works solution.

2. Click the **Product Sales** folder link.

   Notice that the Product Sales folder contains two data sources and three reports, which is what we also viewed in the Report Designer.

3. Click the **Product Profitability** report link and browse the report.

4. Keep **Report Manager** open.

► **Update the Product Profitability report**

1. Return to **Report Designer**. In **Solution Explorer**, double-click the **Product Profitability** report to open the report in Layout view.

2. In the **Toolbox** window, click **Textbox**. In the **Page Footer**, create a text box next to the existing **Company Confidential** text box. Resize the new text box to the right-hand edge of the page.

3. Click inside the new text box and type the following:

   = Globals!ExecutionTime

4. On the **Report Formatting** toolbar, click the **Italic** button and click the **Align Right** button.

5. Click the **Preview** tab, and ensure that the text box displays the current date and time.

6. In **Solution Explorer**, right-click the **Product Profitability** report, and then click **Deploy**.

7. In the **Output** window, scroll up to view the **Product Profitability** report deployment information.

   Even though the build and deploy succeeded, notice the warnings that the data source could not be deployed because it already exists and **OverwriteDataSources** is not specified.

8. To modify the **OverrideDataSources** property, in **Solution Explorer**, right-click the **Product Sales** project, and then click **Properties**.

9. In the **Product Sales Property Pages** dialog box, under **Deployment**, change the **OverwriteDataSources** property to **True**, and then click **OK**.

10. Repeat step 6 to successfully deploy the updated report.

11. Close **Visual Studio .NET 2003**.

▶ **Browse the updated Product Profitability report**

1. In **Report Manager**, browse the **Product Profitability** report.

2. To view the updated report changes, on the **Internet Explorer** toolbar, click the **Refresh** button.

   Notice that the updated report is not displayed.

3. To refresh the report display and see the updated changes, on the **HTML Viewer** toolbar within the report itself, click **Refresh Report**. Confirm that the footer has been updated to display the report execution time.

4. Keep **Report Manager** open.

Exercise 2
Executing Reports

In this exercise, you will execute an on-demand report supplying user credentials. You will also execute reports utilizing cached instances and snapshots. Finally, you will work with report history.

Scenario

With the Adventure Works reports successfully published to the Report Server database, the next step is to specify their execution settings. To choose the most appropriate execution settings, consider the source data characteristics and browsing requirements for the following reports:

- The **Order Details** report uses query and report parameters to retrieve order data for a particular reseller between a user-specified start date and end date. Due to the dynamic data and browsing requirements of this report, it is a strong candidate for on-demand execution.

- The **Product Sales YTD** report is used intermittently to quickly view current sales by product category and subcategory. It is typically hard to predict exactly when analysts browse this report; usually it is right before a staff meeting when everybody is swiftly gathering data. Due to the requirement of multiple users viewing the report at or near the same time, it is a strong candidate for instance caching.

- The **Reseller Sales** report displays sales and margin totals by reseller for the current month. Beginning on the first day of each month, account managers use this report to analyze the contribution of their reseller customers. Even though sales and margin totals can fluctuate over the course of a month, account managers want to view the report as it looked on the first day of each month. They also want to keep that view once the current month has passed. Due to these requirements, this report is a strong candidate for a snapshot report. You will create a monthly snapshot to run at the beginning of each month. To allow users to see these snapshots over time, you will store all report snapshots in history.

▶ **Configure the Order Details report for on-demand execution**

1. In **Report Manager**, on the upper right-hand side of the screen, click the **Home** link.

2. Click the **Reseller Sales** folder link, and then click **Order Details**.

   Notice that the Order Details report requires a start date, end date, business type, and reseller to execute.

3. Click the **Properties** tab, and then click **Data Sources** on the left-hand side of the screen.

   Notice that the custom Adventure Works data source is using Microsoft Windows NT® Integrated Security. This means that the current Windows account is used to log in to the SQL Server database.

4. Under **Connect Using**, click **The credentials supplied by the user running the report**.

Caution   To ensure that the data source connection uses SQL Server authentication, do not select the **Use as Windows credentials when connecting to the data source** check box.

---

5. Click **Apply**.

6. On the left-hand side of the screen, click the **Execution** link.

   Notice that the Order Details report is set up to always run with the most recent data. Execution on demand is the default execution setting.

▶ **View the Order Details report**

1. Click the **View** tab.

2. In the **Log In Name** text box, type **ReportExecution**.

3. In the **Password** text box, type **P@ssw0rd**.

   ReportExecution is a SQL Server account that has read access to the Adventure Works databases. You will use this account throughout the remainder of this module to test report executions.

4. Click the **View Report** button.

   You should now be able to browse the report and select a value from the **BusinessType** and **Reseller** parameter drop-down lists.

▶ **Configure the Product Sales YTD report for cached execution**

1. On the upper right-hand side of the screen, click the **Home** link.

2. Click the **Product Sales** folder link. On the right-hand side of the screen, click **Show Details** to view the details of each of the links.

3. Under the **Edit** column header, click the **Properties** button next to the **Product Sales YTD** report.

4. On the left-hand side of the screen, click the **Execution** link.

5. Click **Cache a temporary copy of the report. Expire copy of report after a number of minutes**, leave the default value of **30** minutes, and click **Apply**.

   Notice the error message that appears, informing you that the credentials used to run this report are not stored. Because of this, the cache configuration has failed.

6. On the left-hand side of the screen, click the **Data Sources** link.

   Notice that /Product Sales/AdventureWorksDW is the data source used by this report. You cannot update the login credentials here because this data source is shared.

7. On the upper left-hand side of the screen, click the **Product Sales** folder link.

8. Click the **AdventureWorksDW** data source link.

9. Under **Connect Using**, select **credentials stored securely in the report server**.

10. In the **User name** text box, type **ReportExecution**.

11. In the **Password** text box, type **P@ssw0rd**.

12. Click **Apply**.

   By storing credentials, you are indicating that the report should use the ReportExecution account to retrieve data for all users browsing the report. Because this is a shared data source, all reports that use the AdventureWorksDW data source will run using these stored credentials. If you want to alter this behavior, you can update these reports to use custom data sources.

13. Now that you have configured the necessary database prerequisites, enable the report for caching by repeating steps 1 to 5.

   Notice that there is no error message and that your report is now configured for instance caching.

▶ **Expire copies of the Product Sales YTD report on a schedule**

1. Click **Cache a temporary copy of the report. Expire copy of report on the following schedule**, and then click **Configure**.

2. In **Daily Schedule**, click **On the following days** and accept the default values to execute on every day of the week.

3. In the **Start time** text box, type **11** click **PM**, and click **OK**.

4. On the **Execution** page, click **Apply**.

   In this scenario, you chose a report-specific schedule to expire the cache at the end of each day. Note that if you have several Reporting Services operations that execute at the same time, such as at the end of each day, you should consider using a shared schedule instead of a report-specific schedule.

5. Click the **View** tab and browse the report.

   By viewing, you have just created a cached instance that will expire at 11:00 P.M. this evening.

Note If you wish to, you can confirm this scheduled action by opening SQL Enterprise Manager and viewing the list of jobs in the SQL Server Agent.

► **Change the Reseller Sales report to use AdventureWorksDW**

1. In **Report Manager**, on the upper right-hand side of the screen, click the **Home** link.

2. Click the **Reseller Sales** folder link.

3. Under the **Edit** column header, click the **Properties** button next to the **Reseller Sales** report.

4. Click the **Data Sources** folder link.

   To create a snapshot for this report, you must store its data source login credentials. Instead of changing the custom data source settings, you will change the report to use the Product Sales AdventureWorksDW shared data source, whose credentials are already stored.

5. Click **A Shared Data Source**, and then click **Browse**.

6. Expand the **Product Sales** folder, click **AdventureWorksDW**, click **OK**, and then click **Apply**.

► **Schedule a snapshot to run at the beginning of the Month**

1. In **Report Manager**, on the upper right-hand side of the screen, click the **Site Settings** link.

2. At the bottom on the screen, under **Other**, click the **Manage shared schedules** link.

3. Click the **New Schedule** button.

4. In the **Schedule Name** text box, type **Beginning of Month**.

5. Under **Scheduled Details**, click **Month**.

6. Under **Monthly Schedule**, configure the following:

   • Click **On calendar day(s)**, and type **1** to execute on the first day of the month.

   • Click **Start Time**, type **05:00** and click **AM**.

7. Click **OK**.

8. In **Report Manager**, on the upper-right hand side of the screen, click the **Home** link

9. Click the **Reseller Sales** folder link.

10. Under the **Edit** column header, click the **Properties** button next to the **Reseller Sales** report.

11. On the left-hand side of the screen, click the **Execution** link.

12. Click **Render this report from an execution snapshot**, select the **Use the following schedule to create execution snapshots** check box, click **Shared schedule**, and then select **Beginning of Month** from the drop-down list.

13. Clear the **Create a snapshot of the report when the apply button is selected** check box, and then click **Apply**.

    The report now will not be available until it executes for the first time on the first day of the next month.

▶ **Store Reseller Sales snapshots in report history**

1. On the left-hand side of the screen, click the **History** link.

2. Select the **Store all report execution snapshots in history** check box.

3. Under **Select the number of snapshots to keep**, select **Limit the copies of report history**, and type **12** in the text box.

   To meet the users' requirements to view snapshots over time, configure all snapshots to be stored in report history. Limit the number of copies to 12 to allow analysts to view the previous 12 months' worth of snapshots. When the number of snapshots stored in report history exceeds this limit, the earlier snapshots will be deleted first.

4. Click **Apply**, and when asked to confirm, click **OK**.

▶ **View the Reseller Sales report and report history**

1. Click the **View** tab.

2. Click the **Properties** tab, and on the left-hand side of the screen, click the Execution link.

3. Click Render **this report from an execution snapshot**.

4. Select the **Create a snapshot of the report when the apply button is selected** check box, and then click **Apply**.

5. At the top of the screen, click the **View** tab.

6. Click the **History** tab.

   Notice there is a snapshot that has been created and is now stored in history.

7. Keep **Report Manager** open.

Exercise 3
Creating Subscriptions

In this exercise, you will create a standard subscription for the Product Profitability report. You will then create a data-driven subscription.

Scenario

The sales analysts want to routinely view the Product Profitability report in Excel format. Each month they want an updated version of the Excel output and they want to save the old reports over time. Because the report can get quite large, you will create a standard subscription that will deliver the report in Excel format to a specific file share.

The sales directors for each of the sales territory groups—North America, Europe, and Pacific—want to view the Actual Vs Quota report on a quarterly basis to analyze sales performance against quotas. The directors each have different delivery, rendering, and parameter requirements. To meet their requirements, you will use a data-driven subscription to customize the delivery for each of the directors.

▶ **Create a new standard subscription**

1. In **Report Manager**, on the upper right-hand side of the screen, click the **Home** link.

2. Click the **Product Sales** folder link, and then click the **Properties** button next to the **Product Profitability** report.

3. Click the **Subscriptions** tab, and then click **New Subscription** to view the subscription options.

4. In the **Delivered by** drop-down list, click **Report Server File Share**.

5. Verify that the **Add a file extension when the file is created** check box is selected.

6. In the **Path** text box, type **\\COMPUTERNAME\workspace**.

Important Replace **COMPUTERNAME** with the name of your local computer. Do not type **localhost**.

---

7. In the **Render Format** drop-down list, select **Excel**.

8. Leave the **Credentials used to access the file share** optionsalone for the moment.

9. Under **Overwrite options**, click **Increment file names as newer versions are added**.

   Incrementing file names adds a number to the file suffix. Each time the subscription executes, the number increments by one.

10. Under **Run the subscription**, click **When the scheduled report run is complete**, and then click **Select Schedule**.

11. Click **Once**, set the **Start time** to be three minutes later than the current time, then click **OK**.

12. Under **Report Parameter Values**, for the **Year** and **Month** parameters, select the **Use Default** check box.

13. For the **Category** parameter, select **All Product**.

14. Under **Credentials used to access the file share**, in the **User Name** text box, type **SalesAnalyst**.

15. In the **Password** text box, type **P@ssw0rd**.

16. Click **OK**.

▶ **View the standard subscription output**

1. Right-click **Start**, and then click **Explore** to open **Windows Explorer**.

2. In the **Address** bar, type **\\COMPUTERNAME\workspace**.

Important   Replace **COMPUTERNAME** with the name of your local computer. Do not type **localhost**.

At the execution time that you specified above, the file should appear. Note that this may take several minutes.

3. Double-click **Product Profitability.xls** to open it in **Excel**.

4. View the **Excel** output, and then on the **File** menu, click **Exit**.

5. Close **Windows Explorer**.

▶ **Change the Actual Vs Quota report to use a shared data source**

1. In **Report Manager**, on the upper right-hand side of the screen, click the **Home** link.

2. Click the **Territory Sales** folder link, and then click the **Actual Vs Quota** report.

   The report requires two parameters to execute: **CalendarYear** and **Group**. When you build the subscription, it is important that the correct **Group** parameter value be linked to its corresponding **Sales Director** value. This information is stored in a database table for each sales director, along with other report delivery information.

3. Click the **Properties** tab, and then click the **Data Sources** link.

4. Click **A shared data source**, and then click **Browse**.

5. Expand the **Product Sales** folder, and click **AdventureWorksDW**. Click **OK**, and then click **Apply**.

▶ **View the SubscriptionGroupDirector table in Enterprise Manager**

1. Click **Start**, point to **All Programs**, point to **Microsoft SQL Server**, and then click **Enterprise Manager**.

2. Under the Console Root, expand **Microsoft SQL Servers**, expand **SQL Server Group**, expand the **(local)** server, expand **Databases**, expand **AdventureWorksDW**, and then click **Tables**.

3. In the right pane, in the table list, right-click **SubscriptionGroupDirector**, point to **Open Table**, and then click **Return all rows**.

   The information should appear as in the following illustration:

4. On the **File** menu, click **Exit** to exit **Enterprise Manager**.

▶ **Create a data-driven subscription**

1. In **Report Manager**, click the **Subscriptions** tab, and then click **New Data-driven Subscription**.

2. In the **Description** text box, type **Actual Vs Quota Subscription**.

3. In the **Specify how recipients are notified** drop-down list, click **Report Server E-mail**.

4. Click **Specify a shared data source**, and then click **Next**.

5. Expand the **Product Sales** folder, click **AdventureWorksDW**, and then click **Next**.

6. In the **query** box, type **SELECT * FROM SubscriptionGroupDirector**.

7. Click **Validate**. Towards the bottom of the page, verify that you receive a **Query validated successfully** message, and then click **Next**.

8. Configure the properties by using the following table.

Property	Option	Value
To	Get the value from the database	To
Cc	No value	None
Bcc	No value	None
Reply-To	Specify a static value	Sales@adventure-works.msft
Include Report	Get the value from the database	IncludeReport
Render Format	Get the value from the database	RenderFormat
Priority	Specify a static value	Normal
Subject	Specify a static value	@ReportName was executed at @ExecutionTime
Comment	No value	None
Include Link	Get the value from the database	IncludeLink

9. Click **Next**.

10. For the **CalendarYear** parameter, select the **Use Default** check box.

11. Under **Group**, click **Get the value from the database**, and in the drop-down list, click **GroupParameter**, and then click **Next**.

12. Click **On a schedule created for this subscription**, and then click **Next**.

13. Under **Schedule details**, click **Once**. Set the start time to execute two minutes later than the current time.

14. Click **Finish**.

▶ **View the e-mails**

1. Right-click **Start**, and then click **Explore** to open **Windows Explorer**.

2. In the **Address** bar, type **C:\Inetpub\mailroot\Mailbox\ adventure-works.msft** and then navigate to the **P3_EuropeDirector.mbx** subfolder.

   The folder should contain an Internet e-mail message or .eml file with an appropriate time and date based on your schedule. Double-click the file to open it with Microsoft Outlook® Express. (If the **Internet Connection Wizard** appears, click **Cancel**, and then click **Yes** in the confirmation dialog box.) View the PDF attachment by double-clicking the attachment.

3. On the **File** menu, click **Close**.

4. Repeat steps 2 to 3 for the **P3_NADirector.mbx** and **P3_PacificDirector.mbx** subfolders to view their e-mails.

Note   The report information for the NADirector might not display properly. The default Outlook Express security settings cause report information to appear in a single, unformatted column.

Course Evaluation

Your evaluation of this course will help Microsoft understand the quality of your learning experience.

At a convenient time before the end of the course, please complete a course evaluation, which is available at http://www.CourseSurvey.com.

Microsoft will keep your evaluation strictly confidential and will use your responses to improve your future learning experience.

Module 6: Administering Reporting Services

Contents

Overview

- Server Administration
- Performance and Reliability Monitoring
- Database Administration
- Security Administration

Introduction

Microsoft® SQL Server™ 2000 Reporting Services requires minimal administration in order to maintain a reliable, scalable, and secure environment. However, knowledge of the issues that an administrator can encounter will help you to keep your report server running smoothly.

In this module, you will learn how to administer the Reporting Services server, how to monitor and optimize the performance of the report server, how to maintain the reporting services databases, and how to keep the system secure.

Objectives

After completing this module, you will be able to:

- Use configuration files to administer the report server.
- Monitor the performance and reliability of the report server.
- Administer the ReportServer and ReportServerTempDB databases.
- Administer the Reporting Services security model.

Lesson: Server Administration

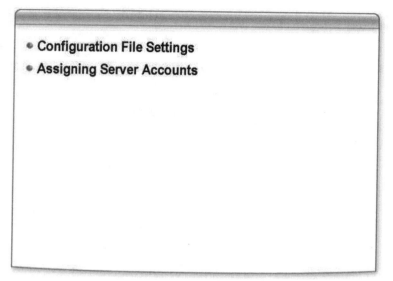

- Configuration File Settings
- Assigning Server Accounts

Introduction

Reporting Services relies on configuration files to control some of the core components of the report server. It also requires configuration of two server accounts in order to operate normally. You will not need to configure these options often, but it is useful to know how to change the settings if required.

In this lesson, you will learn about the configuration files that control the report server and the settings that you can control. You will also learn about the report server accounts that are required for daily operation of the server.

Lesson objectives

After completing this lesson, you will be able to:

- Describe the report server configuration files.
- Assign security accounts for the report server.

Configuration File Settings

Configuration File	Settings
RSReportDesigner	Rendering, data source, and designer extensions
RSWebApplication	Delivery extensions and active user request limits
RSReportServer	Data connection strings, SMTP server settings, rendering, and delivery extensions
ReportingServices Service	Trace level and log files

Introduction

A Reporting Services installation includes several Extensible Markup Language (XML) configuration files that control the behavior of various Reporting Services components. After installation, you may need to modify these configuration files to add or remove particular features, using any XML editor.

RSReportDesigner

RSReportDesigner.config is located in the Microsoft SQL Server\ 80\Tools\Report Designer folder and contains settings for Report Designer. You can configure the options for this file as shown in the following table.

Setting	Description
Render	Configures the possible rendering options for previewing reports using Report Designer. The installed options include XML, comma separated values (CSV), Microsoft Excel, Portable Document Fomat (PDF), and so on.
Data	Configures the connection types available for data sources that provide the data for reports. The installed options include SQL, OLEDB, open database connectivity (ODBC), and Oracle.
Designer	Configures the available query designers for use in Report Designer. A designer normally relates to a particular data source, but all of the provided data sources use a single designer extension.

You can create or add extension classes for all three elements by adding them to the appropriate element within the configuration file.

RSWebApplication

RSWebApplication.config is located in the Microsoft SQL Server\
<SQL Server Instance>\Reporting Services\ReportManager folder and contains settings for Report Manager. You can configure the options for this file as shown in the following table.

Setting	Description
DeliveryUI	Configures the available delivery extensions, which include e-mail or file share delivery. You can set a default delivery extension as well as configure the default rendered report type for each delivery mechanism.
MaxActiveReqForOneUser	Configures the maximum number of active requests that a single user can have. The default value is 20 requests; any additional requests from a user are denied. To remove limits on the number of connections, set the value to 0.

RSReportServer

RSReportServer.config is located in the Microsoft SQL Server\
<SQL Server Instance>\Reporting Services\ReportServer folder and contains configuration settings for the Report Server.

You can configure the options for this file as shown in the following table.

Setting	Description
Database connection strings (various settings)	Configure the connection to the report server database. These settings are encrypted to provide greater security. You must use the rsconfig.exe utility to edit these values.
RSEmailDPConfiguration	Configures the e-mail settings for delivery of reports using SMTP. Allows you to modify the server name, server port number, and connection timeout, among other settings.
Render	Configures the rendering options for reports. These settings should match the Render settings in RSReportDesigner.config.
Data	Configures the connection types available for data sources that provide the data for reports. These settings should match the Data settings in RSReportDesigner.config.

ReportingServices Service

The ReportingServicesService.exe.config configuration file is located in Microsoft SQL Server*<SQL Server Instance>*\
Reporting Services\ReportServer\bin and contains information regarding the level of server tracing enabled on the report server. Tracing configuration is described in more detail in the next lesson.

Assigning Server Accounts

- **Report server database connection account choices**
  - Windows authentication
  - SQL authentication
- **Report server Windows service account choices**
  - Local System account (recommended)
  - Domain account
  - Network service account (Windows Server 2003 only)

Introduction

Some Reporting Services components require specific user credentials in order to function. You will need to modify these settings after installation if you plan to change the user accounts used by Reporting Services.

Connection to report server database

The account used by the report server must have database owner (dbo) privileges in the report server database. You configure this account during the Reporting Services installation. You can choose to connect to the database using either Microsoft Windows® or SQL authentication.

The configuration information for this account is encrypted in the configuration file for security reasons. If you need to edit the settings after installation, use the rsconfig.exe command-line utility. This utility is available when you use the command prompt.

The following example shows how to change the report server connection to use a Windows user account:

```
rsconfig -s localhost -d ReportServer -a windows -u ReportUser
-p P@ssw0rd
```

The following table lists the configuration settings represented by each switch in the preceding example.

Switch	Configuration setting
-s	Computer name
-d	Report server database name
-a	Specified Windows authentication
-u	Username
-p	Password

Report server Windows service

The Report server Windows service can run as any of the following account options:

- Local System account – This is the recommended option because the account only has sufficient permissions to function correctly.
- Domain user account – This option limits the choices for configuring data sources because you cannot use prompted or stored Windows credentials when connecting to a data source.
- Network service account – This option is only available in Microsoft Windows Server™ 2003.

You can set this account using the Windows Services tool as you would for any other Windows service.

google delegate & Impersonate
Service Principal Name

Lesson: Performance and Reliability Monitoring

- Using Trace Files
- Controlling Trace Files
- Logging Report Execution
- Using Performance Counters
- Applying Timeouts
- Suspending Jobs

delegation is done by computer
impersonation is done by person

Introduction

Part of an administrator's role is to monitor the ongoing performance and reliability of a report server to ensure smooth operation. Understanding the different tools that can assist you in monitoring performance and reliability will help you keep track of issues before they become serious. Learning how to adjust the server's settings will help you maintain a fast and reliable system.

In this lesson, you will learn how to use report server trace files and how to log report executions. You will also learn how to use the built-in performance counters to monitor your system performance and how to set execution timeouts. Finally, you will learn how to suspend long-running report server jobs.

Lesson objectives

After completing this lesson, you will be able to:

- Describe the purpose of report server trace files.
- Configure the level of tracing.
- View report execution log information.
- Utilize report server performance counters.
- Apply timeouts to long-running queries or reports.
- Suspend jobs.

-account properties!

SPN
→Service Principal Name

impersonation + delegations -

Configure SQL Agent to Impersonate
SQL Server to delegate

Using Trace Files

- **Records information about Report Server operations**
  - System information
  - Event logging
  - Exceptions and warnings
  - Inbound and outbound SOAP envelopes
  - HTTP header, stack trace, and debug information
- **Different trace files for each component**
- **Created daily but never deleted**

Introduction

Reporting Services provides trace files with which you can monitor the status of the report server. Becoming familiar with these trace files will help you assess reasons for reporting problems if they should occur.

Recorded information

Trace logs contain information about various report server operations, including the following:

- System information
- Events logged in the Application log
- Exceptions and warnings generated by the report server
- Inbound and outbound SOAP envelopes
- HTTP header, stack trace, and debug trace information

You can review trace logs to confirm report delivery, monitor report execution activity, and view error information.

Trace files

There are three trace files that located in the \Microsoft SQL Server\ *<SQL Server Instance>*\Reporting Services\LogFiles folder:

- ReportServerService__<timestamp>.log: Trace log for the report server Windows and Web services
- ReportServerWebApp__<timestamp>.log: Trace log for Report Manager
- ReportServer__<timestamp>.log: Trace log for the report server engine

Created daily

Trace files use the report server's local system time to generate a new log each day or generate a new log when the Reporting Services application restarts. Because trace logs are not automatically removed from the server, you should implement a strategy for archiving and removing old log files if you decide to keep tracing enabled.

Controlling Trace Files

- DefaultTraceSwitch in ReportingServicesService.config controls trace level
- Trace level options:
  - 0 = Disable tracing
  - 1 = Exceptions and restarts
  - 2 = Exceptions, restarts, warnings
  - 3 = Exceptions, restarts, warnings, status messages (default setting)
  - 4 = Verbose mode

Introduction

Tracing can provide different levels of information to suit your needs. You can use *detailed tracing* when you are trying to resolve an error that is difficult to find, and you can use *minimal tracing* information when the system is operating normally.

Set DefaultTraceSwitch

You can control the level of information recorded in the trace logs by altering the **DefaultTraceSwitch** configuration setting in the ReportingServicesService.config file. You can edit this setting using any XML editor.

Trace levels

You can set **DefaultTraceSwitch** to one of the following values:

- 0 = Disables tracing
- 1 = Exceptions and restarts
- 2 = Exceptions, restarts, warnings
- 3 = Exceptions, restarts, warnings, status messages. (This is the default setting.)
- 4 = Verbose mode

The following XML code example shows how to set the **DefaultTraceSwitch** value in the ReportingServices.config file:

```
<system.diagnostics>
  <switches>
    <add name="DefaultTraceSwitch" value="3" />
  </switches>
</system.diagnostics>
```

It is recommended that you do not disable tracing completely, in the interest of at least logging exception information.

Logging Report Execution

- **Report execution logs to the Report Server database, and allows:**
  - Monitoring of execution performance over time
  - Viewing frequency of report requests and the users who request them
- **Logs information including:**
  - Data retrieval, processing and rendering times, and report source
- **Set up execution logging in Report Manager to:**
  - Enable or disable logging globally
  - Specify removal frequency of log entries
- **Use supplied DTS package to browse log information**

Introduction

One of the most important aspects of Reporting Services administration is logging report execution. This type of log information offers troubleshooting and monitoring benefits particularly related to report execution.

Logs to report server database

Report execution information is logged directly in the report server database. The log information allows you to view the frequency of particular report requests as well which users make them.

Types of information

For each report execution, there is a variety of information captured, including:

- Data retrieval time: Time (in milliseconds) spent executing the query
- Processing time: Time (in milliseconds) spent processing the report, including applying filters, subtotals, grouping, sorting, and so on
- Rendering time: Time (in milliseconds) spent rendering the report in a specific format
- Source: Origin of the report execution. Possible values include:
  - Live
  - Cache
  - Snapshot
  - History

Setting up logging

Use Report Manager to set up execution logging by specifying the following options:

- Enable or disable report execution logging.

  Logging is enabled by default in Report Manager. You can disable it by opening **Site Settings** and clearing the **Enable report execution logging** check box.

- Specify removal of log entries.

  Log entries are removed after a specified number of days. The default is 60 days.

Browsing execution logs

Reporting Services stores the log data in the ExecutionLog table in the report server database. The table's data is not easy to understand as is, so Reporting Services provides a Data Transformation Services (DTS) package for exporting logged records to another location for viewing and analysis.

You can also use the DTS package to export records from the execution log on a periodic basis by creating a schedule.

Note A SQL script that creates the DTS target database is included on the Reporting Services installation CD. For the purposes of this course, the database has already been installed.

Using Performance Counters

- **Performance counters provide statistical information about Reporting Services applications**
- **Report server counters include:**
  - Active Sessions
  - Reports Executed/Sec
  - Total Cache Hits
  - Total Requests
- **Scheduling and Delivery Processor counters include:**
  - Deliveries/Sec
  - Total Processing Failures

Introduction

Reporting Services provides a series of performance counters that enable you to monitor server activity, observe trends, and troubleshoot any system bottlenecks. When used with SQL Server performance counters, the Reporting Services counters provide monitoring capabilities for all aspects of the report server.

Statistical information

When reports are executed, statistical information is created in the form of performance counters. This information is viewable through the Performance tool, Performance Logs and Alerts, and Task Manager.

Report server performance counters

There are 18 performance counters that relate to the performance of the report server. These counters are categorized as counters that show current activity or counters that show a total number, counting everything since the server was last started. Deciding which counters you should use will depend on your specific needs.

Report server performance counters include:

- Active Sessions: A count of all active browser sessions

- Reports Executed/Sec: The number of successful report executions per second. Use this counter with Request/Sec to compare execution to report requests that can be returned from the cache.

- Total Cache Hits: The total number of requests for reports from the cache since the service was last started.

- Total Requests: The total number of requests made to the report server since the service was last started.

Scheduling and Delivery Processor performance counters

There are 23 performance counters that relate to the performance of scheduling and delivery. These counters are categorized in the same way as report server performance counters.

Scheduling and Delivery Processor performance counters include:

- Deliveries/Sec: The number of report deliveries per second, from any delivery extension
- Total Processing Failures: The total number of report processing failures since the service was last started. This counter is reset when the application domain recycles—this is an automated way to restart the application.

Applying Timeouts

- • Source query timeouts
  - • Apply to the query execution time
  - • Configured per data set query
  - • Return a failure when timeout is exceeded
- • Report execution timeouts
  - • Apply to the total report execution time
  - • Configured globally or per report
  - • Return a failure when timeout is exceeded

Introduction

Occasionally, a report may take a long time to execute. If reports take too long to execute, users can become impatient, which can often lead them to trying to run the report again, before the original request has been satisfied. This in turn can slow down the system further. You can configure timeouts in order to prevent such problems from occurring.

Source query timeouts

Source query timeouts help you prevent unpredictable source queries from running for an unreasonable length of time. You can also use these timeouts to protect reports from any delays resulting from unanticipated changes in the source database that inadvertently impact query performance.

You can specify the maximum time limit for individual data set queries during report design using the **Dataset** dialog box in Report Designer. When the timeout is exceeded, the execution fails automatically and the user receives an error message in their browser window.

Report execution timeouts

Report execution timeouts help you prevent any long-running report executions that go beyond the acceptable threshold.

You can specify the maximum time limit for overall report execution in **Site Settings** in Report Manager. Alternatively, you can configure a timeout for each report individually in the report execution properties. When the timeout is exceeded, the user receives an error message in their browser window.

Tip   You can also manually cancel long-running queries or subscriptions using the **Manage Jobs** page of Report Manager.

Suspending Jobs

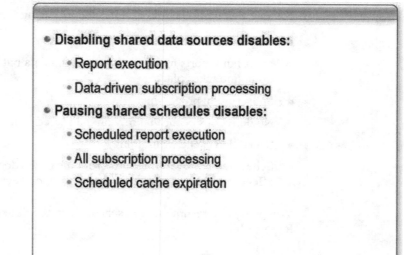

- **Disabling shared data sources disables:**
  - Report execution
  - Data-driven subscription processing
- **Pausing shared schedules disables:**
  - Scheduled report execution
  - All subscription processing
  - Scheduled cache expiration

Introduction

During the life cycle of your Reporting Services implementation, you may need to pause or temporarily suspend the execution of a job, such as a subscription or snapshot execution. Reasons for suspending jobs may include the need to take into account holidays, maintenance, or troubleshooting incorrect data.

Tip The options below are only available for shared data sources, not custom sources. For this reason, as well as the ease of maintenance associated with shared data sources, it is a good practice to use shared data sources whenever possible.

Disabling a shared data source

Disabling a shared data source disables the following functions:

- Report execution

  Users can still view reports based on existing snapshots or cached versions, but no new execution can occur. Report Manager displays an error message if users attempt to execute reports.

- Data-driven subscription processing

  No data-driven subscriptions based on the shared data source can run; however, standard subscriptions can still run.

Pausing a shared schedule

You enable and disable shared data sources in the **General** properties of Report Manager for the individual shared data source.

Pausing a shared schedule disables the following functions:

- Scheduled report execution

  Snapshot reports maintain their existing data but no new scheduled execution takes place.

- Subscription processing

  No deliveries occur that rely on the shared schedule.

- Scheduled cache expiration

  Scheduled removal of reports from the cache does not occur. This does not affect removal based on a timeout value, however.

You pause and resume shared schedules in the **Shared Schedules** section of Report Manager.

Lesson: Database Administration

- Understanding Database Storage
- Determining Disk Space Requirements
- Defining a Backup and Restore Strategy

Introduction

Reporting Services stores reports and report items in SQL Server databases. As with all databases, a small amount of administration may be required in order to ensure that the report server is robust and reliable, and to troubleshoot occasional problems.

In this lesson, you will learn how to administer the report server databases, how to plan for disk space requirements, and what information needs to be backed up and restored.

Lesson objectives

After completing this lesson, you will be able to:

- Describe how the report server stores information.
- Estimate required disk space for a report server installation.
- Plan a backup and restore strategy.

Understanding Database Storage

> - **ReportServer database stores:**
>   - Reports, folders, shared data sources, and meta data
>   - Resources
>   - Snapshots
>   - Report history
> - **ReportServerTempDB database stores:**
>   - Session cache
>   - Cached instances
> - **ChunkData tables consume a large percentage of both databases**

Introduction

Reporting Services requires two SQL Server databases in order to operate: the ReportServer database and the ReportServerTempDB database. Both databases are created automatically during installation. Understanding what information is stored in each database will help you manage the physical files that make up the databases.

ReportServer database

The following items are stored in the ReportServer database:

- Reports, folders, shared data sources, and meta data (includes the actual report and data source definitions)
- Resources (includes images associated with reports)
- Snapshots (includes the current data for snapshot reports)
- Report history (includes previous snapshot reports)

ReportServerTempDB database

The following items are stored in the ReportSeverTempDB database:

- Session cache: The user-specific report cache
- Cached instances: The report cache for multiple users

ChunkData tables

In the ReportServer database, the ChunkData table contains the snapshots and report history. In the ReportServerTempDB database, another ChunkData table contains the report session cache and report cached instances. Both tables store the intermediate format of reports, which means they contain the actual report data and will therefore consume a large percentage of the overall size of each database.

These two ChunkData tables are a main factor in estimating your database sizes, which is described in the following topic.

Determining Disk Space Requirements

> • Steps to estimate database sizes:
>   1. Estimate total number of reports
>   2. Examine intermediate report size
>   3. For ReportServer database, factor in intermediate report persistence
>   4. For ReportServerTempDB database, factor in caching

Introduction

Before installing Reporting Services, you will need to estimate the size of your report server databases so that you can plan any additional hardware requirements.

Steps for estimating database size

To determine disk space requirements for your ReportServer and ReportServerTempDB databases, consider the following general estimation guidelines:

1. Estimate the total number of reports.

2. Examine the intermediate report size.

3. For the ReportServer database, you need to factor in the persistence of the intermediate reports. Consider the following:

   • Snapshot: Only one snapshot is allowed at any point in time

   • Report history: How long is report history maintained and how frequently is history added

4. For the ReportServerTempDB database, you need to factor in session caching. Consider the following:

   • Cached instances: One instance per combination of report parameters according to expiration settings

   • Number of users: Affects the size of the session cache

   • Session cache timeout: Affects the length of time that items are held in the session cache

Defining a Backup and Restore Strategy

- **Data backup and restore**
  - Use SQL Server backup and restore
  - ReportServer database - essential
  - ReportServerTempDB database - optional
- **Encryption key backup and restore**
  - Public and symmetric keys needed for passwords and connections
  - Use encryption key management utility

Tempdb is in Simpler Recovery Mode

Introduction

You will need to implement a backup and restore strategy for your report server databases. Additionally, you must back up the key used to encrypt content stored within each database. This will help you recover from any unexpected failures.

Data backup and restore

Because ReportServer and ReportServerTempDB are SQL Server databases, the primary mechanism for backup and restore is SQL Server backup and restore.

Backup is considered mandatory for the ReportServer database since it contains the report and data source definitions. You can use the SQL Server Maintenance Wizard to schedule the backups. However, the ReportServerTempDB database can be recreated when users return to a report, so backup is not necessary.

Encryption key backup and restore

Each report server database encrypts stored user password and connection information. A symmetric key is used to encrypt this sensitive data.

To manage the cryptographic key, use the encryption key management command line utility, rskeymgmt.exe. This tool captures the key defined during installation and writes it to a file hashed with a password that you provide. Store this file in a secure location—you will need it to restore the report server after certain operations, including:

- Changing the report server Web service user account
- Changing the SQL Server instance name
- Changing the computer name of an installation

- Need full Database Backup nightly
- Logs need to be backed up with full backup model

- Simple Recovery model for DW

Lesson: Security Administration

- **The Reporting Services Authorization Model**
- **Assigning Roles**
- **Working with Item-Level Role Definitions**
- **Securing Items**
- **Working with System-Level Role Definitions**
- **Securing the System**

Introduction

Securing your report server will often be the most important aspect of administration. Whether the report server supplies reports across the Internet or over a company intranet, security is paramount.

In this lesson, you will learn about the Reporting Services authorization model and find out how Reporting Services uses role-based security. You will learn how to apply item security with role assignments, how to create roles, and how to secure the actual report server site.

Lesson objectives

After completing this lesson, you will be able to:

- Describe the Reporting Services authorization model.
- Assign roles.
- Modify and create item-level roles.
- Secure individual items using roles.
- Modify and create system-level roles.
- Secure the report server site.

The Reporting Services Authorization Model

* **Relies on role-based security**
  * Roles categorize user interaction with a specific system or resources into groups
  * Facilitates administration of user permissions
  * Provides flexible management of role membership
* **Requires underlying network authentication**
  * Windows authentication is the default model
  * Custom or third-party authentication via security extensions is supported

---

Introduction

Reporting Services uses authorization to ensure that only appropriate users can view individual reports or author new reports. You will also need to limit access to various features of the Report Manager, such as maintaining shared schedules.

Role-based security

The role-based security model supplied by Reporting Services is similar to that of other role-based security models used in other technologies, such as .NET development and SQL Server. The basic premise of role-based security is the ability to categorize users into groups (or *roles*) according to how they interact with a specific system and its resources.

Report Manager allows you to administer a list of user permissions by linking a user or Windows group to a role. For example, you can add a user to the **Browser** role, which allows the user to view reports. Other Reporting Services roles are described in the following topics.

This approach provides a highly flexible and scalable security framework that allows you to manage the membership of a role instead of managing the security of each user individually.

Underlying network authentication

Reporting Services relies on the authentication capabilities of the underlying network. In other words, Reporting Services does not authenticate users.

By default, Reporting Services integrates with Windows authentication. However, you can replace the default security extension with a custom or third-party module if required.

Assigning Roles

- Base roles on tasks that users can perform
- Tasks are:
  - Predefined within the system
  - Categorized as either *item* or *system*
- Assignment consists of three components:
  - Windows user account or group
  - Role definition - collection of item or system tasks
  - Securable object - item or system-level object
- Use Report Manager to assign roles

Introduction

In Reporting Services, you administer security by creating role assignments in Report Manager. Assigning a role involves choosing appropriate tasks for that role and linking the role to users or groups and securable objects.

Base roles on tasks

A *role assignment* is a security policy that defines the tasks that users or groups can perform on specific items or branches of the report server folder hierarchy. Reporting Services provides predefined roles that you can use; you can also create your own roles.

Tasks are predefined and categorized

Reporting Services defines a list of predefined tasks that you cannot add to or modify. These mutually exclusive tasks cover the full range of user and administrator actions. Some examples of these tasks include:

- Viewing reports
- Managing reports
- Managing report server properties

Tasks fall into one of the following categories:

- Item tasks: Tasks that relate to a report, folder, resource, or shared data source

  Examples of item tasks include managing reports, managing folders, and managing subscriptions.
- System tasks: Tasks that apply to the report server site as a whole

  Examples of system tasks include managing shared schedules and managing jobs.

Role assignment

Role assignment consists of the following three components:

- Windows user account or group: A user will receive permissions from all groups that he or she belongs to, in addition to any permissions granted to the actual user account itself.

- Role definition: The role definition specifies the set of allowable item or system tasks.

- Securable object: This includes an item object, such as a report, or a system-level object, such as a shared schedule.

Use Report Manager

Report Manager provides the ability to modify roles, add new roles, and assign the roles to users or groups and securable objects. The remaining topics in this lesson will describe how to set these security options.

Working with Item-Level Role Definitions

- **New item-level roles can be added**
- **Predefined item-level roles can be modified**

Predefined Role	Description
Browser	View reports, resources, and folders
My Reports	Manage own My Reports folders
Publisher	Add content to the report server database
Content Manager	Deploy reports, manage data source connections, determine how reports are used

Introduction

A *role definition* is a named collection of tasks that defines the type of access available to a user. Working with roles simplifies administration when compared to setting permissions on a user-by-user basis.

New roles

You can create your own roles if none of the predefined roles provides you with your required task grouping. Report Manager allows you to create item-level roles using the following process:

1. Navigate to the **Site Settings** page.
2. Click **Configure item-level role definitions**.
3. Click **New Role**.
4. Enter a role name and description in the **Name** and **Description** text boxes.
5. Select the appropriate tasks from the drop-down list.
6. Click **OK**.

You can then assign this new role to a user or group using the **New Role Assignment** page within the individual item that needs securing.

Tip You can create a new item-level role by copying an existing role. To do this, edit the original role and click **Copy**. You can then follow steps 4 to 6 above.

Predefined roles

Reporting Services provides four predefined item-level roles that you can modify as appropriate by using Report Manager:

- **Browser**: Allows users to run reports and navigate through the folder structure. Examples of tasks included in this role are:
  - Viewing reports
  - Viewing resources
  - Viewing folders
- **My Reports**: Allows users to build reports for personal use or store reports in a user-owned folder. Examples of tasks included in this role are:
  - Creating linked reports
  - Managing folders
  - Managing data sources
- **Publisher**: Allows users to publish content to the report server database. Examples of tasks included in this role are:
  - Managing reports
  - Managing data sources
  - Creating linked reports
- **Content Manager**: Allows users to deploy reports, manage shared data source connections, and set security at the item level. Examples of tasks included in this role are:
  - Creating linked reports
  - Managing subscriptions
  - Managing reports
  - Managing report history

Report Manager allows you to edit these predefined item-level roles and any new roles by using the following process:

1. Navigate to the **Site Settings** page.
2. Click **Configure item-level role definitions**.
3. Click the role that you wish to edit.
4. Change the appropriate information.
5. Click **OK**.

Securing Items

- Secure individual items such as reports, data sources, or resources
- Or group items together by using a folder – simplifies administration
- Link user or group to item-level role for each item
  1. Edit the Security properties of the item
  2. Click **New Role Assignment**
  3. Enter user or group name and select roles

Introduction

When assigning roles you must specify which securable item you intend to grant access to. You can choose to secure items individually or as a group.

Secure individual items

Individual items that you can secure include:

- **Report**: You can control whether a report is visible to users as well as whether they can change the report properties.

  Note that you can only secure snapshots and report history through their parent reports.

- **Data sources**: You can secure shared data sources to limit which users can modify the data source settings.

- **Resources**: Only standalone resources can be secured as individual items.

  Note that you cannot secure embedded resources separately from a report.

Grouping items

Grouping items together into folders provides a simpler mechanism for security, as you do not have to secure several individual items. Folder security will apply to the folder itself as well as the items it contains, including subfolders.

The **Home** folder is the root node of the folder hierarchy. Setting security for this folder establishes the initial security settings for all subsequent folders, reports, resources, and shared data sources in the folder hierarchy.

Link account to role for an item

In order to secure an item, you must link the user or group account to a role (or roles) on an individual item basis. Using Report Manager, follow these steps to secure an item:

1. Open the **Properties** page for the individual item and display the **Security** properties.

2. Click **New Role Assignment**.

3. Enter the user or Windows group name and select the appropriate roles.

   When you click **OK**, Reporting Services validates the user or Windows group name, resulting in an error message if the account is invalid.

Working with System-Level Role Definitions

- **New system-level roles can be added**
- **Predefined system-level roles can be modified**

Predefined Role	Description
System User	View basic information about the report server
System Administrator	Administer report server but not content

Introduction

For system-level security, roles affect the overall security of the report server site, not just individual items. You can administer these permissions by using the predefined system-level roles or creating your own roles.

New roles

You can create new system-level roles by copying one of the predefined roles or by creating a new role. Report Manager enables you to create roles using the following process:

1. Navigate to the **Site Settings** page.

2. Click **Configure system-level role definitions**.

3. Follow the same procedures as for item-level role definitions, as described in the earlier topic Working with Item-Level Role Definitions.

You can then assign this new role to a user or group using the **System Role Assignments** page.

Predefined role definitions

Reporting Services supplies two predefined system roles that you can modify:

- **System User**: Allows users to view schedule information in a shared schedule and view other basic information about the report server. Examples of tasks included in this role are:
  - Viewing report server properties
  - Viewing shared schedules

- **System Administrator**: Allows users to manage features and set defaults, set site-wide security, define role definitions, and manage jobs. Examples of tasks included in this role are:
  - Managing jobs
  - Managing report server properties
  - Managing shared schedules

Using Report Manager, you can edit these predefined system-level roles and any new roles using the following process:

1. Navigate to the **Site Settings** page.
2. Click **Configure system-level role definitions**.
3. Click the role that you wish to edit.
4. Change the appropriate information.
5. Click **OK**.

Securing the System

* Report server site itself is the securable object
* Users or groups
  * Similar to item security - local or domain accounts
  * Local administrators are automatically system administrators
* Link user or group to system-level role
  1. In Site Settings, click **Configure site-wide security**
  2. Click **New Role Assignment**
  3. Enter user or group name and select roles

Introduction

You can secure the report server site through system role assignments. This enables you to determine who has the ability to administer roles, manage jobs, set site properties, and so on.

Report server site is the securable object

The securable object for system security is the actual report server site, and its settings affect the site globally. Site-level tasks include creating shared schedules, managing jobs, and settings various properties. This level of security does not provide any form of control over individual report server items, such as reports.

User or groups

Reporting Services does not create its own user accounts. Instead, it references existing local or domain accounts and groups defined in the operating system

If you inadvertently set role assignments in a way that locks all users out of the system, a local administrator can always reset security. As a precaution against a lockout situation, members of the local Administrators group can always access a report server to change site settings no matter what role assignments are set. These site settings include system role assignments, item-level role definitions, and system-level role definitions.

Note that having access to a report server is not the same as having full access to all the reports and data it contains. To ensure that highly privileged users such as local administrators cannot access confidential reports, you must secure the reports at the data-access level, requiring users to provide credentials to view the report.

Link account to role

In order to secure the site, you must link the user or group account to a system-level role (or roles). Using Report Manager, follow these steps to link an account to a system-level role:

1. Open the **Site Settings** page and click **Configure site-wide security**.

2. Click **New Role Assignment**.

3. Enter the user or Windows group name and select the appropriate roles.

   When you click **OK**, Reporting Services validates the user or Windows group name, resulting in an error message if the account is invalid.

Demonstration: Item Security

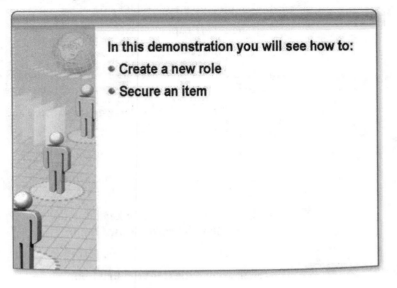

In this demonstration you will see how to:
- Create a new role
- Secure an item

Introduction

In this demonstration, you will see how to create a new role and how to secure a report using role assignment. Note you must complete Exercise 0 of the lab before the demonstration.

Procedures

▶ **Create a new role**

1. Open **Internet Explorer**. If **Report Manager** is not your default home page, then from **Favorites**, click **Report Manager Home**.

2. Click **Site Settings**.

3. Click **Configure item-level role definitions**.

4. Click **New Role**.

5. In the **Name** text box, type **Sales Viewer**. In the **Description** text box, type **Can only view the sales report**.

6. Select only the **View folders** and **View reports** task check boxes.

7. Click **OK**.

▶ **Assign the item permissions**

1. On the upper right-hand side of the screen, click the **Home** link.

2. Click the **Properties** tab.

3. Click the **New Role Assignment** button.

4. In the **Group or user name** text box, type **SalesAnalyst**. This will allow the SalesAnalyst group to access the Home page.

5. Select only the **Sales Viewer** check box, and click **OK**.

6. Click the **Contents** tab.

7. Click the **Module 6 Reports** folder link.

8. On the right-hand side of the screen, click the **Show Details** button to view the details of each of the links.

9. Under the **Edit** column header, click the **Properties** button next to the **Territory Sales Drilldown** report.

10. On the left-hand side of the screen, click the **Security** link.

11. Click the **Edit Item Security** button, and then click **OK** when asked to confirm your action.

12. Select the check box next to the **SalesAnalyst** group, click **Delete**, and click **OK** to confirm your action.

    You have now removed this role assignment for the **Territory Sales Drilldown** report.

13. On the **File** menu, click **Close**.

▶ **Run Internet Explorer as the SalesAnalyst user**

1. Click **Start**, point to **All Programs**, right-click **Internet Explorer**, and then click **Run as**.

2. In the **Run As** dialog box, click **The following user**, type **SalesAnalyst** in the **User name** textbox, type **P@ssw0rd** in the **Password** text box, and then click **OK**. (Enter this information whenever the **Connect to** dialog box appears.)

3. Navigate to **http://locahost/Reports**.

   Note that the **Site Settings** link is not visible.

4. Click the **Module 6 Reports** folder link.

   Note that you can only see the **Company Sales** report.

5. Click the **Company Sales** report link to view the report.

6. Click **Properties**.

   Note that you can only view the **General** properties.

7. On the **File** menu, click **Close**.

Review

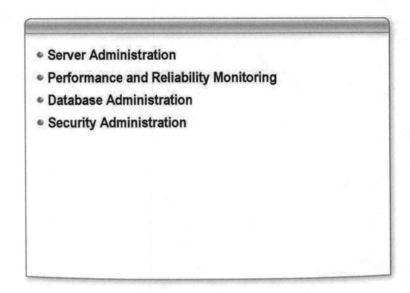

- Server Administration
- Performance and Reliability Monitoring
- Database Administration
- Security Administration

1. Why must you use rsconfig.exe to change the report server database connection information in the RSReportServer configuration file?

2. How do you configure the amount of information recorded in the report server trace files?

3. How can you temporarily stop all reports that are based on a shared data source from executing?

4. What report server information should you back up?

5. What is the difference between system and item-level security?

Lab 6: Administering Reporting Services

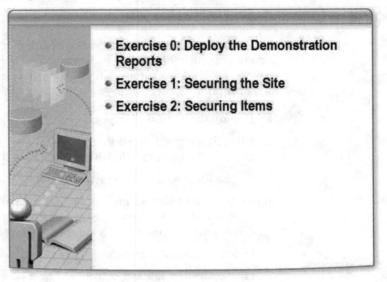

Objectives

After completing this lab, you will be able to:

- Enforce site security using roles.
- Enforce item security using roles.

Estimated time to complete this lab: 45 minutes

Exercise 0
Deploy the Demonstration Reports

In this exercise, you will deploy this module's demonstration reports, which are also required for this lab. If you have already deployed the demonstration reports, proceed to Exercise 1.If you have not already deployed the demonstration reports for this module, follow this required procedure.

▶ **Deploy the Module 6 reports**

1. Click **Start**, point to **All Programs**, point to **Microsoft Visual Studio .NET 2003**, and then click **Microsoft Visual Studio .NET 2003**.

2. On the **File** menu, click **Open Solution**.

3. In the **Open Solution** dialog box, navigate to the C:\Program Files\Microsoft Learning\2030\Democode\Mod06 folder containing the demonstration files. Click **Module 6 Reports.sln**, and then click **Open**.

4. Double-click **AdventureWorks.rds**.

5. On the **Credentials** tab, select the **Use a specific user name and password** check box, type **ReportExecution** in the **Username** text box, and type **P@ssw0rd** in the **Password** text box.

6. Click **OK**.

7. In **Solution Explorer**, right-click the solution, and then click **Deploy Solution**.

8. Close **Visual Studio .NET**.

Exercise 1
Securing the Site

In this exercise, you will secure the Reporting Services site using system-level security. You will create a new role that allows several tasks and link the role to a Windows group. Finally, you will test the role using Internet Explorer.

▶ **Run Internet Explorer as the NADirector user**

1. Click **Start**, point to **All Programs**, right-click **Internet Explorer**, and then click **Run as**.

2. In the **Run As** dialog box, click **The following user**, type **NADirector** in the **Username** combo box, type **P@ssw0rd** in the **Password** text box, and then click **OK**. (Enter this information whenever the **Connect to** dialog box appears.)

3. Navigate to **http://locahost/Reports**.

   Note that the user has no permissions.

4. On the **File** menu, click **Close**.

▶ **Create a new role**

1. Open **Internet Explorer**. If **Report Manager** is not your default home page, then from **Favorites** click **Report Manager Home**.

   Warning   Do not use the **Run As** option here.

2. Click **Site Settings**.

3. In the **Security** section, click **Configure system-level role definitions**.

4. Click the **New Role** button.

5. In the **Name** text box, type **Security Manager**. In the **Description** text box, type **Can set item and site security**.

6. Select only the **Manage Report Server security** and **Manage roles** task check boxes.

7. Click **OK**.

▶ **Assign the new role to the AWSalesDirector group**

1. Click **Site Settings**.

2. In the **Security** section, click **Configure site-wide security**.

3. Click the **New Role Assignment** button.

4. In the **Group or user name** text box, type **AWSalesDirector**.

5. Select only the **Security Manager** role check box.

6. Click **OK**.

▶ **Run Internet Explorer as the NADirector user**

1. Click **Start**, point to **All Programs**, right-click **Internet Explorer**, and then click **Run as**.

2. In the **Run As** dialog box, click **The following user**, type **NADirector** in the **Username** combo box, and type **P@ssw0rd** in the **Password** text box.

3. Navigate to **http://locahost/Reports**.

4. Click **Site Settings**.

    Note that the only the **Security** section is available.

5. On the **File** menu, click **Close**.

Exercise 2
Securing Items

In this exercise, you will add item browsing permissions to the AWSalesDirector group using the Browser role. Finally, you will test the role using Internet Explorer.

▶ **Assign the item permissions**

1. Open **Internet Explorer**. If **Report Manager** is not your default home page, then from **Favorites**, click **Report Manager Home**.

2. Click the **Properties** tab.

3. Click the **New Role Assignment** button.

4. In the **Group or user name** text box, type **AWSalesDirector**.

5. Select only the **Browser** check box, and click **OK**.

6. Click the **Contents** tab.

7. Click the **Example Reports** folder link.

8. Click the **Properties** tab.

9. On the left-hand side of the screen, click the **Security** link.

10. Click the **Edit Item Security button**, and then click **OK** when asked to confirm your action.

11. Select the check box next to the **AWSalesDirector** group, click **Delete**, and click **OK** to confirm your action.

12. On the **File** menu, click **Close**.

▶ **Run Internet Explorer as the NADirector user**

1. Click **Start**, point to **All Programs**, right-click **Internet Explorer**, and then click **Run as**.

2. In the **Run As** dialog box, click **The following user**, type **NADirector** in the **Username** combo box, type **P@ssw0rd** in the **Password** text box, and then click **OK**. (Enter this information whenever the **Connect to** dialog box appears.)

3. Navigate to **http://locahost/Reports**.

   Note that the **Execution Log Reports** folder link is no longer visible.

4. Click the **Module 6 Reports** folder link.

5. Click the **Company Sales** report link to view the report.

6. Click the **Properties** tab.

   Note that you cannot set any properties for the report.

7. On the **File** menu, click **Close**.

Module 7: Programming Reporting Services

Contents

Overview

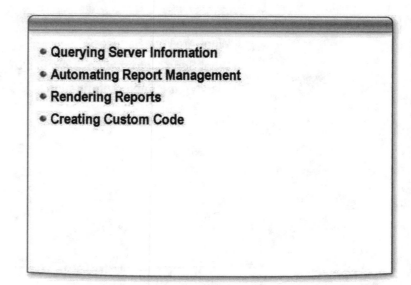

- Querying Server Information
- Automating Report Management
- Rendering Reports
- Creating Custom Code

Introduction

Although Report Manager and Report Designer provide you with much of your required functionality, Reporting Services includes additional features to provide easier administration, report rendering, and custom functionality. These extra capabilities ensure that your report server is used to its full potential.

In this module, you will learn how to query Reporting Services information programmatically and how to automate your report management tasks. You will also learn how to render reports without relying on Report Manager. Finally, you will learn how creating custom code can extend the feature set of your report server.

Objectives

After completing this module, you will be able to:

- Retrieve information about the report server.
- Automate report management tasks.
- Render reports programmatically.
- Create custom code and call the custom functionality from reports.

Lesson: Querying Server Information

- What Are Web Services?
- What Server Information Is Available?
- Discovering Server Information

Introduction

One of the major advantages of Microsoft® SQL Server™ 2000 Reporting Services is that it provides a Web service that you can use to query the report server for information. This Web service enables you to request information about the list of available reports and other items, such as folders.

In this lesson, you will learn how Web services use underlying standards and protocols to allow communication between a host and a client. You will also learn what information is available to a client application and how to query the Report Server Web service for available information about reports.

Lesson objectives

After completing this lesson, you will be able to:

- Describe Web services.
- Describe what information is available using the Report Server Web service.
- Retrieve server information using the Report Server Web service.

What Are Web Services?

* **Platform-independent technology based on established standards**
  * XML, SOAP, HTTP
* **Allows interaction from any type of application**
  * Windows applications, Web applications, etc.

Introduction

Reporting Services uses Web services to enable viewing and managing of reports. Before you look at the individual details of the Reporting Services Web services, you must understand the basics of the underlying technology.

Platform independence

Web services allow communication between applications over open protocols using standard data formats. This enables client and server applications to run on whatever platform is most suitable. Web services do not rely on any one platform. Instead, they rely on the following standards to enable platform independence:

- Extensible Markup Language (XML): Provides a standard data presentation

- SOAP: Provides a standard format for packaging data

- HTTP: Provides a standard protocol for sending and receiving data packets

The above standards are set by the World Wide Web Consortium (http://www.w3c.org). Also know as the W3C, the World Wide Web Consortium is an independent organization composed of around 375 members.

Any platform that can read and write XML and transport data over HTTP can use Web services. This flexibility provides the opportunity for integration with most applications platforms.

Application interaction

Web services can be called from any type of application, including Microsoft Windows® and Web applications. Applications can be developed in any programming language by any vendor as long as they can interact with Web services. The Microsoft .NET Framework also provides underlying technology to communicate with Web services.

What Server Information Is Available?

- Browsing
  - What reports are available?
  - What parameters does this report require?
- Managing
  - What subscriptions are in place?
  - What are the security settings for this report?
- Retrieve information using the Report Server Web service

Introduction

Reporting Services provides a Web service that allows you to request and discover report server information. This information may be useful in a number of custom applications, for both viewing report information and managing the reports themselves.

Browsing

One of the major reasons for retrieving information about items on the server is to facilitate user access to appropriate reports. You can programmatically determine which reports are available for a particular user, whether those reports require parameters, and other pertinent information about the reports. For example, this is how the ASP.NET Report Server Web site works with reports.

Managing

In addition, you can programmatically change a report's attributes as part of an application to manage reports. However, before you change to the new attributes of a report, your application may want to know the current attributes.

You can also work with subscriptions and security settings by retrieving server information.

Retrieve information using the Report Server Web service

The primary mechanism for getting information about Reporting Services items is by communicating with the Report Server Web service, which is accessible via standard SOAP calls. Fortunately, the .NET infrastructure makes it easy to write applications that communicate with a Web service, as you will see in the remainder of this module.

Discovering Server Information

1. **Add a Web reference to the client application**

   http://«server»/reportserver/reportservice.asmx?wsdl

2. **Specify security credentials for the proxy object**

   rs.Credentials = System.Net.CredentialCache.DefaultCredentials

3. **Retrieve information as needed**

   - Information for all server items: reports, resources, and folders

   - Search for items using **FindItems**

   - Navigate hierarchy using **ListChildren**

Introduction

In order to retrieve server information about reports, you must follow some basic procedures. (The following steps assume that you are using a .NET Framework application as the client.)

Add a Web Reference to the service

First, you must add a Web reference to the Report Server Web service. Adding the Web reference creates a proxy class that translates normal method calls into the appropriate SOAP calls that are then sent to the Web service.

To create a Web reference in Microsoft Visual Studio® .NET, open your client project. On the **Project** menu, click **Add Web Reference**. The **Add Web Reference** dialog box requires the URL that contains the programmatic description of the Web service, known as the WSDL (Web Services Description Language). The URL should be in the format http://*server*/reportserver/reportservice.asmx?wsdl.

Specify security credentials for the proxy

The proxy class called **ReportingService** is created automatically for you. However, you must establish security credentials before calling any methods on the Report Server Web service by setting the **Credentials** property of the proxy class. The following code example shows how to use the default credentials of the logged-on user:

```
rs.Credentials = System.Net.CredentialCache.DefaultCredentials
```

Retrieve information as needed

You can now retrieve whatever information you need using the Report Server Web service.

When you retrieve information about reporting items, you are not limited to reports. You can also retrieve information about other items on the server, most notably folders that organize reports. You can search for information using the following methods:

- Search for items using the **FindItems** method of the proxy class.

  This method allows you to filter all or part of the hierarchy by using search conditions. When you create a search condition, you compare certain key attributes of the reporting items, such as name, create date, or modify date. When you search for items, the returned list is filtered by the authenticated user's permissions.

- Navigate items in the hierarchy using the **ListChildren** method of the proxy class.

  This method allows you to navigate through the folder hierarchy by working with each item in the folder structure.

Note   You will see how to use **FindItems** to query server information using a Web service in the following demonstration.

Demonstration: Querying for Server Information

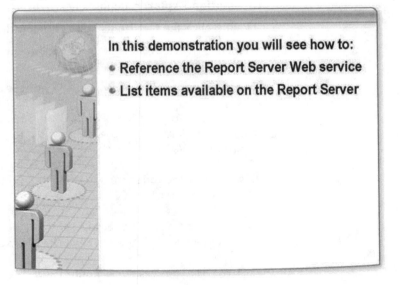

In this demonstration you will see how to:
- Reference the Report Server Web service
- List items available on the Report Server

Introduction

In this demonstration, you will see how to create a simple Windows application that retrieves information using the Report Server Web service. It will search for items on the server that match specified criteria and display the results in the form.

Procedures

▶ **Open the prebuilt solution**

1. Click **Start**, point to **All Programs**, point to **Microsoft Visual Studio .NET 2003**, and then click **Microsoft Visual Studio .NET 2003**.

2. On the **File** menu, click **Open Solution**.

3. In the **Open Solution** dialog box, navigate to the C:\Program Files\Microsoft Learning\2030\Democode\Mod07\GetItems folder containing the demonstration files. Click **GetItems.sln**, and then click **Open**.

▶ **Add a Web reference to the Reporting Services Web service**

1. In **Solution Explorer**, right-click the **References** folder, and click **Add Web Reference**.

2. In the **URL** text box, type the following URL:

```
http://localhost/ReportServer/ReportService.asmx?wsdl
```

3. Click **Go**.

4. After the Web service is located, in the **Web reference name** text box, delete the default value, type **ReportService**, and then click **Add Reference**.

▶ **View the code of the Get Items button and test the solution**

1. In **Solution Explorer**, double-click **frmGetItems.vb**.

2. Double-click the **Get Items** button to view the code window.

   The button click event contains the following code (only relevant code has been shown):

```
Dim myReportService As New ReportService.ReportingService

Dim condition As New ReportService.SearchCondition
condition.Name = "Name"
condition.Value = txtName.Text

Dim mySearchConditions(0) As ReportService.SearchCondition
mySearchConditions(0) = condition

myReportService.Credentials = _
    System.Net.CredentialCache.DefaultCredentials

Dim myCatalogItems As ReportService.CatalogItem()
myCatalogItems = myReportService.FindItems("/", _
    Nothing, mySearchConditions)

For Each cItem As ReportService.CatalogItem In _
 myCatalogItems
    lstResults.Items.Add(cItem.Path)
Next
```

3. On the **Debug** menu, click **Start**.

4. In the text box, type **Sales** and then click **Get Items**.

   The results of the search are displayed in the list box. Resize the form as necessary to view the information in the list box.

5. Close the form.

6. Close Visual Studio .NET.

Lesson: Automating Report Management

- What Can Be Automated?
- Automation Using Web Services
- Using Scripts to Automate

Introduction

Reporting Services provides various options for managing reports. You have already seen how to manage reports and other items using Report Manager, but you can also manage items using automation. Automation greatly reduces the amount of work required when deploying or administering reports.

In this lesson, you will learn how to automate report management tasks, including publishing reports and listing available reports, using Web services and scripting.

Lesson objectives

After completing this lesson, you will be able to:

- Describe report management automation.
- Automate tasks using Web services.
- Automate tasks using scripting.

What Can Be Automated?

- **Any feature Report Manager provides**
  - Add or delete reports and folders
  - Administer security, schedules, etc.
- **Example usage:**
  - Apply identical report settings to multiple servers
  - Apply identical security settings to multiple reports

Introduction

Reporting Services provides automation capabilities using the same Web service described in the preceding lesson for browsing information.

Features Report Manager provides

When you automate report management using the Report Server Web service, you can perform operations identical to those that are performed in Report Manager. This is because Report Manager uses the Web service to carry out all of its tasks. Therefore, you can write custom code to add or delete reports and folders, administer security settings or schedules, or any other task that Report Manager can perform.

Example usage

Any report management task that you must execute multiple times is ideally suited for use as a custom application. Consider the following examples of report management automation:

- Applying identical settings to multiple servers when running a report server farm

- Applying the same security or subscription settings to multiple reports

- Generating report Report Definition Language (RDL) files and then automatically deploying the generated reports

Automation Using Web Services

1. **Add a Web reference to the client application**
2. **Specify security credentials for the proxy object**
3. **Use methods as needed:**
   - Create methods
   - Delete methods
   - Get methods
   - List methods
   - Set methods

Introduction

In order to use the Report Server Web service for automation, you must follow the same steps as for browsing server information. These steps assume you are using a .NET Framework application as the client.

To automate using the Web service

Follow these steps to automate report management using the Report Server Web service:

1. Add a Web reference to the Web service.
2. Specify the security credentials for the proxy object.
3. Use the methods as needed.

   There are over 80 methods that you can use for automating report management. Most of these methods can be broken down into the following categories:

   - Create: Allow creation of items
   - Delete: Allow deletion of items
   - Get: Allow retrieval of item properties
   - List: Return lists of information
   - Set: Update item properties

The following code example shows how to upload a report using the Web service:

```
Dim stream As FileStream = File.OpenRead("MyReport.rdl")
Dim report As Byte() = New Byte(stream.Length) {}
stream.Read(report, 0, CInt(stream.Length))
stream.Close()

Dim rs As New ReportingService()
rs.Credentials = System.Net.CredentialCache.DefaultCredentials
rs.CreateReport("My Report", "/Samples", True, report, _
    Nothing)
```

The preceding code example loads the report file into a **FileStream** object and then opens the Web service. The security credentials are assigned to the proxy object and then the **CreateReport** method is called.

The **CreateReport** parameters are specified as follows:

- Report: The name of the report
- Parent: Which parent folder the report should be located within
- Overwrite: Whether to overwrite an existing report if it is found
- Definition: The byte array containing the report definition
- Properties: Any additional properties the report requires

Important   In a production application, you should use a **Try…Catch…Finally** block to protect the code from errors. This has been omitted above to simplify the code example.

Using Scripts to Automate

- Alternative to creating custom applications
- Use rs.exe to automate tasks
  1. Create Visual Basic .NET function named **Main**
  2. Store in script file with .rss file extension
  3. Pass file as command line argument to rs.exe

Introduction

Windows applications are very useful when you require complex user interaction to manage the report server. Windows applications allow you to use standard Windows controls, such as text boxes, check boxes, and combo boxes, to create a flexible and user-friendly management environment. However, there will be times when you do not need this level of interactivity.

Alternative to custom applications

Rather than write a complete executable application to carry out a management task, you can create a script file and then use the rs.exe utility to execute the script. The rs.exe utility manages the SOAP interface and the connection to the Web service. It also manages the necessary authentication.

Using rs.exe

The rs.exe utility requires a script file in order to manage a report server. You can use rs.exe by following these steps:

1. Create a Visual Basic .NET function named **Main**.

   The function does not need to create a proxy object, connect to the server, or pass authentication.

2. Save the file with the **.rss** file extension.

3. Pass the **.rss** file to **rs.exe** as a command-line argument.

   You can create multiple script files with the extension **.rss** and then execute them in batch processes as command line arguments to **rs.exe**.

The following example shows how to list items in a file called list.rss:

```
Public Sub Main()
    Dim items() As CatalogItem = rs.ListChildren("/", True)

    For Each item As CatalogItem In items
        Console.WriteLine(item.Name)
    Next item
End Sub
```

The **Main** method is executed and the variable **rs** is automatically created to represent the proxy object. Note that no authentication is required, as the call to rs.exe performs this step.

You can execute this script file using the following command:

```
rs.exe -i list.rss -s http://localhost/ReportServer
```

The rs.exe utility expects an input file and a server URL as the minimum information. It will automatically use Windows authentication during the script execution.

Demonstration: Automating Report Management

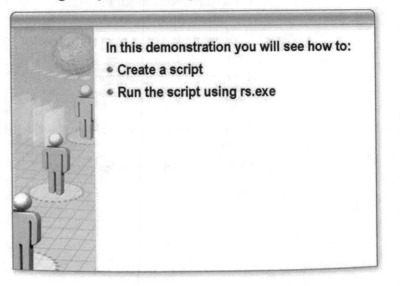

Introduction

In this demonstration, you will see how to create a simple script file that lists information about the items available on the report server. The script will then be run using the rs.exe utility.

Procedures

▶ **Create the script file**

1. Click **Start**, point to **All Programs**, point to **Accessories**, and then click **Notepad**.

2. Type the following code:

```
Public Sub Main()
    Dim items() As CatalogItem = rs.ListChildren("/", True)

    For Each item As CatalogItem In items
        Console.WriteLine(item.Name)
    Next item
End Sub
```

3. On the **File** menu, click **Save**.

4. In the **Save in** combo box, click **My Documents**.

5. In the **File name** text box, type **List.rss**.

6. In the **Save as type** drop-down list, click **All Files**.

7. Click **Save**, and then close **Notepad**.

▶ **Execute the script file**

1. Click **Start**, point to **All Programs**, point to **Accessories**, and then click **Command Prompt**.

2. In the command prompt window, type **cd "My Documents"** and press **Enter**.

3. Type the following command:

```
rs.exe -i List.rss -s http://localhost/ReportServer
```

The command prompt should display the list of reports and folders that exist on the report server.

4. Close the command prompt window.

Lesson: Rendering Reports

- Rendering Reports Using URL Access
- Rendering Reports Using Web Services

Introduction

Often you will want to render reports using tools other than Report Manager. This may involve linking to reports from Web pages located within the company intranet or creating custom applications that display reports.

In this lesson, you will learn how to render reports using URL access in a browser, as well as programmatically using the Report Server Web service.

Lesson objectives

After completing this lesson, you will be able to:

- Render reports from a Web page.
- Render reports programmatically using the Report Server Web service.

Rendering Reports Using URL Access

- **Use a hyperlink from a Web page**
  http://localhost/ReportServer?/Reports/SalesReport&rs:Command=Render
- **Additional parameters allow rendering control**
  http://.../SalesReport&rs:Command=Render&rc:Toolbar=false&rc:Zoom=200
- **URL can include report parameters**
- **URL sent as plain text – use SSL for security**
- **Web service detects appropriate HTML level for browser**

Introduction

Displaying reports from a company Web site is one of the most common requirements for a report server. Any Web page can link directly to reports or folders by using the item URL. This allows both Internet and intranet sites to render reports in a browser.

Use a hyperlink

Accessing reports from a Web page is simple with Reporting Services. Create a hyperlink on a Web page that points to a report or folder URL and users can then easily view report output. You must specify the server location, the report server virtual directory, and the report name, including the folder hierarchy as appropriate. You must also append the special parameter rs:Command=Render to the URL to render the report.

The following URL example shows the server name as **localhost**, the report server virtual directory as **ReportServer**, the folder as **Reports**, and the report as **SalesReport**:

```
http://localhost/ReportServer?/Reports/SalesReport&rs:Command=
Render
```

If you specify a folder rather than a report, it displays a simple page with available subfolders and reports.

Additional parameters allow rendering control

You can control how a report renders in the browser by using various URL access parameters. These parameters can control features such as whether to display the report toolbar in the browser and the zoom value of the report.

The following URL example shows a report without the report toolbar increased to a zooming level of 200%:

```
http://localhost/ReportServer?/Reports/SalesReport&rs:Command=
Render&rc:Toolbar=false&rc:Zoom=200
```

Report parameters

If a report requires query parameters, you can directly insert parameter values into the URL. A report parameter is entered into a URL without the rs:Command= prefix, as shown in the following example:

```
http://localhost/ReportServer?/Reports/SalesReport&rs:Command=
Render&SalespersonID=1232
```

URL sent as plain text

Remember that a browser sends URLs to the Web server as plain text by default. If you include anything in the URL that is confidential, such as parameters, be sure to connect to the Web server using a secure, encrypted protocol such as Secure Sockets Layer (SSL).

Automatic browser detection

When you use a URL to render a report, the Web service automatically detects the browser you are using and issues the appropriate Hypertext Markup Language (HTML) for that browser. Reporting Services supports both HTML 4.0 and 3.2, but reduced functionality will apply when the browser only supports HTML level 3.2. For example, features such as Document Maps are unavailable in a 3.2 browser.

Rendering Reports Using Web Services

1. **Add a Web reference to the client application**
2. **Specify security credentials for the proxy object**
3. **Use the Render method**
   - Specify report path, render format, and other options
   - Returns byte array as result
   - Save byte array to file or display manually

Introduction

Using a URL is clearly the simplest way to render a report, but there are times when you want more control programmatically. You can render a report using the Report Server Web service in essentially the same way that you get report item information from the Report Server Web service.

To render using the Web service

Follow these steps to render reports using the Report Server Web service:

1. Add a Web reference to the Web service.
2. Specify the security credentials for the proxy object.
3. Use the **Render** method.

   The **Render** method has many parameters, including the full path for the report and the rendering format. You can also pass any report parameters or other options as arguments to the method call.

   The function returns the rendered report as a byte array so that you can display the report in whatever way you require. For example, you can display an HTML rendered report in a literal Web control, or you can save the report output to a file.

The following example renders a report to a PDF file for viewing in Adobe
Acrobat Reader:

```
Dim rs As New ReportingService
rs.Credentials = _
    System.Net.CredentialCache.DefaultCredentials

Dim result As Byte() = Nothing
result = rs.Render("/Reports/SalesReport", "PDF", _
    Nothing, Nothing, Nothing, Nothing, Nothing, _
    Nothing, Nothing, Nothing, Nothing, Nothing)

Dim stream As FileStream = File.Create("report.PDF", _
    result.Length)
stream.Write(result, 0, result.Length)
stream.Close()
```

The first two required parameters are the report path and the rendering
format. All the other parameters can be left as default values of Nothing (in
Microsoft Visual Basic® .NET) or null (in Microsoft Visual C#®).

Tip   For more information about these parameters, view the
ReportingService.Render method definition in the Reporting Services
Books Online.

Demonstration: Rendering a Report Using a Web Service

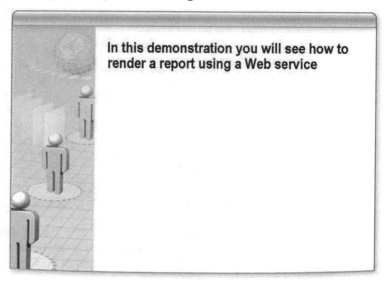

In this demonstration you will see how to render a report using a Web service

---

Introduction

In this demonstration, you will see how to render a report as a PDF and then view the file in Adobe Acrobat Reader.

Procedures

▶ **Open the prebuilt solution**

1. Click **Start**, point to **All Programs**, point to **Microsoft Visual Studio .NET 2003**, and then click **Microsoft Visual Studio .NET 2003**.

2. On the **File** menu, click **Open Solution**.

3. In the **Open Solution** dialog box, navigate to the C:\Program Files\Microsoft Learning\2030\Democode\Mod07\RenderReport folder containing the demonstration files. Click **RenderReport.sln**, and then click **Open**.

▶ **Add a Web reference to the Reporting Services Web service**

1. In **Solution Explorer**, expand the **Web References** folder and delete the **ReportService** web service.

2. Right-click the **Web References** folder, and click **Add Web Reference**.

3. In the **URL** text box, type the following URL:

```
http://localhost/ReportServer/ReportService.asmx?wsdl
```

4. Click **Go**.

5. After the Web service is located, in the **Web reference name** text box, delete the default value, type **ReportService**, and then click **Add Reference**.

▶ **View the code in the Render button and test the solution**

1. In **Solution Explorer**, double-click **frmRender.vb**.

2. Double-click the **Render** button to view the code window.

   The button click event contains the following code (only relevant code has been shown):

```
Dim rs As New ReportService.ReportingService
rs.Credentials = _
   System.Net.CredentialCache.DefaultCredentials

Dim result As Byte() = Nothing
result = rs.Render(lstResults.SelectedItem.ToString(), _
   "PDF", Nothing, Nothing, Nothing, Nothing, Nothing, _
   Nothing, Nothing, Nothing, Nothing, Nothing)

Dim stream As FileStream = _
   File.Create("ReportOutput.PDF", result.Length)
stream.Write(result, 0, result.Length)
stream.Close()
```

3. On the **Build** menu, click **Rebuild Solution**.

4. On the **Debug** menu, click **Start**.

5. In the text box, type **Sales** and then click **Get Items**.

   The results of the search are displayed in the list box. Resize the form as necessary to view the information in the list box.

6. Select one of the reports from the list box, and then click **Render**.

   The report is rendered and Acrobat Reader displays the results. This may take several seconds to occur.

7. Close the form.

8. Close **Visual Studio .NET**.

Lesson: Creating Custom Code

- Extending Reporting Services
- Why Create Custom Assemblies?

Introduction

In addition to automating day-to-day operations, such as creating and customizing reports, facilitating user access to reports, and managing reports, you can automate Reporting Services in other ways, such as by adding extensions to the report server and by creating custom assemblies.

In this lesson, you will learn about Reporting Services extensions and about custom assemblies.

Lesson objectives

After completing this lesson, you will be able to:

- Describe Reporting Services extensions.
- Describe the uses for custom assemblies.

Extending Reporting Services

- **Create "add-ins" for Reporting Services**
  - Proprietary data sources
  - Enhanced rendered output
    (for example, 3-D view, link to diagrams)
- **Extension types:**
  - Data processing
  - Rendering
  - Delivery

Introduction

Reporting Services provides you with most of the reporting features that you will require on a day-to-day basis. Occasionally, you might require functionality that the default installation does not provide. Fortunately, you can create additional functionality yourself, since Reporting Services is designed as an extensible architecture.

Creating add-ins

The use of custom extensions allows you to create seamless "add-ins" to Reporting Services. These are particularly useful if you are a third-party developer using Reporting Services to create a specialized solution.

For example, if you have a specialized application with a proprietary data source, you can create a custom data processing extension to retrieve data from your application. Alternatively, you might want to create a reporting visualization tool that links to three-dimensional views of data.

Extension types

All of the major tasks that Reporting Service implements are extensions. Therefore, you can add additional customized extensions that integrate seamlessly with the native functionality of the report server.

Currently, you can create new extensions based on the following extension types:

- Data Processing

  All data connections rely on a data processing extension. You can add your own data processing extension for your own data sources or, alternatively, you can add additional functionality to the existing Reporting Services data processing extensions.

- Rendering

  Each report render option is implemented as an individual rendering extension. You can create your own rendering extension to produce report output that matches your file types.

- Delivery.

  Delivery extensions are responsible for delivering rendered reports. You can create your own delivery extension, such as an extension for a queuing application.

Note   Most reporting needs can be met with the native extensions that ship with Reporting Services. Creating custom extensions should only be considered by developers with advanced knowledge of the Reporting Services programming model.

Why Create Custom Assemblies?

- Create complex calculations and call from within a report
- Access the full capabilities of the .NET platform
- Logic is secure and reusable

Introduction

Reporting Services can take advantage of custom .NET assemblies written by you or third-party developers. If you already have experience in programming in any .NET language, you will immediately be able to create custom .NET assemblies for use in reports.

Create complex calculations

Custom functions can be used to encapsulate complex or detailed expressions. Rather than build all of the logic for a complex statistical calculation in a text box expression using Report Designer, you can encapsulate the complexities in a custom function and then call the function from the report.

Full capabilities of .NET

Custom functions in an assembly can use the full capabilities of the .NET Framework. For example, the custom code can be procedural and not just a single expression, allowing you to make use of sophisticated programming structures such as conditionals (like **IF** and **CASE** statements) and loops (like **FOR** and **WHILE** constructs).

Logic is secure and reusable

Putting custom functions in an assembly allows you to be confident that the code is secure. (You must provide a strong key for the assembly so that no one, either maliciously or inadvertently, can change the code in the function.) Another benefit of placing logic in a custom assembly is that you can reuse the function in multiple reports.

Review

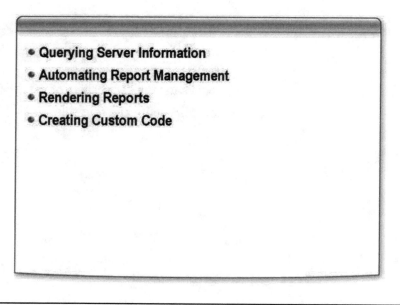

- Querying Server Information
- Automating Report Management
- Rendering Reports
- Creating Custom Code

1. Why are Web services an ideal choice for interacting with the report server?

2. What steps should you follow to use the Report Server Web service?

3. How can you automate report management tasks?

4. When should you use SSL to secure report rendering?

5. What are the benefits of creating custom assemblies?

Lab 7: Programming Reporting Services

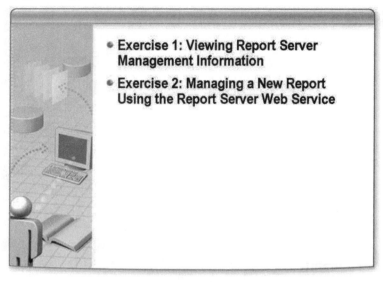

Exercise 1: Viewing Report Server
Management Information

Exercise 2: Managing a New Report
Using the Report Server Web Service

Objectives

In this lab, you will create a custom application that uses the Report Server Web service to view and manage report information. You will also create a custom .NET assembly, install it into the GAC, and use it from a report.

After completing this lab, you will be able to:

- View report server management information within a custom application.

- Manage a new report from a custom application.

Estimated time to complete this lab: 60 minutes

Exercise 1
Viewing Report Server Management Information

In this exercise, you will create an application that retrieves information from the report server by calling the Report Server Web service.

▶ **Open the starter application**

1. Click **Start**, point to **All Programs**, point to **Microsoft Visual Studio .NET 2003**, and then click **Microsoft Visual Studio .NET 2003**.

2. On the **File** menu, click **Open Solution**.

3. In the **Open Solution** dialog box, navigate to the C:\Program Files\Microsoft Learning\2030\Labfiles\Lab07\Exercise01\Starter folder containing the starter files. Click **ReportManager.sln**, and then click **Open**.

▶ **Add a Web reference to the Report Server Web service**

1. In **Solution Explorer**, right-click the **References** folder, and then click **Add Web Reference**.

2. In the **URL** text box, type the following URL:

```
http://localhost/ReportServer/ReportService.asmx?wsdl
```

3. Click **Go**.

4. After the Web service is located, in the **Web reference name** text box, delete the default value, type **ReportService** and then click **Add Reference**.

▶ **Add code to the form to retrieve server information**

1. In **Solution Explorer**, right-click **frmManage.vb**, and then click **View Code**.

2. At the very top of the file, add an **Imports** statement to the **ReportManager.ReportService** namespace, as shown in the following code:

```
Imports ReportManager.ReportService
```

3. After the **Inherits** statement, create a class-level variable called **rs** that references the **ReportingService** proxy class. Your code should appear as follows:

```
Private rs As New ReportingService
```

4. Locate the **frmManage_Load** event, and before the call to the **LoadInformation** method, add the following code to set the credentials:

```
rs.Credentials = _
    System.Net.CredentialCache.DefaultCredentials
```

5. Locate the **LoadInformation** method.

6. Modify the code as shown here:

```
Private Sub LoadInformation()
  lstView.Items.Clear()
  Dim myCatalogItems As CatalogItem()

  myCatalogItems = rs.ListChildren("/", True)

  For Each cItem As CatalogItem In myCatalogItems
      Dim strValues(3) As String
      strValues(0) = cItem.Name
      strValues(1) = cItem.Path
      strValues(2) = cItem.Type.ToString()
      strValues(3) = cItem.CreatedBy

      lstView.Items.Add(New ListViewItem(strValues))
  Next
End Sub
```

The code creates a list of all the items on the report server. It then loops through the list and displays the information in the list view control.

▶ **Add code to retrieve individual item information**

1. Locate the **DisplayCurrentInfo** method.

2. Modify the code as shown here:

```
Private Sub DisplayCurrentInfo()
  Me.Cursor = Cursors.WaitCursor

  Dim item As ListViewItem = lstView.SelectedItems(0)
  Dim strName As String = item.SubItems(0).Text
  Dim strPath As String = item.SubItems(1).Text

  Dim properties As [Property]()
  properties = rs.GetProperties(strPath, Nothing)

  Dim sb As New System.Text.StringBuilder

  For Each prop As [Property] In properties
      sb.Append(prop.Name & ": " & prop.Value & vbCrLf)
  Next

  MessageBox.Show(sb.ToString(), _
      "Properties of " & strName)
  Me.Cursor = Cursors.Default
End Sub
```

The code retrieves information from the server about the item selected in the list view control. The information is then displayed in a message box.

▶ **Test the application**

1. From the **Debug** menu, click **Start**.

   When the form loads (this could take a few seconds), it should display the list of all available items on the report server.

2. Select one of the reports from the list view, and then click **Get Info**.

   Examine the properties displayed in the message box before closing it.

3. Select one of the folders from the list view, and then click **Get Info**.

   Examine the properties displayed in the message box before closing it.

4. Click **Close**.

Exercise 2
Managing a New Report Using the Report Server Web Service

In this exercise, you will upload a new report by calling the Report Server Web service. A starter application has been provided in case you did not finish Exercise 1.

▶ **Open the starter application (if you did not complete Exercise 1)**

1. On the **File** menu, click **Open Solution**.

2. In the **Open Solution** dialog box, navigate to the C:\Program Files\Microsoft Learning\2030\Labfiles\Lab07\ Exercise02\Starter folder containing the starter files. Click **ReportManager.sln**, and then click **Open**.

▶ **Add a Web reference to the Reporting Services Web service**

1. In **Solution Explorer**, expand the **Web References** folder and delete the **ReportService** web service.

2. Right-click the **Web References** folder, and click **Add Web Reference**.

3. In the **URL** text box, type the following URL:

```
http://localhost/ReportServer/ReportService.asmx?wsdl
```

4. Click **Go**.

5. After the Web service is located, in the **Web reference name** text box, delete the default value, type **ReportService**, and then click **Add Reference**.

▶ **Add code to upload a report**

1. In **Solution Explorer**, right-click **frmManage.vb**, and then click **View Code**.

2. Locate the **UploadReport** method.

3. Within the **If...End If** block, add the following code:

```
Dim stream As FileStream = _
    File.OpenRead(ofdBrowse.FileName)
Dim report As Byte() = New Byte(stream.Length) {}
stream.Read(report, 0, CInt(stream.Length))
stream.Close()
```

This code opens the report definition file and loads it into a byte array.

4. Immediately after the code you just typed, create a **Try...Catch...Finally** block with the following code:

```
Try
    Me.Cursor = Cursors.WaitCursor

    rs.CreateReport("My New Report", "/", True, report, _
        Nothing)
    LoadInformation()

Catch ex As Exception
    MessageBox.Show(ex.ToString(), "Could not load report")
Finally
    Me.Cursor = Cursors.Default
End Try
```

This code asks the report server to create the new report based on the byte array. It then redisplays the list view information and checks for any errors.

▶ **Add code to delete an item**

1. Locate the **DeleteItem** method.

2. Modify the code as shown here:

```
Private Sub DeleteItem()
    Dim item As ListViewItem = lstView.SelectedItems(0)
    Dim strPath As String = item.SubItems(1).Text
    Dim strQuestion As String = _
    "Are you sure you want to delete " & strPath & "?"

    If MessageBox.Show(strQuestion, "Confirm Deletion", _
        MessageBoxButtons.YesNo, MessageBoxIcon.Question) = _
        DialogResult.Yes Then
        Try
            Me.Cursor = Cursors.WaitCursor

            rs.DeleteItem(strPath)
            LoadInformation()

        Catch ex As Exception
            MessageBox.Show(ex.ToString(), _
            "Could not delete item")
        Finally
            Me.Cursor = Cursors.Default
        End Try
    End If
End Sub
```

This code confirms that the user wants to delete the item and then asks the report server to delete the item. The **Catch** block deals with any errors.

▶ **Test the application**

1. From the **Debug** menu, click **Start**.

    When the form loads (this could take a few seconds), it should display the list of all available items on the report server.

2. Click **Upload**.

3. In the **Choose Report To Upload** dialog box, navigate to the C:\Program Files\Microsoft Learning\2030\Labfiles\Lab07\Exercise02 folder, select **Product Profitabity.rdl** and then click **Open**.

4. When the list view has refreshed, locate **Product Profitability** located under **/ProductSales/Product Profitability** in the list view, and click the item.

5. Click **Delete**.

6. When asked to confirm your deletion, click **Yes**.

7. When the list view has refreshed, confirm that the **Product Profitability** item located under **/ProductSales/Product Profitability** is no longer visible.

8. Click **Close**.

Course Evaluation

Your evaluation of this course will help Microsoft understand the quality of your learning experience.

To complete a course evaluation, go to http://www.CourseSurvey.com.

Microsoft will keep your evaluation strictly confidential and will use your responses to improve your future learning experience.